THE GREAT LOVER
and other plays

ALEX

THE

ADAPTED, WI

DRE DUMAS, PÈRE
GREAT LOVER
and other plays

INTRODUCTION, BY BARNETT SHAW

Frederick Ungar Publishing Co.
New York

Library of Congress Cataloging in Publication Data

Dumas, Alexandre, 1802–1870.
   The great lover and other plays.

   CONTENTS: The great lover (Mademoiselle de Belle-Isle).—Kean.—Young King Louis (La jeunesse de Louis XIV).—Three interludes for Molière's The love doctor (Trois entr'actes pour l'amour-médecin).
   I. Shaw, Barnett. II. Title.
PQ2223.S5   842'.7   78-20925
ISBN 0-8044-2147-1

CONTENTS

INTRODUCTION

Alexandre Dumas was the son of a mulatto general, Thomas-Alexandre Dumas, who served under Napoleon. His grandfather was the Marquis Davy de la Pailleterie, who had married a native named Marie-Cessette Dumas while running a plantation on the island of Haiti. Both Dumas and his father ignored the title to which they had a right, preferring to use the name Dumas.

Dumas was born in Villers-Cotterets, forty miles from Paris, on July 24, 1802. After finishing his schooling he went to Paris and obtained a position as clerk for the Duke of Orleans. It was not long before he had a mistress, and in 1824, a son. The son, Alexandre Dumas fils, was destined to become a writer like his father and even for a time to surpass him in popularity as a dramatist. For Dumas père, still in his twenties, a farce written with a friend had a modest success and started young Alexandre on a serious career as a dramatist.

Dumas swept through nineteenth-century Paris like a whirlwind. He was the uncrowned "King of Paris" who—according to a contemporary—could have filled every theatre if all other dramatists had stopped writing. Victorien Sardou called Dumas the best man of the theatre of his century. His influence in the field of drama has been enormous, although often overlooked by writers of theatre history. His *Henri III et sa cour* (1829) was the first great triumph of the Romantic movement. His *Antony* (1831) was the first romantic drama in modern dress, attacking the accepted idea of marriage and proclaiming the rights of love. The play created a sensation in Paris, and it became the inspiration for hundreds of "triangle" plays that persist to this day.

The intense passion and power of *Antony* were again put to work in *Kean* (1836), a play whose hero was ostensibly the English actor Edmund Kean, but in reality Dumas himself. The play has never left the stage in France, and a movie version was made many years ago.

Dumas created the historical drama, the play of "cape and sword,"

first in the most popular melodrama of all time, *La tour de Nesle**
(1832), and later in the dramatizations of his *Les trois mousquetaires,**
*Le Chevalier de Maison Rouge,** and other novels. Dumas, who became
as popular a novelist as he was dramatist, put most of his novels on
the stage, and even built his own *Théâtre Historique* where they were
presented. It was also in this theatre that Dumas first produced his
verse translation of *Hamlet,* to be the standard version of that Shakespeare play in France until 1916, racking up 207 performances at
the Comédie-Française. One of the big events in Paris during Febru-
ary, 1848, was the performance of *Monte Cristo,* a play so long that it
had to be produced on two successive evenings. To critics who said
the play was too long, Dumas replied: "There are neither long nor
short plays, only amusing plays and dull ones."

Dumas also tried his hand at comedy, and was very successful.
Three of his comedies, *Les demoiselles de Saint-Cyr, Un mariage sous
Louis XV,** and *Mademoiselle de Belle-Isle,* played in repertory at the
Comédie-Francaise for many years.

The playwright's travelogues were as widely popular as his novels
and plays. His accounts of his trips to Switzerland, Russia, and
Algeria are like no other travel books ever written. English editions
of these travel books appeared in the United States in the 1960s.

Dumas monopolized Parisian society as he did the theatre and the
novel. When he entered a room, women sighed and men grew envious. When he spoke, the most eloquent held their breath to listen.
Not the most modest of men, he was quite aware of his magnetism
and charm. Once, when asked if he had enjoyed a certain gathering,
he replied: "I should have been quite bored if I hadn't been there."

With unbounded enthusiasm Dumas could draw an astounding
number of facts from the depth of a phenomenal memory. He
usually wrote fourteen hours a day, in a perfect hand, seldom making a correction, and without groping for a word. Very often he had
a novel or play complete in his head before he sat down to write. He
wrote the first volume of *Le Chevalier de Maison Rouge* in sixty-six
hours on a bet.

But in 1845 Dumas met with ill luck; he was attacked as a plagia-
rist by a disgruntled writer named Mirecourt. The accuser was sen-
tenced to two weeks in prison for libel, but much damage was done
to Dumas's reputation. For many years in France, Dumas was belit-
tled as an improvisor. Writers were jealous of this giant of a man
who dominated every field of literature. Today, the true genius of

Alexandre Dumas is recognized more than ever; new editions of his works appear constantly in France, and as translations in other lands.

Fiorentino, with whom Dumas collaborated on some works dealing with Italy, said: "Dumas is not a dramatic writer, he is the drama incarnate. And how many believed themselves to be his collaborators who were only his confidants! In his books, but above all in his plays, his collaborators had only the slightest share. He remodeled the scenarios, changed the characters, added or cut down scenes, and wrote all in his own hand."

George Bernard Shaw, in his *Dramatic Criticism,* said: "Dumas père was what Gounod called Mozart, a summit of art. Nobody ever could, or did, or will improve on Mozart's operas, and nobody ever could, or did, or will improve on Dumas's romances and plays."

It was the revolution of 1848 that hastened the decline of Dumas. Shortly after the *coup d'état* of 1851 with which Louis-Napoleon declared himself emperor, Dumas fled to voluntary exile in Brussels. His theatre went into bankruptcy, and creditors seized his cherished chateau of Monte Cristo at Port-Marly, a mansion into which he had poured vast sums.

A few years later he returned to Paris in an attempt to recoup his fortune. He tried his hand at the editorship of several newspapers, and he continued to write at a furious pace. He had plays on the boards every year until 1869, the year before he died. But the quality of his work declined under the intense pressure. Plays on the level of *Antony, Kean,* and *Mademoiselle de Belle-Isle* did not come again from his pen. The two exceptions were a one-act gem called *Romulus,* which he wrote for the Comédie-Française, and a full-length historical comedy-drama called *La jeunesse de Louis XIV*. This play, which in many ways surpasses *Les trois mousquetaires,* was accepted by the Comédie-Française, but was stopped by the censors. It had a successful run in Brussels, however, and played in Paris after the death of Dumas, well into the twentieth century.

Dumas died in December, 1870, at the home of his son near Dieppe, as Bismarck's troops were invading France. Four years earlier, in his novel titled *La terreur prussienne,** he had warned of the danger of Prussian imperialism. The writer was buried in the cemetery of Villers-Cotterets, beside his mother and father.

Both Dumas, father and son, were dramatists. The father became a novelist, but never stopped writing plays. The son started as a novelist but eventually devoted himself to the theatre. His chief claim to fame today resides in one play, *La dame aux camélias,* called *Camille* in English-language versions, which was also the basis for Verdi's opera *La traviata.* Neither as novelist nor dramatist was the son capable of creating heroic characters like those that dominate the father's work: d'Artagnan, Edmond Dantes, Chicot the jester, Bussy d'Amboise, Porthos, Athos, Aramis, Annibal de Coconnas, and Cagliostro. All of those men except Edmond Dantes had actually lived, but they had been long forgotten until Dumas père immortalized them. Dumas put himself into his heroes.

In 1883 a statue of Dumas père, designed by Gustave Doré, was unveiled in Paris, on the Place Malesherbes. Dumas is seated at the summit; on one side a group of people is reading one of the romances that have been printed and reprinted in every language, and on the other side is a bronze of D'Artagnan with drawn rapier. At the statue's inauguration, one speaker said that if every person who had been thrilled by *The Three Musketeers* or *The Count of Monte Cristo* had contributed a penny to the memory of Dumas, the statue could have been cast in solid gold.

Published posthumously, with the help of Anatole France, was Dumas's *Grand dictionnaire de cuisine.* Culinary art was just another interest in the life of the irrepressible Alexandre Dumas. Far from being a dull collection of recipes, his cookbook is an amazing series of anecdotes, with interesting treatises on food, dining, wine, and even mustard.

The fabulous chateau of Monte Cristo, about which Dumas wrote in only one book, his charming *Histoire de mes bêtes,* has been declared a national monument by the French government, and an organization called *L'association des amis d'Alexandre Dumas,* founded by the popular French writer Alain Decaux, is engaged in restoring the chateau and the spacious gardens to their former splendor.

Meanwhile the name of Alexandre Dumas père survives—on the printed page, on the stage, and in more than three hundred films based on his plays and novels, in France, England, the United States, and even in Japan, where thirty movies have been made from his works.

His future remains unlimited.

Barnett Shaw

The Great Lover

ABOUT THE PLAY

Mademoiselle de Belle-Isle, as the French version is called, opened on April 12, 1839 at the Comédie-Française, where it remained in repertory for nearly one hundred years, having more than five hundred performances. Sarah Bernhardt and Rachel were among the great actresses to take the role of Gabrielle. The play moves with surprising grace and agility, and there is a delicate weaving of comedy and drama. The author's genius becomes more amazing when we learn that he recited the play to the committee of the Comédie-Française and had it accepted by acclamation before one word of it was down on paper.

In this adaptation, some lengthy speeches have been shortened, some historical references have been deleted, and a few "asides" have been cut.

MARQUISE DE PRIE, *favorite of the Duke de Bourbon*
MARIETTE, *her maid*
A SERVANT
DUKE DE RICHELIEU, *a notorious nobleman*
GABRIELLE DE BELLE-ISLE, *a young girl from Brittany*
COUNT D'AUMONT, *Captain of the King's Guards*
CHEVALIER CHAMBLAY, *Officer of the King's Constabulary*
LIEUTENANT SEVRAN, *in love with Gabrielle*
CHAMILLAC, *a gentleman of the court*

The action takes place in 1726, in the chateau of Chantilly, France.
Scenes 1, 2, 3, 4, 5: The apartment of the Marquise
Scene 6: A game room in the chateau
Scene 7: Same as first scenes

Because of the rapid development, it is possible for the seven scenes to be played without interruption. If an intermission is required, it should come after Scene 4.

Costumes and decor: Louis XV period

SCENE 1

The apartment of the Marquise de Prie. Gaudy Louis XV style. A center arch-
way gives access to a corridor that leads at left to other rooms of the apart-
ment, and at right to the main entrance. In the right wall is a window that
looks down on street below. In the left wall is a door leading to the private
quarters of the Marquise. It is morning. The MARQUISE *is seated while*
MARIETTE *stands at a table, opening letters that she tosses into a burner.*

[Note: In a recent European revival of the play, each scene opened with
period music of a music-box quality. The characters on stage remained mo-
tionless like porcelain figures for a few moments, starting to talk when the
music stopped.]

MARQUISE: Go directly to the signatures, Mariette. I know what the
letters say without boring myself by reading them.

MARIETTE: Madame the Marquise is very indifferent today.

MARQUISE: Don't you see, my dear, that all these declarations of love
and devotion are sham? Do you think I receive them because of
myself?

MARIETTE: Why, then?

MARQUISE: Because I happen to be the favorite of the Duke of Bourbon.

MARIETTE: Oh!

MARQUISE: And the Duke of Bourbon happens to be the first minister of Louis XV.

MARIETTE: Oh!

MARQUISE: And Louis XV happens to be—must I tell you?

MARIETTE: The King of France.

MARQUISE: Then I make myself clear. Burn the letters—burn them.

9

MARIETTE: Even this one from the Count D'Aumont?

MARQUISE: Especially that one from the Count D'Aumont. Burn! Burn!

MARIETTE: So much love going up in smoke.

MARQUISE: Not love, but drivel! Is that all of them?

MARIETTE: Yes, Madame.

MARQUISE: Nothing from the Duke de Richelieu?

MARIETTE: Nothing.

MARQUISE: That's odd.

MARIETTE: May I be allowed to say that I'm a little worried?

MARQUISE: Why? Because there's no letter from the Duke?

MARIETTE: Oh, no—not that exactly—I mean that Madame seems to be really in love.

MARQUISE: And why does that worry you?

MARIETTE: It's the Duke de Richelieu that worries me. In fact, it frightens me to think of your being in love with him. Many women have died of it.

MARQUISE: Nonsense!

MARIETTE: That's what they say! Just the same, you should be careful.

MARQUISE: What makes you think I'm in danger?

MARIETTE: You're concerned when there is no letter from the Duke. You're indifferent when there are letters from others. And worst of all, you've been faithful to him for three weeks now.

MARQUISE: It seems much longer than that.

MARIETTE: No—precisely three weeks.

MARQUISE: I could tell you something that would surprise you.

MARIETTE: Tell me!

MARQUISE: You're very curious, aren't you?

MARIETTE: I beg your pardon, but it's been a long time since anything surprised me.

MARQUISE: I'll tell you the secret. The Duke de Richelieu is faithful to me.

MARIETTE: May I be permitted to have some doubts about that?

MARQUISE: Doubt as much as you like. I'm sure of it.

MARIETTE: Did you give him a love potion?

MARQUISE: No—I made him give his word, that's all. See this?

(She holds up half of a gold coin, which she takes from a small purse on the table.)

MARIETTE: Half of a gold coin?

MARQUISE: Correct. The Duke has not yet returned the other half.

MARIETTE: And what does that signify?

MARQUISE: That he still loves me.

MARIETTE: I'm sorry—this is over my head.

MARQUISE: I'll explain. You know, we often become unhappy in love, not simply because we love someone who does not love us, but because we do *not* love someone who still loves us.

MARIETTE: I'll have to think about that. Yes—there's truth in what you say, I believe.

MARQUISE: Well, when I became involved with the Duke, after his return from Vienna, we decided that our affair should never have a dismal ending. Each of us took half of a gold coin and we resolved that the moment either of us, for any reason, lost interest or had a change of heart, he would send his half of the coin to the other.

MARIETTE: Do you mean—with no questions asked?

MARQUISE: No questions—no reproaches—no scenes.

MARIETTE: And since the Duke has not sent his half of the coin—?

MARQUISE: It's certain that he still loves me.

(*She puts the coin into the purse on the table.*)

MARIETTE: It's a very ingenious plan.

MARQUISE: Yes.

MARIETTE: If it works. It's too bad the gold coin can't come back to you by itself. I could trust a gold coin, but I don't trust men, especially the—

(*She is interrupted by a* SERVANT.)

SERVANT: The Duke de Richelieu requests the honor of presenting himself to Madame the Marquise.

MARQUISE: Have him come in. (*To* MARIETTE) Now I understand why I had no letter.

(*The* DUKE *enters from the right.*)

DUKE: I'm honored that you didn't make me cool my heels in the corridor.

MARQUISE: Did you think I would?

DUKE: Would I appear conceited if I said "no"?

(*He kisses her hand.*)

MARQUISE: You won't mind if Mariette makes a few adjustments?

DUKE: Not at all.

(MARIETTE *works on the* MARQUISE's *hair.*)

MARQUISE: Did you just arrive from Paris?

DUKE: Ten minutes ago.

MARQUISE: What's new there?

DUKE: They're praying for the sun as usual. They don't know that you are the one who makes the weather fair.

MARQUISE: When you talk like that, you're irresistible.

DUKE: I try.

MARQUISE: Did you see Madame Alainville?

DUKE: Yes.

MARQUISE: How is she?

DUKE: Getting thinner.

MARQUISE: Impossible—she was already impalpable.

DUKE: Well, she'll become invisible, that's all. And what goes on here?

MARQUISE: Nothing even worth gossiping about.

DUKE: I was thinking Chamblay was here.

MARQUISE: He is.

DUKE: Still trying to prevent duels, I suppose. Did he come alone?

MARQUISE: No—with the Count D'Aumont.

DUKE: Really? That dear Count! He always looks as if he had combed his hair two days ago and shaved two weeks ago. Without a doubt, he's the most unkempt gentleman in France.

MARQUISE: That's his particular charm. (*To* MARIETTE) That will do now, Mariette. You may go.

(MARIETTE *exits center, to left.*)

DUKE: At last—we're alone.

(*Kisses her hand and arm as he sits beside her on sofa.*)

MARQUISE: After eight days of absence, when you should have been away only five.

DUKE: After two years exile in Vienna, is that too long to make my court to the King?

MARQUISE: And to Madame Villars, Madame de Duras, Madame Villeroy, Madame de Sabran, Madame de Mouchy, Mademoiselle Santerre, Mademoiselle—

DUKE: My dear, that roll-call sounds suspiciously like a reproach.

MARQUISE: If it were, what would you say?

DUKE: That you aimed your reproach before I had the opportunity of doing the same.

MARQUISE: What is yours, please?

DUKE: During those eight days, not one little letter from you. Do you know that I have never seen your handwriting?

MARQUISE: My sweet Duke—for a diplomat you are not thinking at all. Can the favorite of the first minister write letters to her lover, especially when her lover is the notorious Duke de Richelieu?

DUKE: Well, my magnificent Marquise, even though you cannot write to *me,* I hope you will enjoy these writing tablets that I bought for you in Paris. They seemed to suit you.

MARQUISE: I'm grateful, my delightful Duke.

DUKE: I'm glad.

MARQUISE: And let me say that although I didn't write, my hands were busy. I embroidered this purse just for you. I hope you like it.

DUKE: That was charming of you, my marvelous Marquise. I shall cherish it.

MARQUISE: (*Looking at the tablets*) My coat of arms! I can't deny that you bought these especially for me, my darling Duke.

DUKE: (*Looking at purse*) My initials! I must truthfully say that you were thinking of me when your little fingers worked at this, my mellow Marquise. (*She starts to open the tablets. The* DUKE *rises.*) Don't open them now. Later—when I'm gone.

MARQUISE: Are you leaving already?

DUKE: I must pay my respects to the Duke de Bourbon.

MARQUISE: Shall I see you soon?

DUKE: Need you ask? (*Takes her hand.*) My incomparable Marquise loves me as much as ever?

MARQUISE: Need you ask? (*The* DUKE *exits.*) The Duke is more infatuated than ever. There must be a love letter with these tablets. He didn't want me to open them. (*She opens them, picks up half of the gold coin.*) Oh! The other half of the gold coin!

(*The* DUKE *reappears, holding the purse in one hand the half of coin in the other.*)

DUKE: Marquise!

MARQUISE: (*Holding tablets in one hand, the coin in other.*) Duke!

(*They both break into laughter.*)

DUKE: Our hearts beat as one, I swear it.

MARQUISE: We do have an uncanny rapport.

DUKE: So you don't love me any longer?

MARQUISE: Of course—I'll always love you. And you?

DUKE: Until death!

BOTH TOGETHER: As a friend!

(*They laugh again.*)

MARQUISE: Then you have a new love?

DUKE: I'm working on it—and I'm counting on your help. But tell me about yours.

MARQUISE: I've completely lost my head.

DUKE: (*Sits.*) Who is it?

MARQUISE: A young soldier from Brittany for whom I just obtained a commission as lieutenant in the King's Guards.

DUKE: What is his name?

MARQUISE: Raoul Sevran.

DUKE: Does he know how fortunate he is?

MARQUISE: Not yet. He doesn't even know he owes his commission to me.

DUKE: He must believe that a good fairy is watching over him.

MARQUISE: He's also quite aware that I'm watching him.

DUKE: Where is he now?

MARQUISE: Here in Chantilly.

DUKE: The devil! Why didn't you send this purse to me sooner?

MARQUISE: He's only been here a few days.

DUKE: Good! I don't like to see time wasted where love is concerned.

MARQUISE: I don't intend to waste any. Now tell me your story—and be as frank as I was.

DUKE: I shall. Let me describe a most charming female—

MARQUISE: Spare my pride, please! I didn't give you a shining description of my lieutenant.

DUKE: Excuse me—I got carried away. She's the daughter of a nobleman from Brittany, and this nobleman is at this moment lodged in the Bastille on some trivial charge. She has come to ask pardon for her father. She went first to the King but he directed her to the Duke de Bourbon. I met her in Paris, followed her to Versailles, and met her again here.

MARQUISE: She's here now?

DUKE: Like your lieutenant. A charming coincidence for us both. This promises to be amusing, though complicated.

MARQUISE: You've forgotten something.

DUKE: What?

MARQUISE: The name of your charmer.

DUKE: (*Eloquently*) Mademoiselle Gabrielle de Belle-Isle.

SERVANT: (*Entering from right*) Mademoiselle Gabrielle de Belle-Isle!

MARQUISE: Was that an echo? (*To* SERVANT) Why did you announce her without informing yourself if I am receiving?

SERVANT: But I thought—

DUKE: Please see her.

MARQUISE: I can't refuse you anything, my dear Duke. (*To* SERVANT) Allow her to come in.

DUKE: You're adorable.

MARQUISE: You said you wanted help. How can I refuse you?

(GABRIELLE *enters.*)

GABRIELLE: Madame, you're so generous to receive me on my first request.

MARQUISE: If you want to thank someone, thank the Duke de Richelieu.

GABRIELLE: The Duke?

MARQUISE: He told me about your very urgent business.

GABRIELLE: Then I thank the Duke. I had the pleasure of meeting him in Paris, and again at Versailles. And thank you, Madame, for your kindness in receiving me.

MARQUISE: Tell me how I may be useful.

GABRIELLE: My father has been imprisoned in the Bastille for three years.

MARQUISE: I had no idea it was so long. How dreadful.

GABRIELLE: Since then my mother died. I find myself floundering helplessly between a tomb and a prison. My father is old, and he is guilty of no crime.

MARQUISE: Then he should be released.

GABRIELLE: But no one will listen to me. I tried to see the King but I was told to see the first minister. That's why I am here.

MARQUISE: Have you seen him?

GABRIELLE: No. My intuition told me to see you first. You are a woman and you will understand my problem, and you will help me, I know.

DUKE: You are right, Mademoiselle. The Marquise will do all that is possible. I promise you in her name.

GABRIELLE: I'll be eternally grateful.

SERVANT: (*Entering*) Madame the Marquise, the Count D'Aumont and the Chevalier Chamblay have requested the honor of presenting themselves.

MARQUISE: Have them wait at least five minutes and then bring them in.

(SERVANT *goes out.*)

DUKE: The devil! Can't you put them off?

MARQUISE: But I've been expecting them.

DUKE: But Mademoiselle's story is very important for you to hear.

MARQUISE: Of course. (*To* GABRIELLE) You see, my dear, as much as I should like to hear your story, I must get ready to receive these gentlemen. Later today, we can resume our talk.

GABRIELLE: My story won't take long. Won't you please listen now?

MARQUISE: I'm afraid that is impossible.

DUKE: Nothing is impossible! I have an idea.

MARQUISE: And what is that, please?

DUKE: I have an excellent plan. Take Mademoiselle de Belle-Isle into another room, and I'll receive your visitors in your name.

MARQUISE: This is a day when I can refuse you nothing. Come, my dear.

GABRIELLE: Oh, Madame—thank you!

(*She goes out with* MARQUISE, *down corridor to left.*)

DUKE: (*Alone*) If I get her father freed, there should be some recompense for me. (*He hums and goes into a little dance.*) I've been good to you, Mademoiselle, Now you be good to me, Mademoiselle. (*Pauses a moment.*) It's only fair!

Blackout

SCENE 2

The same. Five minutes later.
(SERVANT *enters.*)

SERVANT: The Count D'Aumont and the Chevalier Chamblay.

(D'AUMONT *and* CHAMBLAY *enter.*)

DUKE: (*To* SERVANT) I am receiving for Madame the Marquise. That will be all. (*The* SERVANT *leaves.*)

D'AUMONT: My fond greetings, Duke.

DUKE: Good morning, D'Aumont. Good morning, Chamblay.

CHAMBLAY: Good morning.

DUKE: (*To* CHAMBLAY) I haven't seen you since you arrested me for starting an asinine duel. Really, I have no hard feelings. Do you know I might have been killed?

CHAMBLAY: Happy to hear you have no hard feelings. I'm sorry that D'Aumont and I can't say the same.

DUKE: What do you mean?

CHAMBLAY: (*Smiling*) Simply that you've been in here with the Marquise for heaven knows how long, while we can't even get a glimpse of her.

DUKE: I assure you that as far as I am concerned, the Marquise is fair game. Happy hunting!

D'AUMONT: Did she request you to speak to us for her?

DUKE: Yes, she did. And I'd like to give you some wise advice in her name.

D'AUMONT: Advice? To me?

DUKE: Yes—to you.

D'AUMONT: Give it, then.

DUKE: (*His hand on D'Aumont's shoulder*) Listen, D'Aumont, I speak as a friend—

D'AUMONT: I'm listening.

DUKE: God made you a gentleman, the King made you a Count, your wife made you Captain of the Guards, and I pinned a medal on your chest once. Remember?

D'AUMONT: Very well.

DUKE: Then you remember that I had to embrace you. It was part of the ceremony.

D'AUMONT: What about it?

DUKE: It was like embracing a porcupine, D'Aumont. Why don't you shave?

D'AUMONT: What do you want of me? Women used to love beards.

DUKE: But that's not a beard—it's a thicket.

D'AUMONT: The devil take all the new fashions. We haven't changed—it's the women. You don't realize the change that has taken place while you were in Vienna.

DUKE: What change?

D'AUMONT: France is getting so prudish that it's unbearable.

DUKE: Really?

D'AUMONT: We're having a real epidemic.

DUKE: Epidemic?

D'AUMONT: Yes—of virtue.

DUKE: Chamblay, have we changed as much as he says?

CHAMBLAY: I hate to admit that he is right. False morality and false sentiment are what we endure these days. We're like the people in the paintings of Watteau that are so much in favor now. Do you know them?

DUKE: Of course.

CHAMBLAY: Nothing but gods, goddesses, cupids and shepherds, in attitudes of nauseating affectation, looking at sunsets.

DUKE: That sounds gruesome. Then the good old days are gone?

CHAMBLAY: Vanished.

DUKE: But surely women have not stopped being women—God bless the dear creatures.

CHAMBLAY: My dear Duke, women used to have one confessor for two lovers, now they have two confessors for one lover.

DUKE: Bah! You've always been a misanthrope, Chamblay.

D'AUMONT: It's true. He got it from a good source—it was his wife who told him.

CHAMBLAY: You're wrong, D'Aumont—it was your wife.

D'AUMONT: All the more reason to believe it. And look at the way women dress. They look like walking pyramids.

CHAMBLAY: And mountains of hair. How can they find time for lovers when they spend four hours a day arranging their coiffures?

D'AUMONT: Duke, you gave me some advice, now let me give you some: if you want to retain your title of the Great Lover, go back to Vienna where life is still exciting.

(SERVANT *enters.*)

SERVANT: Lieutenant Sevran to see Madame the Marquise.

DUKE: Have him come in. (SEVRAN *enters.*) I'm doing the honors for Madame the Marquise. You gentlemen know each other? (*They nod.*) I want to congratulate you on your commission as lieutenant.

SEVRAN: Thank you. Please don't let me disturb your conversation.

DUKE: Not at all. Now, D'Aumont—you were saying?

D'AUMONT: You should return to Vienna.

DUKE: Why?

D'AUMONT: Because there is nothing to do here.

DUKE: Speak for yourself, my friend.

D'AUMONT: I know—you're very sure of yourself, but you'll see— you'll go back to Vienna of your own accord.

DUKE: I'd like to make a bet with you gentlemen.

D'AUMONT: What bet?

DUKE: I'll put up a thousand. Each of you will put up five hundred. (*To* SEVRAN) Lieutenant, you may participate if you care to.

SEVRAN: It's possible. What is the wager?

CHAMBLAY: Yes—what's the wager?

DUKE: You say that in my absence women have become ferociously virtuous.

D'AUMONT: That is our opinion.

DUKE: I'm going to prove to you that vice is eternal, and virtue is only a passing fashion.

CHAMBLAY: How do you intend to do it?

DUKE: I'll bet that the first woman that we see—either here or when we leave the chateau—the first woman—married or single—will grant me a rendezvous within twenty-four hours.

D'AUMONT: What sort of rendezvous?

DUKE: What sort? What sort do you think? A satisfying rendezvous, of course.

D'AUMONT: Be more exact.

DUKE: I'll be more than exact—I'll be explicit. I'll make love to her. You know what that is, of course.

CHAMBLAY: I think so. But where?

DUKE: In her bedroom, naturally.

D'AUMONT: What time?

DUKE: Between ten and midnight. Does that suit you?

D'AUMONT: Yes. How will the results be proved?

DUKE: I'll throw a message from her bedroom window.

D'AUMONT: What if her bedroom window looks out on a river?

DUKE: Hire a boat. As for the details, you'll have to take my word as a gentleman.

D'AUMONT: The bet is on.

CHAMBLAY: And half is mine.

DUKE: Agreed! (*To* SEVRAN) You, sir?

SEVRAN: I pass.

DUKE: (*Shaking hands with* D'AUMONT *and* CHAMBLAY) It's understood then—the first woman that we see—either in the chateau or after we leave here.

CHAMBLAY: Correct.

DUKE: I must make one condition, though.

D'AUMONT: I was waiting for that.

DUKE: But this condition will only make it more difficult for me.

D'AUMONT: What is it?

DUKE: She must be pretty. The first *pretty* woman that we meet.

CHAMBLAY: That's all right with us, and it does make it more difficult for you.

DUKE: But much more pleasant.

(SERVANT *enters from left.*)

SERVANT: Madame the Marquise de Prie.

(*He goes out.*)

DUKE: Gentlemen—she doesn't count. I would be stealing your money.

(*The* MARQUISE *enters.*)

MARQUISE: Gentlemen, I hoped I would be able to see you now, but I had forgotten that I must go to mass. Tomorrow night there will be a ball at the chateau and I shall see all of you there. Good-day, gentlemen. (*She starts out and calls down the hall.*) This way, Mademoiselle de Belle-Isle—we'll go together.

(*She goes out right.*)

D'AUMONT: You see how things are? Four men are waiting to see the Marquise, and she is going to pray.

CHAMBLAY: Gentlemen! You're not paying attention!

(*He indicates* GABRIELLE *who passes in the corridor and exits right without glancing into the room.*)

DUKE: Gabrielle!

(SEVRAN *makes a movement.*)

D'AUMONT: That seems to trouble you. But she's the first pretty woman we've seen.

CHAMBLAY: You won't be stealing our money this time.

DUKE: No—but I hope to win it from you.

D'AUMONT: You can try. The bet stands.

SEVRAN: Just a moment!

DUKE: What is it, Lieutenant? Do you want to take part? There's still time.

SEVRAN: I'll take all the bet. This will be between the Duke and me.

D'AUMONT: All of it? You?

SEVRAN: Yes—I!

CHAMBLAY: But why all of it?

SEVRAN: Because I have the right. The girl the Duke de Richelieu hopes to dishonor within twenty-four hours is to become my wife in three days.

Blackout

SCENE 3

The same. Afternoon of the same day. The MARQUISE *and* DUKE *are seated.*

MARQUISE: Did you really make such a ridiculous bet?

DUKE: I certainly did.

MARQUISE: You're foolish.

DUKE: Was I ever accused of being wise?

MARQUISE: You will lose.

DUKE: I have until tomorrow morning. It's only five o'clock now.

MARQUISE: But who accepted the bet?

DUKE: That would interest you, and I'll tell you after I've won. But let me assure you that it will help you with your young lieutenant.

MARQUISE: It will?

DUKE: Very much. So you must give me your word to help me, and to promise not to tell Gabrielle.

MARQUISE: You have my word.

DUKE: Good. Now I must go look over the scene of my conquests.

MARQUISE: Where is she staying?

DUKE: Hotel du Soleil.

MARQUISE: Oh, yes, I remember. She told me this morning.

DUKE: The hotelkeeper never refuses me anything. I'll keep you informed.

MARQUISE: Until later, then.

DUKE: Au revoir.

(*He exits.*)

MARQUISE: Mariette! (MARIETTE *enters from corridor.*) I rather expected to find you there.

MARIETTE: I wasn't listening.

MARQUISE: Which means that you heard everything.

MARIETTE: I did—in spite of trying not to listen.

MARQUISE: What do you think of the Duke now?

MARIETTE: He doesn't seem to be broken-hearted because you returned your half of the coin.

MARQUISE: What did you expect? Tears?

MARIETTE: But you wouldn't be a woman if you weren't a little jealous.

MARQUISE: Imagine his conceit. He tells me the whole story of his lecherous bet, and then makes me promise not to tell Mademoiselle de Belle-Isle.

MARIETTE: I hope you don't intend to keep your word.

MARQUISE: I'll keep my word, but I also intend to protect that young girl from the Duke.

MARIETTE: I'm glad. I hope you teach him a good lesson while you do it.

MARQUISE: I intend to work on it.

MARIETTE: Have you an idea?

MARQUISE: Almost.

SERVANT: (*Entering from right*) Mademoiselle de Belle-Isle.

MARQUISE: She couldn't have come at a better time. Have her come in.

(SERVANT *exits and* GABRIELLE *enters.*)

GABRIELLE: I hope you will forgive my impatience. Have you seen the Duke de Bourbon?

MARQUISE: Yes—but I'm sorry to say I had no success.

GABRIELLE: Oh, if only I could convince you that my father never harmed anyone.

MARQUISE: It's not I that you must convince—it's the first minister.

GABRIELLE: Then it's hopeless.

MARQUISE: Perhaps not. I have an idea. There is a man who has a great deal of influence here, and if he were to plead your cause, I'm sure he would win.

GABRIELLE: Who is this man? Where can I find him? What is his name?

MARQUISE: The Duke de Richelieu.

GABRIELLE: Then I'm saved. He's been very good to me already—during my journey, and even here this morning.

MARQUISE: That's true. Well—you must write to him and request a meeting.

GABRIELLE: That's exactly what I have already done. After his kindness this morning, I thought that was the right thing to do.

MARQUISE: Have you sent the letter?

GABRIELLE: Not yet. I wanted to ask you if you thought it was proper—and if I used the right words. This letter is very important to me.

MARQUISE: Don't worry about it. I'm sure you used the right words. I'll take the letter and deliver it to the Duke myself.

GABRIELLE: Oh, thank you, Madame, thank you.

MARQUISE: You can meet the Duke here in my house.

GABRIELLE: Here?

MARQUISE: Why not? I have a bedroom that can be your very own. Why should you stay in a dreary hotel, among strangers, when you can be with a friend?

GABRIELLE: Oh, Madame, your kindness overwhelms me.

MARQUISE: The important thing is not to lose time. Go to your hotel and get all your baggage, and bring it here. My servants will take it to your room. (*She rings for* MARIETTE, *who appears.*) Tell them to prepare a carriage for Mademoiselle de Belle-Isle, and then send someone for the Duke de Richelieu.

MARIETTE: Yes, Madame.

(*She goes out.*)

MARQUISE: I'll take care of the letter.

GABRIELLE: (*Hands her the letter.*) I don't know how to thank you.

(*She tries to kiss her hand.*)

MARQUISE: What are you doing? We're friends. (*Kisses* GABRIELLE *on both cheeks.*) I'll be here when you return. (GABRIELLE *exits.* MARQUISE *reads the letter.*) How dull! This needs a complete revision. Short and tantalizing. (*She tears up* GABRIELLE's *letter, crumpling it in her hand.*) Mariette! (MARIETTE *enters.*) Stay here, and if the Duke de Richelieu should come in, tell him to have patience, and that I'll be here in less than five minutes.

MARIETTE: Yes, Madame, I'll take care of him.

MARQUISE: I'm sure you will.

(*She goes out left.*)

MARIETTE: I think he's coming now.

(*She looks out window.*)

DUKE: (*Offstage, cooing*) Is that you, my magnificent Marquise?

(MARIETTE *opens door as* DUKE *thrusts his head in and kisses her.*)

MARIETTE: (*Flabbergasted*) But I'm not the Marquise!

DUKE: I knew that.

MARIETTE: She'll be back in a moment.

DUKE: Meanwhile you don't mind my kissing you, do you?

MARIETTE: No, sir.

DUKE: Have I given you a present lately?

MARIETTE: Oh, yes—you gave me three gold pieces the first time you came through the secret door.

DUKE: Is that all?

MARIETTE: And you gave me this ring the last time you left through the secret door.

DUKE: That miserable little ring? Well, this occasion calls for something better.

(*He hands her a purse of money and then puts his arm around her neck.*)

MARIETTE: Oh, thank you.

DUKE: It's nothing. If you help me, there will be more.

MARIETTE: I'll do whatever you say.

MARQUISE: (*Entering with a new letter.*) What are you doing to Mariette?

DUKE: Just giving her a present.

(*He pats* MARIETTE *on her behind as she exits.*)

MARQUISE: Things seem to be going very well with you.

DUKE: What makes you think so?

MARQUISE: You're not so generous when you're in a bad humor.

DUKE: The fact is that I'm very happy.

MARQUISE: Perhaps I can make you still happier.

DUKE: How?

MARQUISE: By telling you something, and by giving you something.

DUKE: Don't keep me in suspense.

MARQUISE: Gabrielle just left here.

DUKE: Really?

MARQUISE: She was looking for you—and not finding you—she left this.

DUKE: For me? And she left it with you? What does she want?

(*He takes the letter.*)

MARQUISE: A rendezvous. Someone told her that you have influence with the Duke de Bourbon, so she wants you to speak to him.

DUKE: I already have.

MARQUISE: Any success?

DUKE: Very little.

MARQUISE: It takes the Duke an eternity to make up his mind.

DUKE: Perhaps not. I expect to hear from him very soon.

MARQUISE: Why don't you wait here? I have some things to take care of. A friend of mine is coming to spend some time here.

DUKE: Please go about your business. I'll wait.

MARQUISE: Make yourself comfortable, my dear Duke.

(*She goes out door at left.*)

DUKE: Let's see what dear Gabrielle has to say. (*Reads the letter.*) "Would the Duke be kind enough to meet me soon? I have a great favor to ask, in exchange for which the Duke will have my abundant gratitude—and I repeat—abundant." (*He smiles.*) Direct and uncomplicated. I like it. "Abundant gratitude." Very nice, if true. It's almost *too* direct. How can I be sure she wrote this? The Marquise looked at me in a strange way when she handed me the letter. I must find out if it really is from Gabrielle. (*Paces, looks at letter again.*) Is it from Gabrielle?

GABRIELLE: (*Entering*) I thought I heard you speak my name.

DUKE: Yes—I heard your footsteps, and I said "That must be Gabrielle." What's the matter? You seem to be trembling.

GABRIELLE: A little, I'm afraid.

DUKE: How should I interpret that?

GABRIELLE: (*Close to him, looking at him much more innocently than the* DUKE *imagines.*) It's very simple. I can't look at you without thinking: "This is the man who is going to solve all my problems."

DUKE: Who knows—perhaps you can help me solve some of mine.

GABRIELLE: How strange it was that I met you in Paris and again at Versailles. Do you believe in premonition?

DUKE: I believe in whatever brought you to me, and I assure you I'll be very unhappy if my premonition—or whatever it was—deceives me.

GABRIELLE: Did Madame the Marquise give you a letter?

DUKE: Yes—which she says is from you. Of course you understand that I cannot help you directly. I can only be an intermediary between beauty and power. But I will do all I can.

GABRIELLE: I can't ask more than that.

DUKE: First of all, I should like a brief petition—in your own words—which I can present to the first minister this very day. In fact, while you are writing it I shall send my servant to request an interview.

GABRIELLE: What shall I say?

DUKE: What you said to the Marquise this morning—that your father is in prison unjustly. Make it very simple. Just write as you would speak to me.

GABRIELLE: I'll write it. (*She sits at desk.*) How can I thank you?

DUKE: (*Smiling lecherously*) It won't be difficult. But, later! I'll return in a few minutes.

(*He goes out.*)

GABRIELLE: (*Writing*) "Your Highness"

MARQUISE: (*Entering*) What are you doing, my dear?

GABRIELLE: I'm writing a petition to the Duke de Bourbon.

MARQUISE: Who told you to do that?

GABRIELLE: The Duke de Richelieu.

MARQUISE: Are you to send it directly to the first minister?

GABRIELLE: No—the Duke is going to present it himself.

MARQUISE: When?

GABRIELLE: Very soon. He's returning in a few minutes to get it.

MARQUISE: Then we can't waste time. Let me see what you've written. (*She takes the paper.*) This won't do at all. There are certain rules you must follow in cases like this.

GABRIELLE: Will you help me?

MARQUISE: I'll do better. I'll write it for you.

GABRIELLE: Really? (*She rises and the* MARQUISE *sits at desk.*) But what if the first minister discovers that it is your handwriting?

MARQUISE: Do you think that would damage your cause? I assure you it would be better that way. Watch for the Duke, and tell me the moment he arrives. He must not know that I'm rendering you this little service.

GABRIELLE: (*Looking down corridor*) I don't hear anyone.

MARQUISE: Good. What is your father's full name?

GABRIELLE: Charles-Louis-Auguste Fouquet de Garonne.

MARQUISE: His titles?

GABRIELLE: Marquis de Belle-Isle, Count de Vernon.

MARQUISE: How long has he been in prison?

GABRIELLE: Three years.

MARQUISE: We'll put an end to that.

GABRIELLE: Do you really think so?

MARQUISE: Of course. (*She writes a few more words.*) It's done—and according to all the rules of court etiquette.

MARIETTE: (*Entering from left center*) The bedroom is at Mademoiselle's disposal whenever she wishes it.

MARQUISE: In a short while. Mademoiselle is waiting for someone. Don't go too far away.

MARIETTE: I'll be here. (*She starts to go.*) The Duke is coming, Madame.

(*She exits.* MARQUISE *picks up a book quickly and sits on sofa pretending to read, after pushing* GABRIELLE *into desk chair.*)

MARQUISE: I do believe that's the Duke.

DUKE: Sorry to have kept you waiting, Gabrielle.

GABRIELLE: You were not too long. The ink is scarcely dry. (*Hands him the letter.*) Here it is.

(*He takes it, turns away from her, holds the other letter next to it, examines them closely, then smiles with satisfaction. The* MARQUISE, *watching him, also smiles. The* DUKE *turns to* GABRIELLE.)

DUKE: Now, Gabrielle, we must set a time for our meeting.

GABRIELLE: As soon as possible.

DUKE: I agree. This evening.

GABRIELLE: But you must ask Madame for permission.

DUKE: Why?

GABRIELLE: Because she has graciously given me lodging here while I'm in Chantilly.

DUKE: Ah, ha! (*To* MARQUISE) Then the friend you were expecting—?

MARQUISE: Was Gabrielle.

DUKE: You didn't tell me that.

MARQUISE: Didn't I? I thought I did. You see, it was dreadful for her to be isolated in a hotel, all alone as she is.

DUKE: Of course—I understand. But that won't change anything, I hope. May I see Gabrielle here this evening?

MARQUISE: Why not? This is her home. She may receive you when she likes.

DUKE: Then I ask your permission, Gabrielle.

GABRIELLE: Come when you like, Duke. You will always be received as a friend and savior.

DUKE: It may be rather late before I can return. I must see the Duke de Bourbon first, and give him your petition.

GABRIELLE: For three years I have sat up many nights in tears. I'll be only too happy to have a night of joy.

DUKE: I too! Until tonight, then, my dear Gabrielle.

GABRIELLE: Until tonight, Duke.

DUKE: Our rendezvous must be very confidential. I should not like witnesses.

GABRIELLE: There will just be the two of us, I promise.

DUKE: You are charming.

GABRIELLE: I must go to my room now.

(*She leaves.*)

DUKE: (*Turning abruptly, he leans on the* MARQUISE's *chair.*) So that's the way you keep your word, my machinating Marquise?

MARQUISE: In what way have I failed you, my doubting Duke?

DUKE: By confounding my entire plan.

MARQUISE: A plan based on the cooperation of a low-class hotelkeeper? That wasn't worthy of the great lover.

DUKE: It wasn't?

MARQUISE: Of course not. Here you can be comfortable, and there will be no surprises, no misunderstandings. Here you will get results.

DUKE: Do you think so?

MARQUISE: Unless your two years in Vienna have dulled your usual skill.

DUKE: I did get a trifle rusty in Vienna. It was too easy. Thanks for making me call upon my vast resources.

MARQUISE: Do you really think you will succeed in winning your bet?

DUKE: With a little additional help from you, I'm sure of it.

MARQUISE: What help can I be?

DUKE: What I want of you most of all is your absence.

MARQUISE: Thank you.

DUKE: It's essential. At ten o'clock tonight, you will leave here.

MARQUISE: You needn't have asked. I am leaving for Paris tonight—at ten o'clock.

DUKE: Good. Then Gabrielle will be alone.

MARQUISE: Very much alone.

DUKE: Very well. That's all I require.

MARQUISE: But you must promise me something.

DUKE: That's fair. What?

MARQUISE: No servant in the chateau is to know of your project, or to be bribed into helping you.

DUKE: I promise.

MARQUISE: Good. I could see that you were beginning to work on Mariette. But I'm taking her to Paris with me.

DUKE: You're overly suspicious.

MARQUISE: How could I not be when I know you so well? Another thing—you must promise not to use any potions, beverages, or aphrodisiacs.

DUKE: How can you imagine such a thing?

MARQUISE: From your past record, naturally.

DUKE: That was in my youth. Youth never has any faith in its own primitive power.

MARQUISE: You haven't answered my demand.

DUKE: I promise! No drugs of any kind. Not even a small sniff.

MARQUISE: One more thing. You will return the key to my secret door.

DUKE: I should be happy to oblige, but in my haste to follow Gabrielle, I left the key in my apartment in Paris.

MARQUISE: Honestly?

DUKE: Word of honor.

MARQUISE: You're adorable, my charming Duke.

DUKE: You spoil me, Madame the Marquise.

MARQUISE: Excuse me a moment. I must tell my servant to prepare a carriage so I may leave for Paris tonight.

DUKE: Please do. (*As soon as the* MARQUISE *has left, the* DUKE *dashes to window, calls to his servant below.*) Germain! Germain! Listen carefully. Ride at once to Paris and bring me a small gold key that is in an amethyst cup on the fireplace in my bedroom. Kill as many horses as you need to, but have the key here before ten o'clock tonight. Understand? On your way! (*Walks away from window.*) That takes care of that. I didn't promise the Marquise that I wouldn't send for the key. (MARQUISE *enters.*) I must be leaving, my charming Marquise.

MARQUISE: Are your battle plans well laid?

DUKE: In detail.

MARQUISE: Do you think you will win?

DUKE: Experience versus youth! What do *you* think?

MARQUISE: May the most worthy win.

DUKE: Pleasant trip, my dear Marquise.

MARQUISE: Thank you. And may you have a rewarding—

DUKE: Victory?

MARQUISE: Let us only say—may you get your just deserts. Au revoir.

DUKE: Au revoir. (*The* DUKE *starts out.*)

Blackout

SCENE 4

The same. Nine o'clock the same night. The MARQUISE *is seated.* MARIETTE *has entered from left.*

MARIETTE: I told Mademoiselle de Belle-Isle that you wished to speak to her.

MARQUISE: Good.

MARIETTE: Have you figured out a way to outwit the Duke?

MARQUISE: It's simple. The Duke left his key to the secret door in Paris. The wretch! He was always careful to have it on other occasions. I'll lock all the doors. Our roué of a Duke will spend the night in the street. That will be good for him.

MARIETTE: Here is Mademoiselle de Belle-Isle, Madame.

(She exits as GABRIELLE *enters from left.)*

MARQUISE: Come in, my dear. I have something to tell you. I've been thinking about your father. How long since you've seen him?

GABRIELLE: Three years—since he was put in prison.

MARQUISE: Haven't you tried to visit him in the Bastille?

GABRIELLE: I've begged a hundred times, but I am always refused.

MARQUISE: You would be happy to see him, wouldn't you?

GABRIELLE: Need you ask?

MARQUISE: If someone could obtain that privilege for you, could he count on your complete confidence?

GABRIELLE: To see my father for only a moment, I would place my heart and soul as bond.

MARQUISE: Then listen—and listen well—because we are playing with the existence of several people.

GABRIELLE: I know this is grave and serious, but you can trust me. Please, go on.

MARQUISE: The governor of the Bastille is one of my very good friends. I can give you a letter to him.

GABRIELLE: And with that letter?

MARQUISE: You would be able to see your father.

GABRIELLE: Oh, dear God!

MARQUISE: It will take two hours to go to Paris. You can leave here at ten o'clock. You will arrive in Paris about midnight. You may stay with your father until three in the morning, and be back here before anyone is awake.

GABRIELLE: Tonight? I can see my father this very night? Oh, Madame, I am trembling with happiness.

MARQUISE: It all depends upon one very important condition.

GABRIELLE: Please tell me.

MARQUISE: There must be no misunderstanding, Gabrielle.

GABRIELLE: Yes, go on.

MARQUISE: I am going to open a prison that only the signature of the King can otherwise open.

GABRIELLE: I understand.

MARQUISE: The Duke de Bourbon is very jealous of his authority as first minister. If he ever learned of this, I would be ruined forever.

GABRIELLE: I see.

MARQUISE: And you would be ruined, and that isn't all. Your father would lose all chance of ever being released. It might even cost him his life.

GABRIELLE: Good God!

MARQUISE: You see how serious it is. I want you to swear that as long as the Duke de Bourbon is first minister, no one will know that

you saw your father, and no one will know that you left the chateau tonight.

GABRIELLE: I swear!

MARQUISE: No one! Is that clear?

GABRIELLE: I swear—on the life of my father—that as long as the
Duke de Bourbon is first minister, no one will know that I have
seen my father or left here tonight.

MARQUISE: No matter who asks—no matter what his rank or position—you must say you were in your room here all night.

GABRIELLE: I swear it.

MARQUISE: There's not much time. A carriage is waiting below. You
must be back here, and in your bedroom, before six o'clock tomorrow morning.

GABRIELLE: I'll do exactly as you say. Thank you, thank you. What
have I done to deserve this kindness?

MARQUISE: Nothing. I love you, that's all. Remember—discretion.

GABRIELLE: Don't worry.

MARQUISE: I want to see if everything is in readiness. Be prepared to
leave at any time.

(*She exits door left.*)

SERVANT: (*Entering from right*) Lieutenant Sevran to see Mademoiselle.

GABRIELLE: Oh! (*A pause*) Have him come in. (SEVRAN *enters. Kisses*
GABRIELLE.) Raoul.

SEVRAN: What's the matter? You seem excited.

GABRIELLE: Because I'm full of joy. For the first time in three years I
have hope that my father will be released. I have met wonderful
people who are helping me.

SEVRAN: I wish I could be as joyful as you, but my mind is filled with
doubts.

GABRIELLE: But you shouldn't be gloomy at such a moment.

SEVRAN: I only need to be reassured. Tell me—who are the people that are helping you?

GABRIELLE: Madame de Prie, for one. She has been goodness itself. She has even insisted that I stay here with her.

SEVRAN: Her goodness is what disturbs me. Have you spoken to her about our marriage?

GABRIELLE: No. She doesn't even realize that I know you.

SEVRAN: Good. Let it remain that way. Now, tell me—did you see anyone else today?

GABRIELLE: Oh, yes, Raoul, I saw someone who may be even more helpful than the Marquise.

SEVRAN: Who is that?

GABRIELLE: The Duke de Richelieu.

SEVRAN: The Duke de Richelieu?

GABRIELLE: What's the matter?

SEVRAN: You saw him today?

GABRIELLE: He has scarcely left here all day.

SEVRAN: Are you to see him again?

GABRIELLE: Only when he comes to tell me the result of his interview with the first minister.

SEVRAN: (*Holding her*) Oh, Gabrielle!

GABRIELLE: You frighten me.

SEVRAN: Haven't you heard about the Duke de Richelieu?

GABRIELLE: I've heard what everyone has heard.

SEVRAN: And you still believe that he has no motive in helping you?

GABRIELLE: Raoul, I may be wrong, but I can't see evil when it's not there. Up to now, the Duke has been a wonderful friend. If he tries to become something else, you have enough faith in me to know I would never allow it.

SEVRAN: You're too naive. Once he makes up his mind, he uses every means at his disposal. Women who are much more experienced than you have been unable to escape from him. Every moment of his life is devoted to his desire.

GABRIELLE: What must I do, Raoul? Please, tell me.

SEVRAN: Promise me not to meet the Duke here or anywhere else tonight.

GABRIELLE: I promise.

SEVRAN: I'm counting on you. If you fail me it will bring misfortune on both of us.

GABRIELLE: But I won't see him tonight. You have my word. Does that reassure you?

SEVRAN: Yes.

GABRIELLE: Then I must ask you to leave.

SEVRAN: But it's not yet ten o'clock.

GABRIELLE: I have some letters to write, and I'm very tired.

SEVRAN: Just one hour, and I'll leave.

GABRIELLE: Impossible, Raoul. Please leave now—please.

SEVRAN: You're almost begging me to leave. Good God, what is going on?

GABRIELLE: Nothing! It isn't strange that I should be tired after an eventful day, is it? You act as if you're jealous. I've never seen you like this.

SEVRAN: (*Coldly*) Very well—I'll leave!

GABRIELLE: You sound so cruel. You found me happier tonight than I've been since you've known me. Does that displease you? Would you prefer me to be sad?

SEVRAN: Pardon me, Gabrielle. I love you so much that I can't believe my good fortune. I seem to think everyone is conspiring against us. I was wrong. I'll leave. What time may I see you tomorrow?

GABRIELLE: As early as you like—eight o'clock, or even seven o'clock.

SEVRAN: Eight o'clock. Good night, my darling. (*They kiss.*) And don't see the Duke.

GABRIELLE: I've already given you my word.

SEVRAN: (*As he exits*) That was just a reminder.

GABRIELLE: (*Goes to door left, knocks.*) Madame the Marquise! (MARQUISE *enters with* MARIETTE.) I was getting anxious. It's ten o'clock.

MARQUISE: Here is the letter. Guard it. The carriage is waiting. Follow Mariette.

GABRIELLE: How can I ever repay you?

MARQUISE: By absolute secrecy.

GABRIELLE: Can you doubt me?

MARQUISE: If I had the slightest doubt, I wouldn't be doing this.

GABRIELLE: (*Hugs her.*) Thank you, Madame.

MARQUISE: Hurry now, you have no time to waste. (GABRIELLE *goes out right, followed by* MARIETTE.) The Duke should be on his way soon to storm the fortress. He'll find it won't be easy. (*Rings for* SERVANT, *who appears.*) See that every door and window is securely locked.

SERVANT: I have already seen to that, Madame.

MARQUISE: Good. Admit no one tonight. No one! Look out the window and see if anyone is in the street.

SERVANT: (*At window*) There's a man down there. He's coming to the door. He's trying to open it. Now he's going away. There's another man standing below the window.

MARQUISE: You may go now. (SERVANT *goes out.*) My dear Duke won't get in tonight. He'll be chilled to the bone before the night is over. It's very satisfying to do a good deed and get revenge on a cold lover at the same time. And I haven't broken my word. I left Gabrielle at ten o'clock, and Gabrielle is accounted for between ten and midnight. (*She rubs her hands and grins.*) It's been a good day.

(MARIETTE *runs in, very excited.*)

MARIETTE: Madame! Madame! You said the Duke left his key in Paris. But he just came in by the secret door. I saw him from the top of the stairs and I ran here as fast as I could. He's coming up now.

MARQUISE: That calls for new strategy. Turn out every light, Mariette. Go to your room quickly and don't make a sound.

(*She goes out as* MARIETTE *puts out the candles and then dashes out. There is a moment of silence before the* DUKE *enters at right.*)

DUKE: Luckily, I got the key to the secret door in time. Otherwise that witch of a Marquise would have locked me out. Everything is dark. That's the way I like it. (*Calling.*) Gabrielle!

VOICE: In the bedroom!

DUKE: Ah! In the bedroom! That's the way I like it. (*Goes to window.*) There he is—or perhaps it's a friend of his. (*Calling, in half-whisper*) Monsieur—if you're Lieutenant Sevran, or if you know him—here is a note for him. Tell him exactly where and how you got it. (*He drops the note.*) And now to my fair lady's bedroom for the important work of the evening. (*He tiptoes out center and down hall to left.*)

Blackout

SCENE 5

Same as first four scenes. Early next morning. (SERVANT *and* SEVRAN *are discovered at door.*)

SERVANT: But Lieutenant, it's only seven o'clock. Nobody is up yet.

SEVRAN: That doesn't matter—I'll wait. I must speak to Mademoiselle de Belle-Isle as soon as she awakens.

(*The* SERVANT *leaves.* SEVRAN *paces.* GABRIELLE *comes in from left.*)

GABRIELLE: I'm awake, Raoul, and I was expecting you. I'm so happy to see you, Raoul.

SEVRAN: As happy to see me as you were anxious to get rid of me last night.

GABRIELLE: Is your head still full of silly suspicions?

SEVRAN: What do you expect? I can't help thinking how you suddenly became so tired last night.

GABRIELLE: What are you thinking? What's come over you?

SEVRAN: Nothing has come over me. I'm glad to see you so happy this morning. Did you perhaps find some new source of joy?

GABRIELLE: I had a beautiful dream. I dreamed that a magic carpet carried me to the Bastille, right into my father's cell. I kissed him, I hugged him, and I talked to him for hours. He spoke about you, saying that the thought of our marriage was the only thing that gave him consolation.

SEVRAN: I had a dream too—but mine was a nightmare.

GABRIELLE: What was it?

SEVRAN: I dreamed that you met the Duke de Richelieu—in spite of your promise to me.

GABRIELLE: I'm sorry that you had such a dream.

SEVRAN: You told me your dream, so I told you mine.

GABRIELLE: But yours was a ridiculous dream.

SEVRAN: But very vivid. I dreamed I was in the street below this window when a man opened it and threw me a note. And to prove that my dream was even more real than yours, here is the note which I found in my bed when I woke up this morning.

GABRIELLE: A note?

SEVRAN: Read it!

GABRIELLE: "I'm in Gabrielle's apartment. I will tell you tomorrow what time I left. Duke de Richelieu." What does this mean?

SEVRAN: It means that yesterday the Duke made a revolting bet with me—and it means that last night he won the bet.

GABRIELLE: I don't understand a word you're saying.

SEVRAN: I'll make you understand. The Duke came here soon after I left. He was with you in this room. He opened the window and threw me this note. Now do you understand?

GABRIELLE: What are you really trying to tell me?

SEVRAN: What you already know, that's all—except that you were unaware that I knew everything that was going on. I waited until dawn but I never saw the Duke leave. I tried every window and door to see if I could force my way in. Luckily they were all barred. I'm sure I would have killed you both if I could have found you.

GABRIELLE: You must be insane to say such things. You say I spent the night with the Duke?

SEVRAN: Yes.

GABRIELLE: Are you Raoul? Am I Gabrielle? Are you speaking like that to your fiancée?

SEVRAN: I don't want to believe it. I would gladly say my eyes deceived me. But how can I deny the existence of this note? How can you explain it?

GABRIELLE: I can't explain it—even to myself. Someone must have been here at this window, but it has nothing to do with me.

SEVRAN: A man came in without your knowing it? The doors were locked and guarded by servants. If anyone came in it was because he was invited to come in.

GABRIELLE: I don't know what happened.

SEVRAN: I'll tell you. Because of your great desire to have your father released, you didn't dare refuse the Duke whatever he wanted.

GABRIELLE: Raoul!

SEVRAN: You had to choose between loyalty to me and submission to him—and you made your choice.

GABRIELLE: You believe that?

SEVRAN: Yes! But I'm not judging you. I pardon you, because I know the choice wasn't easy to make.

GABRIELLE: Thank you. But I don't accept your pardon because I did nothing wrong. If I had been with the Duke last night—after giving you my word that I would not see him—I wouldn't be worthy of your love or your pardon. I would not want you to have me for your wife.

SEVRAN: I want to believe you, but how can I?

GABRIELLE: But you must. I did not see the Duke last night! It will be simple enough to prove it.

SEVRAN: How?

GABRIELLE: You say that note is from the Duke?

SEVRAN: It's his handwriting—and I heard his voice at the window.

GABRIELLE: We'll call the Duke. You can hide somewhere and listen to what he says. If he declares that he saw me after five o'clock yesterday afternoon, you can believe whatever you like.

SEVRAN: Since it's your idea, I'll do it. I want to believe you.

GABRIELLE: Then believe.

SEVRAN: But you'll admit there is something mysterious about all this.

GABRIELLE: We'll solve the mystery. Then you'll see how silly this has all been.

(*She goes to him and holds him.*)

SEVRAN: I don't believe you could possibly have deceived me.

GABRIELLE: Of course not.

(*They embrace again.*)

SERVANT: (*Entering*) The Duke de Richelieu.

GABRIELLE: Heaven sent him. Now hide! Go behind the cabinet in the corridor. You can hear everything. Promise not to come out. (*He rushes into corridor and left.*) Have the Duke come in. (SERVANT *leaves and* DUKE *enters.*) You don't know how glad I am to see you.

DUKE: And I'm glad to see you, and in good voice. I didn't expect to see you up so early, and so full of vitality.

GABRIELLE: As a matter of fact, I was about to send for you.

DUKE: Yes? Then I've reached the summit of success.

GABRIELLE: Please! I have a very serious question to ask you, and the answer will touch on my honor.

DUKE: Your honor? Who would besmirch your honor? Tell me his name and I'll deal with him.

GABRIELLE: There is no one to be punished. I'm speaking of a bet that you made yesterday.

DUKE: Oh, that? I'm sorry that you learned of it, but I'll explain. I loved you very much before the bet. Ever since I saw you in Paris I've been following you. The bet was made before a group of men. You were not the object of it—your name was not even mentioned. The bet involved the first woman who passed. You happened to be the first. I wish it could have been someone else. But my honor was at stake. Unfortunately, my honor was at odds with my love. That's the whole truth. If I did wrong, I'm sorry, and I hope you will pardon me.

GABRIELLE: I willingly pardon you the bet, but I refuse to pardon any effort you might be making to maintain your amorous reputation.

DUKE: What do you mean?

GABRIELLE: By insinuating that you succeeded in winning your bet.

DUKE: Insinuating?

GABRIELLE: I used a mild word. I should have said "lying." Explain why you wrote this note and threw it from this window last night. Here—read it!

DUKE: No need. I know its contents.

GABRIELLE: What? You know?

DUKE: Isn't it my handwriting?

GABRIELLE: You wrote this?

DUKE: I can't deny it.

GABRIELLE: And you threw it from this window?

DUKE: Yes—from that window.

GABRIELLE: Then you were in this room?

DUKE: Naturally.

GABRIELLE: But you did not see me.

DUKE: What do you mean—I didn't see you? (*A slight pause, then laughs*) Oh! You mean that the lights were out? True, true—I didn't see you, but—

GABRIELLE: Don't play with words. I mean that you were not near me after I spoke to you about five o'clock in the afternoon in the presence of the Marquise.

DUKE: I was not near you? My dear, we were as one from eleven o'clock until—I have no idea what time it was.

GABRIELLE: You're lying.

DUKE: I'm lying?

GABRIELLE: Yes! You're telling a wicked, horrible lie.

DUKE: Pardon me, Gabrielle, but when a woman speaks like that, there is nothing to do but leave.

(*He starts out.*)

GABRIELLE: Oh, no! You're not getting out so easy. Just because you're the Duke de Richelieu, you can't heap dishonor on a girl just to prove to your friends that you won a filthy bet.

DUKE: I care nothing about that bet.

GABRIELLE: Then why lie? Is your reputation as a great lover more precious to you than being a man? Isn't there some honesty in you? A little dignity? Tell the truth! You sneaked in here—I don't know how—and you threw that note out the window. But you did not see me or talk to me. Tell the truth!

DUKE: I'm afraid the truth is not what you want. But I'll say anything you want me to say. Do you want me to write to your lieutenant? I'll tell him I was lying. I'll tell him I lost the bet and I'll pay him the thousand. I'll do whatever you like—and lie—any fabrication.

GABRIELLE: There's something infernal in what you're saying. I didn't know perversity could go so far. I want no lies, I want no stories—I want the truth—the simple truth. Tell me the truth and I'll pardon you for all the pain you've caused me.

DUKE: (*Drawing* GABRIELLE *downstage and in stage whisper*) I've been an idiot. I'm sorry! Why didn't you give me a sign that someone was listening? I understand now. Don't worry—I know just what to say now.

GABRIELLE: (*Exploding*) No one is listening! No one is hidden! Say it to me! There is no one here but me!

DUKE: Very well, my dear, since there is no one here but you, I'll tell you that I thought I knew something about women, but I was a complete fool. Just when I think I have nothing more to learn, they teach me something new. And last night, Gabrielle, you had the honor of giving me the most complete, the most original, the most invigorating lesson I have ever received.

(*He beams as he tries to embrace her.*)

GABRIELLE: (*Repulsing him violently.*) Get out of here! Get out of here at once!

DUKE: I obey. But I haven't lost hope. I'll be here tonight at the same time as last night. I'm afraid your mornings are not your best time.

(*He bows and leaves.*)

GABRIELLE: Oh, my God! My God!

SEVRAN: (*Coming in.*) Well, I did what you said. I hid—I listened—and I heard. Are you satisfied?

(SEVRAN *crosses to leave*)

GABRIELLE: (*Trying to stop him.*) Raoul!

SEVRAN: Let me go!

GABRIELLE: Raoul—listen. You can't leave like this. I can't blame you for your suspicions, but there is something frightful working against me—a terrible trick of fate. Raoul, you don't believe I could become a low, vulgar woman overnight.

SEVRAN: What do you want me to believe? The Duke was in this room.

GABRIELLE: I can't deny that.

SEVRAN: From here he went to your bedroom.

GABRIELLE: Perhaps.

SEVRAN: Perhaps? You're not sure? You were not in the bedroom?

GABRIELLE: No.

SEVRAN: Then where were you?

GABRIELLE: I can't tell you. I made a solemn oath. I can tell you nothing.

SEVRAN: There must be someone who can release you from your oath—out of pity for us both.

GABRIELLE: You are right. When she sees what terrible accusations are being thrown at me, she will allow me to tell everything. You will see—you will see. (*She rings and* SERVANT *appears.*) Where is Madame the Marquise? I must speak to her.

SERVANT: She left for Paris this morning with the Duke de Bourbon, and she will not return until this evening.

(SERVANT *exits.*)

GABRIELLE: What bad luck! Nothing goes right. It's very strange, Raoul, I know, but wait until this evening and you'll know everything. (*He starts to leave.*) Raoul, don't go.

SEVRAN: You are right—everything is strange. Yesterday at noon you left the hotel, last night I found you here but you insisted that I leave. I made you swear you would not see the Duke, yet he was in this room. You admit he could have spent the night in your bedroom, but you say that *you* were not in your bedroom. Yet you can't tell me where you were. You swore a sacred oath, you say, and the one person who can release you from your oath has left town. Yes, it's all very strange—too strange to believe—and I refuse to believe it!

GABRIELLE: What can I say? Everything is against me. What will happen to me, I don't know. But it won't be as frightful as what would happen to others if I broke my oath.

SEVRAN: But Gabrielle, what do you expect me to think?

GABRIELLE: Follow your own convictions, Raoul. I won't detain you any longer.

(SEVRAN *starts to leave.* GABRIELLE *falls into a chair. He turns back.*)

SEVRAN: Listen, Gabrielle, I know that the Duke uses any means to get what he wants. Admit that he used force or that he gave you some sort of narcotic. Admit that, and it will not change my love for you. I will kill him, that's all. Tell me something I can understand and believe, but don't talk to me of a sacred oath. I want to believe you, I want to trust you, I want to love you. If you don't want me to lose my mind, tell me something I can believe.

GABRIELLE: (*Weakly.*) I can't tell you more than I have. I was not in that bedroom. I did not see the Duke de Richelieu between five o'clock yesterday afternoon and this morning.

SEVRAN: Again! I'm tired of hearing that. I know what I must do now.

(*He starts out, she tries to hold him.*)

GABRIELLE: Please!

SEVRAN: Let me go! Let me go!

GABRIELLE: Raoul!

SEVRAN: One last time—do you want to tell me the truth?

GABRIELLE: There's nothing more I can tell you.

SEVRAN: Then heaven forgive you. But one thing I know—I never will!

(*He goes out.*)

GABRIELLE: (*Collapsing in chair.*) Please, God—help me!

Blackout

SCENE 6

A gaming room adjoining the ballroom of the chateau. In the ballroom there is music and dancing. Several people including D'AUMONT, CHAMBLAY, CHAMILLAC *are at a table playing a card game. The* MARQUISE *and the* DUKE *are strolling and conversing.*

DUKE: There's nothing much to tell, I give you my word. There was no struggle. She was in bed and I joined her, that's all. I left at three or four o'clock this morning. Of course there are some exquisite details which I am omitting for fear they might excite you unduly.

MARQUISE: But how did you enter the chateau?

DUKE: By your secret door.

MARQUISE: But you gave me your word that the key was in Paris.

DUKE: It was. You can be sure of that.

MARQUISE: You sent for it?

DUKE: Yes. And it cost me two of my best horses.

MARQUISE: A plague on both your horses. I'm not a bit sorry.

DUKE: I have no regrets. Last night was worth a stable of horses.

MARQUISE: Those are words I'm going to remember all my life. And now, my dear Duke, I have a little story to tell *you*.

(She is grinning widely.)

DUKE: Wait—I haven't finished.

MARQUISE: Then finish.

DUKE: You haven't heard the best part.

MARQUISE: I can't imagine what more you can add.

DUKE: A great deal. Do you know the name of the man who bet against me?

MARQUISE: D'Aumont, I suppose.

DUKE: No, it was Lieutenant Sevran.

MARQUISE: Oh, that's a fairy story you're telling me.

DUKE: Not at all. And do you know why he wanted to take the bet?

MARQUISE: I can't imagine.

DUKE: Because Gabrielle is his fiancée and they were to be married in three days.

MARQUISE: No!

DUKE: It's true.

MARQUISE: I can't believe it.

DUKE: Word of honor.

MARQUISE: I knew I was being too kind to that girl. Imagine, sheltering an enemy in my own home.

DUKE: You see how foolish it was for you to try to make me lose my bet? Not only did I want to win, but I was helping you get revenge.

MARQUISE: So she's going to marry the lieutenant! The witch!

DUKE: It's partly due to your own generosity. The marriage was a long way off. The boy had no decent livelihood until you dropped a lieutenant's commission in his lap—and without even telling him he owed it to you. Gabrielle came here, not only to help her father, but to be near her husband-to-be. They would have been married secretly, three days from now, if I hadn't stirred things up last night. But you don't seem very grateful for what I did.

MARQUISE: I'm grateful, I assure you.

DUKE: I'm glad. But you said you had something to tell me—what was it?

MARQUISE: I have nothing to tell you now.

DUKE: Why not?

MARQUISE: It might change things, and I prefer the way matters stand right now. How did the lieutenant take last night's escapades?

DUKE: Very tragically, from all appearances.

MARQUISE: Really?

DUKE: He left his name at my apartment three times today, but I was out. So, I await developments. I'm sure they will materialize. (*Passes by* D'AUMONT) Are you having good luck, D'Aumont?

D'AUMONT: I have an atrocious hand.

DUKE: You know what they say: "Unlucky in cards, a devil with the women."

D'AUMONT: I lose in both games.

MARQUISE: You picked the wrong time to pity yourself, D'Aumont. Dance with me in the third quadrille.

D'AUMONT: Why not the first one?

MARQUISE: I'm engaged for the first two. (*To* CHAMBLAY.) Chamblay, give your cards to the Duke. I have something to tell you.

CHAMBLAY: (*To the* DUKE) Do you mind?

DUKE: It will be a pleasure. When you come back you will find D'Aumont beaten and happy—

(CHAMBLAY *gives his cards to* DUKE *and strolls off with* MARQUISE.)

CHAMBLAY: I'm delighted that you have something confidential to tell me.

MARQUISE: Don't let your self-love get carried away. It's not that kind of confidence. If you see Lieutenant Sevran come in—he's the young officer who arrived a few days ago—don't let him out of your sight.

CHAMBLAY: I met him yesterday. What's he done?

MARQUISE: Nothing yet—but I have reason to believe that he will try to provoke a duel with the Duke de Richelieu.

CHAMBLAY: Madame, you know it's my public duty to prevent duels, but the Duke de Richelieu causes me more trouble than all the other nobles in France put together.

MARQUISE: Small wonder—almost everyone wants to kill the Duke at some time or other.

CHAMBLAY: What is the cause of this duel you fear?

MARQUISE: I have no idea, but whatever it is, you must prevent it.

CHAMBLAY: I'll do what I can.

MARQUISE: That's all I have to tell you. Will you escort me to the ballroom?

(*They pass the table.*)

DUKE: Look, Chamblay—what I've won for you.

CHAMBLAY: Continue—continue.

(*He goes into ballroom with* MARQUISE.)

DUKE: I told you not to play against me, D'Aumont. I bring you bad luck.

D'AUMONT: I double the stakes.

DUKE: Good! Double!

(SEVRAN *enters, stands by door, sees* RICHELIEU.)

SEVRAN: At last!

DUKE: Oh, it's you, Lieutenant.

SEVRAN: I would like two words with you.

DUKE: Of course, Chamillac, will you take my hand? It's good. (CHA-MILLAC *takes his place as he rises and walks off with* SEVRAN.) At your service.

SEVRAN: I waited in the street until four this morning.

DUKE: I'm sorry—I didn't know. I left by a secret door on the other side of the chateau.

SEVRAN: I came by your apartment three times today.

DUKE: I know that. I'm sorry I was out all day.

SEVRAN: There's no need to tell you my reason for coming here.

DUKE: I can guess.

SEVRAN: You understand that it's a question of the honor of a young girl whose father is in the Bastille.

DUKE: I understand perfectly. I am at your orders.

(CHAMBLAY *enters and approaches cautiously.*)

SEVRAN: I would not like the cause of our fight to be known. I want no seconds or witnesses.

DUKE: I accept. Be at a certain place at a certain time. I will come there alone.

SEVRAN: The small woods by the Porte Royale, then.

DUKE: At what time?

SEVRAN: Eight in the morning, if that is agreeable to you.

DUKE: Perfect. And the arms?

SEVRAN: We must not attract notice. It must be swords.

DUKE: Tomorrow at eight, then, by the Porte Royale.

SEVRAN: Agreed.

CHAMBLAY: (*Striking shoulders of both men lightly with a black baton tipped in white*) In the name of the King, you are forbidden, under pain of imprisonment, to engage in combat with each other.

SEVRAN: He was listening.

DUKE: Chamblay, can't two men have a little discussion without being tapped by your little black stick?

CHAMBLAY: This is no joke, Duke. If you gentlemen have any grievances, a court will hear them—but you must give me your word that there will be no duel between you.

DUKE: It's not for me to answer first.

SEVRAN: Monsieur Chamblay, you have my word there will be no duel.

DUKE: You have mine too, then.

CHAMBLAY: Very well. I shall hold you to it.

(*A* SERVANT *enters and goes to* COUNT D'AUMONT.)

SERVANT: A courier from Paris wishes to speak to the Count D'Aumont immediately—on the part of his Majesty the King.

D'AUMONT: Gentlemen, will you allow me?

(*He rises.*)

CHAMILLAC: Why not? The service of the King before gambling.

(D'AUMONT *follows the* SERVANT *out.*)

DUKE: Lieutenant, I'm terribly sorry.

SEVRAN: Do you think everything is settled?

DUKE: But we gave our word.

SEVRAN: Not to fight. But if a man is to avenge an insult, there are a thousand ways. The only requirement is that his adversary must be loyal enough to accept defeat if it comes to him.

DUKE: I flatter myself on being that kind of adversary. Name your terms.

SEVRAN: We will take the dice. Each of us will have three rolls. The one with the largest total is the winner.

DUKE: That sounds simple. What about the loser?

SEVRAN: The loser blows out his brains. In that sort of duel the law cannot interfere.

DUKE: Very ingenious to say the least.

SEVRAN: Do you hesitate?

DUKE: It's a very unusual proposition.

SEVRAN: You refuse, then?

DUKE: No, but I'm thinking it over.

SEVRAN: Are you waiting for someone to come to your rescue again?

DUKE: I am waiting for no one! I accept.

SEVRAN: Good! I expected that you would.

DUKE: But I ask for eight hours interval in case I lose. I always like to arrange a few things when I expect to be gone for a long time.

SEVRAN: Eight hours—so be it.

(*They approach the dice table.*)

DUKE: Enchanted to join the group.

CHAMBLAY: So you're going to play dice? That's more reasonable.

DUKE: Yes, we're going to have a few throws. Would you like half of my bet, Chamblay?

CHAMBLAY: But you're not putting up any money.

SEVRAN: No, we're playing on our word. Your throw, Duke.

DUKE: You first—I insist.

CHAMBLAY: I'll bet fifty on Richelieu.

CHAMILLAC: I take it.

(SEVRAN *throws the dice.*)

SEVRAN: Five!

DUKE: (*Throwing dice*) Eight!

CHAMILLAC: I lose, but I want revenge.

CHAMBLAY: Are you gentlemen continuing?

DUKE: Yes.

SEVRAN: You won the first throw, Duke, so you can go first.

DUKE: I accept. It will bring you luck. (*He throws*) Nine!

SEVRAN: Chamillac, you may have done wrong to bet on me again. (*He throws dice.*) Eleven! No, I was mistaken.

CHAMILLAC: We're even, Chamblay. Once more.

DUKE: Your throw, lieutenant.

SEVRAN: (*Throwing*) Seven!

DUKE: (*Throwing*) Seven!

CHAMBLAY: Dead throw! Try again.

SEVRAN: (*Throwing*) Nine!

DUKE: (*Throwing*) Eleven!

SEVRAN: (*Rises and walks away.*) I lose.

CHAMILLAC: There's your fifty, Chamblay.

(CHAMILLAC *and* CHAMBLAY *exit into ballroom.*)

DUKE: Lieutenant, I hope you're not going to take that ridiculous game seriously.

SEVRAN: Why not?

DUKE: It's impossible to carry out such terms.

SEVRAN: If you thought it was impossible, you shouldn't have accepted it.

DUKE: I know, but if I had lost, I—

SEVRAN: You would have kept your word, just as I am going to keep mine. This is not a gambling debt, it's a debt of honor.

DUKE: But I beg you to forget the whole thing. In a few days nothing will seem as serious as it seems now.

SEVRAN: All I know is that my life has been torn apart since you walked into it. By eight o'clock tomorrow morning you will be paid according to contract.

(*He starts out.*)

DUKE: You are completely mad if you go through with this. (SEVRAN *turns, clicks his heels and goes out.*) Don't lose your head.

(D'AUMONT *enters*.)

D'AUMONT: A lot of people are losing their heads in Paris.

DUKE: What happened?

D'AUMONT: I just got the news. A complete chaos in the cabinet. Bishop Fleury has been named first minister.

DUKE: And the Duke de Bourbon?

D'AUMONT: Arrested. And that's not all. I received an order which exiles the Marquise de Prie to her estate.

DUKE: Why was the order sent to you?

D'AUMONT: As Captain of the Guards, I am to conduct her.

DUKE: How much time does she have?

D'AUMONT: Not a minute.

DUKE: Here she comes now. She has this dance with you.

D'AUMONT: I wish I were a hundred feet underground.

MARQUISE: What are you doing here, D'Aumont? I'm waiting to dance with you.

DUKE: What is he doing? Ask him rather what he intends to do. I'm convinced he can't make up his mind.

MARQUISE: What do you mean?

D'AUMONT: Marquise, I am desperate at this moment. I am a very unhappy man.

MARQUISE: You? Unhappy? Why?

D'AUMONT: Marquise, whatever happens, count on me as one of your friends.

MARQUISE: But what has happened?

D'AUMONT: You know it is impossible to disobey the King.

MARQUISE: Who is thinking of disobeying the King?

DUKE: This poor D'Aumont would like nothing better, but he's forced to carry out the order he received.

D'AUMONT: Please don't be frightened, Madame. It will be only a temporary disgrace.

MARQUISE: You're going to kill me with all your preparation. I have courage—tell me what you have to say.

DUKE: I'll tell you. The Duke de Bourbon has been arrested.

MARQUISE: And as the first minister goes, so goes his favorite Marquise.

DUKE: That is right. You've been exiled to your estate. D'Aumont must conduct you immediately.

D'AUMONT: Here is the order.

MARQUISE: Good God! The King's signature. Could I write to him?

DUKE: What good would it do? The new first minister would intercept it.

MARQUISE: Then I'll write to the Queen.

DUKE: That's different.

MARQUISE: She will remember that I helped her when she was in exile. But who will deliver my letter?

DUKE: I will, and in person.

MARQUISE: Thank you, Duke. Please find me a pen and some paper. D'Aumont, it's good of you to allow me this time.

D'AUMONT: I'm at your service, Madame the Marquise.

(DUKE *returns with pen and paper, puts it on table, and* MARQUISE *writes hurriedly.*)

DUKE: Don't be nervous—lean against me. (*She tries to steady herself but her hand trembles.*) Here—let me hold the paper steady. (*Leans over her to hold the paper, looks at the letter.*) That handwriting!

MARQUISE: What?

DUKE: Is that your handwriting?

MARQUISE: Of course it is—can't you see?

DUKE: But—but—wait a moment. (*He takes* GABRIELLE's *two letters from his pocket.*) These letters were not written by Gabrielle, they were written by you.

MARQUISE: Yes, they were.

DUKE: If they were from you, then who was in bed last night—that I thought was Gabrielle?

MARQUISE: Ungrateful wretch! After the finest performance of my career.

DUKE: It's not true.

MARQUISE: But it is.

DUKE: I can't believe it. I must have proof. (*The* MARQUISE *whispers in his ear.*) Yes—it was you! Good God! There's no time to lose.

(*He starts out.*)

MARQUISE: But my letter! Wait for my letter!

DUKE: Leave your letter here for me. There's no time now. Within eight hours, one of the bravest men in France is going to blow his brains out and you will be to blame if I don't arrive in time.

MARQUISE: He's gone mad!

(*Returns to her writing*)

CHAMBLAY: Pardon me, Duke, but I am forced to ask for your sword.

DUKE: Why?

CHAMBLAY: Order of his Majesty the King.

DUKE: I'm a prisoner.

CHAMBLAY: Ordered immediately to Paris by the King in order to give his Majesty full explanation of your conduct.

DUKE: Madame the Marquise, if anything happens to that young man I will never forgive you as long as I live.

(*He goes out with Chamblay.*)

Blackout

SCENE 7

The apartment of the MARQUISE *again. Next morning.* GABRIELLE *is at the desk, finishing a letter. The* SERVANT *stands near her.*

GABRIELLE: Do you remember Lieutenant Sevran who has been here twice in the last two days?

SERVANT: Very well.

GABRIELLE: Please, look for him until you find him. Give him this letter and bring him here. And before you go, send Mariette in.

SERVANT: She's not here. She left last night with Madame the Marquise.

GABRIELLE: Madame is not in the chateau?

SERVANT: She left with Monsieur the Count D'Aumont last night before the ball was over.

GABRIELLE: When will she return?

SERVANT: I have no idea. I'll let you know when I find out.

GABRIELLE: But first find the lieutenant—that's most important.

(SERVANT *starts out but returns quickly.*)

SERVANT: Someone to see you, Mademoiselle.

GABRIELLE: I'm not seeing anyone.

SERVANT: (*Smiling.*) But it's the lieutenant.

GABRIELLE: Have him come in. And let me know the moment Madame returns. (SEVRAN *appears.*) Come in, Raoul, I was writing to you, and I was waiting for you, but I didn't expect to see you.

SEVRAN: An unforeseen circumstance led me here.

GABRIELLE: Whatever the circumstance, you are welcome, my dear Raoul.

SEVRAN: I came to ask a favor.

GABRIELLE: Please ask.

SEVRAN: You know I have only you, Gabrielle. My mother and father are dead. I have no brothers or sisters. I have some papers of certain importance that I would like to leave in your hands.

GABRIELLE: But why can't you keep these papers yourself?

SEVRAN: Because they concern what little fortune I possess. I am leaving, and I want them to be safe.

GABRIELLE: You are leaving?

SEVRAN: Yes, I am separating myself from you. It may be a long time—a very long time.

GABRIELLE: What are you telling me?

SEVRAN: I don't want to frighten you, but you know the uncertainties of life. We've had only too many of them during the last two days. When misfortune strikes again, I want to be prepared and resolute.

GABRIELLE: Do you think you are the only one who suffers? Your accusations yesterday were like knives in my heart.

SEVRAN: I know, and before leaving, I want you to forgive me for the way I spoke yesterday. I've loved you for four years, Gabrielle, and it wasn't easy to see a dream of four years broken to bits. But I thought to myself—when I die, she'll think I died with a heart full of reproaches, and that will torment her for the rest of her life. That's why I came here, to leave you my last testament, and to take leave of you—not as your fiancé, but simply as your brother.

GABRIELLE: Raoul, someday you will bitterly regret those words.

SEVRAN: Would you rather that I left you thinking I was full of hate? Wouldn't you prefer to know that I had pardoned you?

GABRIELLE: Pardoned me for what: Listen to me once more, Raoul. I swear on my mother's memory, on my father's life, that I have done nothing wrong.

SEVRAN: You told me that before, but things have gone too far now. Didn't I hear the Duke's words when I was hidden?

GABRIELLE: I know, I know—but in spite of what the Duke said, he is either lying or he is the victim of some horrible misunderstanding, just as I am. Listen to me, Raoul—

SEVRAN: I'm listening.

GABRIELLE: It's wrong for me to tell you this—but that night—when the Duke pretended he was with me—I was not even in the chateau.

SEVRAN: You didn't spend the night in the chateau?

GABRIELLE: No! I left at ten o'clock and returned at five in the morning.

SEVRAN: But where were you all night, in heaven's name? Where were you?

GABRIELLE: That is what I cannot tell you. Only Madame de Prie can tell you that. I've already told you part of what I promised not to reveal. The rest I simply can't tell you.

SEVRAN: You were not here?

GABRIELLE: I told you—it's true. You must wait until the Marquise comes back. She will tell you the true facts.

SEVRAN: You are grasping for straws, Gabrielle. You know very well you will not see the Marquise again.

GABRIELLE: Why not?

SEVRAN: She was taken away last night—banished to her estate.

GABRIELLE: Banished? But why?

SEVRAN: The Duke de Bourbon was dismissed and arrested—it was only to be expected that she also would be disgraced.

GABRIELLE: Do you mean the Duke de Bourbon is no longer first minister?

SEVRAN: Not since yesterday. But you know these things as well as I do.

GABRIELLE: How could I know? I've been closed up in this house for two days like a recluse. Raoul—on your honor—is the Duke de Bourbon no longer first minister?

SEVRAN: Why would I make up such a story? The Duke de Bourbon is in prison.

GABRIELLE: Raoul! We're saved!

(*She rushes to him, embraces him.*)

SEVRAN: What's come over you? What do you mean "saved"?

GABRIELLE: Don't you understand? The night before last! Oh, I'm so happy!

SEVRAN: What about the night before last?

GABRIELLE: That night the Marquise gave me a letter to the governor of the Bastille, put me in a carriage and sent me to Paris. I left at ten o'clock, spent three hours with my father, and was back here at five o'clock in the morning.

SEVRAN: You spent three hours in the Bastille?

GABRIELLE: Raoul—my own father will swear on his gray head that I'm telling the truth.

SEVRAN: You don't have to say that.

GABRIELLE: Now you understand why I was in such a hurry to have you leave when you came to see me. My carriage was waiting. And I couldn't explain anything to you because I gave my word to the Marquise that as long as the Duke de Bourbon was in power I would never mention that I went to the Bastille, or it might cause my father's death.

SEVRAN: I see.

GABRIELLE: But now the Duke de Bourbon is gone and my father will be free and I can tell you everything.

SEVRAN: My dear Gabrielle.

GABRIELLE: Yes—"my dear Gabrielle." Your dear Gabrielle is now the judge and you are the defendant. Remember those false accusations? Remember the rude remarks you made? Remember the frightful things you said? Now it's your turn to ask for pardon.

SEVRAN: Will you pardon me?

GABRIELLE: I'll consider it.

SEVRAN: Please, pardon me.

GABRIELLE: I pardon you! I can't blame you for believing what you did. The evidence was getting so substantial that I was beginning to believe it myself.

SEVRAN: Yes, I've been thinking about that evidence. The Duke swears he spent the night with someone.

GABRIELLE: It might have been the Queen of Sheba but it wasn't me.

SEVRAN: I think he was lying, and he was diabolically convincing.

GABRIELLE: I've never known such a liar.

SEVRAN: He'll pay for it! And he must pay for it before eight o'clock. I have thirty minutes.

(*He starts out.*)

GABRIELLE: Raoul, I don't understand. I'm here—everything is clarified now. Why do you think about that terrible man? Forget him, as I have. We'll be married, we'll go back to Brittany, and we'll be happy.

SEVRAN: Gabrielle, it's your turn not to understand. Let me find the Duke before eight o'clock.

(GABRIELLE *stands between him and the door.*)

GABRIELLE: You're not leaving! Raoul! I don't know what you're talking about or what you want to do, but you're not leaving. I'll call for help! I'll scream!

SEVRAN: Do you know that if I hadn't come here this morning, I would have been dead by eight o'clock?

GABRIELLE: Dead?

SEVRAN: Yes! I would have put a bullet in my own head, but in reality it would have been the Duke de Richelieu who was assassinating me.

GABRIELLE: What are you talking about?

SEVRAN: Last night I provoked a duel with the Duke but we were stopped by an officer of the King. Then I offered to play his life against mine on three rolls of the dice.

GABRIELLE: Raoul! Is that all you think of your life?

SEVRAN: It was an affair of honor. And I lost.

GABRIELLE: Oh!

SEVRAN: I have until eight o'clock to pay my debt. That's why I must kill him. If I don't, he'll tell the world that I was a coward.

GABRIELLE: Raoul, why do you silly men always give only half of your heart to love and the other half to pride? You're not going to shoot yourself, and you're not going to kill the Duke. If he had lost the bet, do you think he would have shot himself?

SEVRAN: Yes, I think he would have.

GABRIELLE: Not while there are so many women waiting to be seduced. The Duke would have laughed it off as a joke, and that's what you must do.

SEVRAN: But it's no joke.

GABRIELLE: It is now! When we see the Duke again, we'll tell him the facts about that night. He can't possibly carry on his lies any longer.

SEVRAN: That won't remedy the terrible damage he has done.

DUKE'S VOICE: (*offstage*) Lieutenant Sevran! Are you there?

SEVRAN: There is justice in the world! He came just in time. Now, you are the one who is going to hide and listen.

GABRIELLE: In the name of heaven, Raoul, promise you won't do anything rash.

(*She goes into door at left.*)

DUKE: (*Just outside entrance.*) I tell you he's in there and I want to see him.

(*He bounds into room. He is wearing boots and is covered with dust, perspiring, with hair in disorder.*)

SEVRAN: At last! I have you!

(*Pulls out his sword.*)

DUKE: Yes, and you don't know how happy that makes me. And put away that sword before you make the most idiotic mistake of your life.

SEVRAN: You lied to me and you lied to Gabrielle.

DUKE: I know I lied.

SEVRAN: And you'll pay for it.

DUKE: I have paid for it! I rode twenty-five miles on horseback to tell you that I know I lied. I would have told you six hours ago if I hadn't been arrested and hauled off to Paris. Fortunately I was able to speak to the King and justify myself.

SEVRAN: So you admit you lied? Do you think that admission makes you blameless?

DUKE: But you're not understanding me. I lied, but I didn't know I was lying—I thought I was telling you the truth. But now I am speaking the truth, and the truth is that I know I was telling brazen lies—but innocent lies—because I didn't know they were lies—and at the time I was stupidly convinced that I was telling the simple truth and nothing but the truth. (*A slight pause.*) Do I make myself clear?

SEVRAN: No!

DUKE: I was duped, hoodwinked, hoaxed, made a fool of by the Marquise de Prie.

SEVRAN: What has the Marquise to do with this?

DUKE: She decided to make me lose that ridiculous bet I made with you. The letters I thought were from Gabrielle were from the Marquise. And the woman in bed—that I thought was Gabrielle—was the Marquise. She fooled me most shamelessly. (*He groans.*) You have no idea how she fooled me! (*Pause.*) But it was delightful at the time. That's what made me such a lecherous liar.

SEVRAN: I begin to understand.

DUKE: It's about time. Your Gabrielle is as pure as an angel—at least as far as I am concerned. You must take me to her so I can hear her pardon from my own lips, because I insulted her, and I am deeply ashamed and repentant.

(GABRIELLE *appears.*)

GABRIELLE: Monsieur the Duke, everything is said—everything is finished. You have a noble heart. Raoul and I have much happiness to share. (*She embraces* RAOUL *and then says to* DUKE) Do you know that this poor fellow was going to kill himself?

DUKE: How could anyone be so damned noble? Yes, that was the bet I won. But I lost the other one and I owe you a thousand.

SEVRAN: I won't hear of it. I consider that we're even.

DUKE: At least I may presume that peace is established?

SEVRAN: (*Presenting* GABRIELLE.) Mademoiselle de Belle-Isle, my wife. (*Presenting the* DUKE.) The Duke de Richelieu, my best friend. (GABRIELLE *hugs them both.*)

Blackout

The End

Kean
OR
Disorder and Genius

ABOUT THE PLAY

Edmund Kean was born in 1789, the illegitimate son of an apprentice architect and an itinerant actress. The infant Kean was looked after by his uncle's mistress after the mother had abandoned him and the father had committed suicide during an alcoholic mania. Both sides of his family had theatrical backgrounds, and his aunt gave him a thorough training in theatre. His mother reclaimed him when he was eight, and he followed the lowest of careers with her, working in circuses and barns, and doing acrobatics as well as acting. By the time he was fourteen he was a young prodigy, but adult success did not come easily. It was achieved finally in 1814 when Kean portrayed Shylock at Drury Lane.

From then on Kean was the most famous actor in England, perhaps in the world. He triumphed as Richard III, Lear, Macbeth, and Othello. It was as Othello that he made his last appearance, opposite his son Charles, struggling through the third act and saying: "I am dying—speak to them for me." He died later that year, 1833.

It was of Kean, who had splashed deeply into drink and debauchery during his life, that Coleridge said: "To see him was like reading Shakespeare by flashes of lightning."

Three years after the death of Kean, Alexandre Dumas the elder wrote his play. It was an immediate triumph and a lasting milestone in French theater. Though the setting of *Kean* is English, Dumas put much of himself into the role of Kean, making him much more French than in real life. Dumas's violent onslaught on the critics in *Kean* was based on his own quarrels with the gentlemen of the press. Parisian critics did not forget Dumas's accusations. His next play, *Charles VII,* was deliberately panned, but Dumas had the last word when the play was performed at the Comédie-Française several years later.

In all fairness, it must be stated that all critics did not turn against Dumas. One of the most famous, Theophile Gautier, wrote that "the life of a critic would not be so intolerable if he could always review plays of papa Dumas."

Characters

ELENA, *Countess Koefeld, wife of the Danish Ambassador*
A SERVANT
AMY, *Countess of Gossville*
COUNT KOEFELD, *Danish Ambassador to England*
PRINCE OF WALES
EDMUND KEAN
SOLOMON, *Kean's prompter*
PISTOL, *a young acrobat*
TOM, *an actor*
DAVID, *an actor*
BARDOLPH, *an actor*
ANNA DAMBY, *a young heiress*
JOHN COOK, *a sailor*
FIRST DRINKER
SECOND DRINKER
THIRD DRINKER
PETER PATT, *a tavern owner*
LORD MELVILLE
CONSTABLE
KITTY
Various members of the acrobatic troupe
WINE BOY, *employee at the tavern*
WAITER, *at the tavern*
DARIUS, *wigmaker at the theatre*
STAGE MANAGER, *at the theatre*
JULIET, *actress*
NURSE, *actress*
MERCUTIO, *actor*
CAPULET, *actor*
GIDSA, *Elena's maid*

The play takes place in London in 1820.

ACT I: A salon in the Danish Embassy, London
ACT II: A room in Kean's home

ACT III: The Coal Bin, a waterfront tavern
ACT IV, Scene 1: Kean's dressing room in Covent Garden
Scene 2: The stage of Covent Garden
ACT V: Kean's home, same as Act II

Act I

A salon in the Danish Embassy in London. A door where guests appear, another door to dining rooms. COUNTESS ELENA KOEFELD *is seated, writing, and at same time giving instructions to a servant.*

ELENA: Have you prepared the card tables?

SERVANT: Yes, Countess. Two for whist—one for Boston.

ELENA: And you have notified the musicians?

SERVANT: They will arrive at nine-thirty.

ELENA: Very well. And of course, the punch, and the tea, and—

SERVANT: All taken care of—and cigars for the gentlemen.

ELENA: Very good. But please don't stray far away during the evening.

(SERVANT *goes out, returns immediately, followed by* AMY.)

SERVANT: The Countess of Gossville.

(*He exits.*)

ELENA: Oh, come in, come in. How are you, dear? It was lovely of you to come early. I have so many things to tell you. We scarcely see each other any longer.

AMY: (*Simpering*) Yes, isn't it miraculous that I contrived to arrive before anyone? At least we'll have half an hour of chatter. And I have a thousand things to tell you, my fascinating Venetian, because you know quite well that wherever one sees my blue eyes, or your bewitching brown eyes, one can always find the latest and the best of whatever is going on in the parlors of London.

79

ELENA: Of course that could mean that white neck, those dainty hands, that slender and supple body. You make me think of the words of our great poet, that England is a nest of swans in the middle of a vast pool. But see here, are you afraid our guests will descend on us? Sit down.

AMY: With pleasure, because I'm tired—terribly tired. (*She sits.*) There was a race at Newmarket and I couldn't resist going. I had to get up at ten in the morning, and when I commit such stupidities, it takes me all day to adjust. If it hadn't been for you, I wouldn't have dragged myself out tonight. What have you been doing?

ELENA: Nothing but making plans for this evening.

AMY: Didn't you go out last night?

ELENA: Yes—to Drury Lane.

AMY: What was playing?

ELENA: Hamlet.

AMY: Who was doing Hamlet? Young?

ELENA: No. Edmund Kean.

AMY: Why didn't you tell me? I would certainly have asked for a place.

ELENA: And I would have given it to you. Kean was really superb.

AMY: Superb?

ELENA: Sublime, I should have said.

AMY: What enthusiasm.

ELENA: Does that surprise you? You know we Italians have no half-emotions. We're unable to hide either hate or admiration.

AMY: Promise not to thrash me too hard, and I'll tell you something.

ELENA: Tell me.

AMY: Prepare to hear the most absurd thing that was ever invented.

ELENA: Tell me, please.

AMY: I really don't know how to tell you—it's so ridiculous.

ELENA: Good heavens—what is it?

AMY: No one can hear us?

ELENA: Do you know you're frightening me? If you don't tell me immediately, I'll faint.

AMY: Well, people are beginning to remark that you are a very assiduous spectator at Drury Lane. A very devoted spectator.

ELENA: Really? Well, it should flatter your countrymen that a foreigner should be so devoted to Shakespeare.

AMY: Yes, but they add that you go to church, not to pray, but to adore the priest.

ELENA: Brixon?

AMY: Heavens, no!

ELENA: Macready?

AMY: No.

ELENA: Kemble?

AMY: No. Kean! Edmund Kean!

ELENA: Ridiculous! (*Biting her lips*) Who says that?

AMY: Does anyone know who says such things? They fall from the sky.

ELENA: And there is always a devoted friend nearby to pick them up. Then, I love him?

AMY: Madly—they say.

ELENA: And do they blame me?

AMY: They pity you! To love such a man as Kean! You, the wife of the Danish ambassador!

ELENA: Just a moment, Countess, I haven't admitted it yet. But why shouldn't one love a man like Kean?

AMY: First of all because he is an actor, and since that sort of person is not being received in our parlors—

ELENA: (*Cutting her*) He ought not to be received in our bedrooms. However, I have met Mr. Kemble at the Duke of York's.

AMY: That's true.

ELENA: Can you close the door to one and open it to another?

AMY: But his frightful reputation, my dear.

ELENA: Really?

AMY: Do you mean to say you don't know about it? Kean is a veritable hero of debauchery and scandal. He's trying to surpass Casanova by the number of his love affairs. One moment he competes with royalty, and then—revealing his true origin—he throws off the costume of Othello or Lear and puts on the garb of a sailor, running from one tavern to another. And they tell me he is carried home more often than he walks.

ELENA: I'm listening—go on. You make him sound fascinating.

AMY: He's loaded with debts, and depends entirely upon the caprice of certain great ladies to escape the creditors who constantly pursue him.

ELENA: And you mean to say that people could think I would love such a man? A man such as you've been describing? You're not speaking seriously. Of course you *are*.

AMY: Very seriously, indeed. But you don't think I believe it, do you? Or that Lord Delmours believes it—or the Duchess of—

ELENA: (*Cutting her sharply*) By the way, I forgot to ask you about him? How is he?

AMY: Who?

ELENA: Lord Delmours.

AMY: (*Embarrassed*) How would I know how he is—what he's doing—what's become of him—?

ELENA: Excuse me, but I hear of him from everyone—that he's a handsome man, a clever man—but very, very indiscreet. And that's too bad, because he mentions you constantly.

AMY: (*Alarmed*) Indiscreet?

ELENA: Yes. But who believes what he says? Nobody! But pardon me, I was interrupting you—you were speaking of—

AMY: I can't remember. Oh, yes, I was speaking of the last ball the Duke of Northumberland gave. It was delightful. I was surprised not to see you there, in fact I looked for you everywhere. I wanted to present you to the Duchess of Devonshire. She would have loved to have met you, I'm sure.

ELENA: Thanks for thinking of me—so often—but I met her a long time ago. You see, my husband, in his position of ambassador from Denmark, was invited to her home very soon after we arrived in London.

AMY: Won't we see the dear ambassador?

ELENA: Don't tell me you have a magic wand, and that your wishes become orders. Look!

(*She indicates* COUNT KOEFELD *who has come to door and is speaking to his secretary who is unseen.*)

KOEFELD: Send a messenger to get the first boat that sails. Those dispatches must not lose a minute.

(*He comes into the room.*)

AMY: Does my dear ambassador at last have a moment's freedom from European politics?

KOEFELD: Your dear ambassador has put off all the sovereigns of Europe until tomorrow in order to consecrate his evening to the true queen of England, the lovely Countess of Gossville.

AMY: What a pity I don't believe a word of all that.

ELENA: Why not? Didn't he just say he has cast off diplomacy until tomorrow?

AMY: Yes, but his habits are second nature.

KOEFELD: If that's so, I'm going to say some terrible things about you.

AMY: Well?

KOEFELD: Who makes your clothes? That gown fits you terribly, and why did you ever choose that color with a complexion like yours? If you at least had blonde hair and black eyes, that severe beauty might compensate for your other faults—but, no— nothing like that. On my honor, after being so mistreated by nature, you should be jealous of the whole world. Well, does that sound more sincere?

AMY: No more than the first.

KOEFELD: What will you believe, then?

AMY: Everything you don't tell me.

KOEFELD: It's too bad women are not ambassadors.

AMY: Why?

KOEFELD: Because there are very few secrets that can be hidden from them.

ELENA: (*Looking knowingly at* AMY) And I hope they also know how to protect those whose secrets have been revealed to them.

AMY: Oh, what a pretty fan.

ELENA: A present from the Prince of Wales.

AMY: Let me see it.

KOEFELD: (*To* AMY) Won't Lord Gossville be here?

AMY: He can't come. At this moment he is helping Lord Melville make an improper marriage.

KOEFELD: That's right, it's today that Lord Melville marries that rich heiress whose dowry he hopes will revive his family fortune. What's her name? Anna—?

AMY: Anna Damby, I believe. It's one of those names that is difficult to retain because there's nothing to make you remember them.

KOEFELD: (*To* ELENA) You know, she's the same pretty little person we see in the box just opposite ours at Drury Lane, the one you remarked came to every performance. She must have made the same comment about you.

ELENA: Yes, I know.

AMY: My dear ambassador, you'll never guess that I asked Elena for a place in your box the next time Kean plays. He's such a great actor—a man of such genius.

KOEFELD: You'd like to see him?

AMY: More than you can imagine—and especially at close range. Your box is so near the stage that it must be marvellously easy to catch every expression of his face, and every movement of his body.

KOEFELD: Well, since you're so anxious to see him face to face, I'll let you see him today—even more closely than from my box.

AMY: Really? And from where?

KOEFELD: From across the table—at dinner. I invited him to dine with us.

ELENA: What? You did that without a word to me?

AMY: Invited Kean!

KOEFELD: Why not? The royal prince invites him. Besides, I've invited him as one invites such people—in the quality of a buffoon. We'll have him play a scene from Falstaff after dinner—it will amuse us—we'll laugh.

ELENA: But why did you do it without telling me?

KOEFELD: It was a surprise I was planning for the Prince. My instructions are to be very attentive to him. But now you have my secret. Tell me that I'm a diplomat!

SERVANT: (*Entering*) A letter for his excellency the Count.

KOEFELD: (*Taking letter from servant, who then leaves*) Permit me. (*Glances at it, then aloud.*) Listen! "I am disconsolate at not being able to accept your gracious invitation but an engagement that I cannot avoid forces me to deprive myself of the honor of being your guest. Be good enough to place my humble regrets before the Countess."

(ELENA *gives a sigh of relief.*)

ELENA: Kean?

KOEFELD: We're living in a strange age, you'll have to admit. A mountebank refuses the invitation of an ambassador.

AMY: It appears to me to be an excuse, not a refusal.

KOEFELD: Oh, it's a refusal, and well in order. I'm well versed in such matters. I negotiated the marriages of three royal highnesses.

ELENA: But was your invitation proper?

KOEFELD: Judge by the reply.

SERVANT: (*Announcing*) His royal highness, the Prince of Wales.

PRINCE: (*Entering, laughing heartily*) May the Lord damn me if it's not a marvellous thing! Pardon, Countess, if I enter so joyously, but you see I just heard the wildest tale that's running the streets of London.

ELENA: Certainly, we shall pardon your highness, but only on condition that you tell us the story.

PRINCE: Will I tell you? I should tell it to the reeds along the Thames, as King Midas did, if I had no one to tell it to.

ELENA: I'm stating in advance—I won't believe a word of it.

AMY: Tell us just the same, your highness. Even if we don't believe it, that won't prevent our spreading it around.

PRINCE: Do you know Lord Melville?

KOEFELD: Who was to marry the rich little nobody?

PRINCE: Who *was* to marry is correct.

AMY: But the marriage was to be today, I thought.

PRINCE: Lord Melville thought so, too, and consequently he left home at nine this morning, ready for the happy event. Unfortunately, when the moment came to march to the altar, there was no bride. Someone went to look for her and found the door open and the girl gone. The cage was there, but no bird.

ELENA: Poor child! Someone wished to sacrifice her, no doubt, but she loved someone else. Something dreadful might have happened to her.

PRINCE: You might add that she lives but a hundred steps from the Thames.

(*He laughs.*)

KOEFELD: She might have thrown herself in—the continual view of the water, you know.

(*The* PRINCE *still laughs.*)

AMY: My God, does that make you laugh, your highness?

PRINCE: Reassure yourselves, the continual view of the water gave her a desire to travel on the sea, nothing more. But since it's tiresome to travel alone, she chose a good companion, and one who will not leave her during the voyage, you can be sure.

AMY: Do you know the name of the ravisher?

PRINCE: One of the most illustrious names in England.

AMY: (*Thinking the* PRINCE *means himself*) Oh, prince, prince—please—

KOEFELD: Don't press his highness too hard, you might embarrass him.

PRINCE: Bad joke, Count! Rest easy—I don't bother the common people. I would be too afraid of failing. No, ladies and gentlemen, it's a much more illustrious name than mine, a forehead that has been crowned a long time, while mine is still waiting for a crown. And may it rest yet for many years on my brother's head.

ELENA: But who, then?

PRINCE: You can't guess with all the hints I've given you? Who else could it be, if not the Faublas, the Richelieu, the Rochester of three kingdoms—Edmund Kean.

ELENA: Edmund Kean? That's impossible!

KOEFELD: Impossible? Why, that explains his refusal. It would take an affair of that importance to keep him away. Now, I'm glad he refused. If he had come tonight, and this thing had happened tomorrow, people would have sworn that I was his accomplice.

PRINCE: And that would have embroiled England with Denmark. Ladies, we must celebrate this event, which has prevented war abroad, and which brings peace to the homeland.

AMY: Were we in danger of a revolution?

PRINCE: Why, yes—we were in a permanent state of civil war—matrimonially speaking. There wasn't a husband in the land who could answer for his wife, sweetheart, or mistress with Kean around. It's a boon to public morale. I shouldn't be astonished if half of London was illuminated tonight.

AMY: Is he really such a fearful person? And is it true that certain fine ladies have had the goodness to raise him to their level?

PRINCE: Wrong! They didn't raise him to their level—they descended to his. There's a wee bit of difference, it seems to me.

KOEFELD: It's amusing that you hear of things like this only in England.

PRINCE: Be careful, Count—ambassadors are half-naturalized.

ELENA: Your highness!

PRINCE: I beg your pardon, Countess.

AMY: Do you believe the news is true, your highness?

PRINCE: Do I believe it? I'll wager a hundred pounds that right now Kean is on the way to Liverpool.

SERVANT: (*Entering, announces*) Mr. Edmund Kean!

ELENA: Mr. Kean?

AMY: Mr. Kean?

KOEFELD: Mr. Kean!

PRINCE: (*Annoyed*) The wager is off! This complicates matters.

KOEFELD: Show him in.

(SERVANT *leaves.* KEAN *enters a moment later.*)

KEAN: Countess! Your excellency! I am daring to hope that you will excuse the contradiction between my letter and my actions, but an unexpected circumstance upset my plans, and has made what

I am doing quite mandatory. (*Turns to* PRINCE.) Will your highness receive my respects?

KOEFELD: I shall admit that I was not expecting you, first, on account of your letter, and then because of strange tales which are being circulated on your behalf.

KEAN: Those tales are precisely what bring me to your doorstep, because those tales are as exaggerated as they can be—except for one circumstance: Miss Anna came to my house. But, not finding me there, she left this letter. The scandalmonger who saw her go in did not have the patience to wait for her to come out, that is all. But, Miss Anna's reputation is compromised, and I have decided that the best way of thanking you for your kind invitation is to choose you as the one to make London hear her justification and mine.

KOEFELD: Your justification? You're either innocent, or you are guilty. If you're innocent, a formal contradiction by you will be sufficient.

KEAN: A formal contradiction by me, you say? Do you think I don't know the calumnies to which my position expose me? My word would be sufficient for the artists who know Kean as a man of honor, but it would carry little weight for people who know me only as a man of talent. They must hear from a person whose high position and spotless reputation command their confidence and respect—by the Countess Koefeld, for example—and she would be willing to do it if she would glance at this letter.

PRINCE: Come to the point.

KOEFELD: Read it yourself—we shall listen.

KEAN: Pardon me, but a secret that means the happiness and the future—perhaps even the existence—of a woman can be revealed only to a woman. There are mysteries and delicacies which masculine hearts cannot comprehend. If this secret were mine alone, I would shout it to the world. But permit me to give the secret of Anna Damby to the Countess. She will promise not to reveal it, but only to say to the world: "Edmund Kean is not guilty of the abduction of Anna Damby." And the world will believe.

PRINCE: Does my rank allow me to share the confidence?

KEAN: Your highness, all men are equal before a woman's secret. (*To* KOEFELD) Your excellency, I beg you once more.

KOEFELD: If the Countess consents, and since you seem to attach so much importance to it, I see no objection.

KEAN: Does the Countess agree?

ELENA: But I am really—

KEAN: I beg of you.

AMY: (*Taking* KOEFELD *by arm*) Once your wife knows the secret, you will easily guess it. You're a diplomat.

PRINCE: (*Taking his other arm*) And when you guess it, you'll share it with me, won't you? Unless of course, it's contrary to your government's instructions.

(*They lead him towards the fireplace.*)

ELENA: (*Downstage,* KEAN *behind her*) Give me the letter, if that is what will vindicate you.

PRINCE: In the presence of this international intrigue, I suggest that we three withdraw.

KOEFELD: Into the next room, then.

(*They go out, still arm in arm.*)

KEAN: Read it.

ELENA: Read it to me. I might not be able to suppress a desire to tear it to pieces.

KEAN: (*Reading*) "Sir, I came to see you but I did not find you in. Although I do not have the honor of being known to you, I will tell you that an interview with you will effect my future happiness. Will I have the good fortune to meet you tomorrow? Signed, Anna Damby."

ELENA: Thanks a thousand times. And what reply did you make?

KEAN: Listen. (*Takes another letter, and pretends to read.*) I didn't know how to see you, Elena. (ELENA *looks up, startled.*) I didn't dare write to you. Opportunity came and I seized it. You know that the rare moments you steal for me pass so quickly that they become but a memory. I have often searched for a way in which a woman in your position could pass an hour with me without compromising herself, and here is what I have found.

ELENA: Yes, yes, go on. (*Looks more closely at letter he is holding.*) But there is nothing written there!

KEAN: It's written! Let me go on. If this woman loved me enough to grant me an hour—for which I would give my life—she could go to the box-office at Drury Lane, pretending to buy a ticket. The man in the box-office is devoted to me. I have given him orders to open a secret door to my dressing room—to a woman dressed in black and veiled—on the next day I play a role.

ELENA: Is that all?

KEAN: That is all. My deepest thanks for listening. (*Goes to door where others left.*) Your highness! Your excellency! You may come in now.

(*The three enter.*)

AMY: Well, Elena?

PRINCE: Well, Countess?

KOEFELD: Well, Elena?

ELENA: I am certain that Edmund Kean is not guilty of the abduction of Anna Damby.

KEAN: (*Preparing to leave*) Thank you, Countess.

PRINCE: Mr. Kean, you've given us a riddle, and I give you my word, I'm going to solve it.

(KEAN *leaves. The* PRINCE *offers his arm to* ELENA, KOEFELD *gives his arm to* AMY, *they enter door from which waltz music is heard.*)

Curtain

End of Act I

Act II

A room of KEAN's *house. Rear, a window that overlooks the Thames. Door at right leads to hall, exterior door, and other parts of house. Door down left to* KEAN's *bedroom. Door, up left to another room. The room is dark.*

There are traces of an orgy. Many bottles about the room. KEAN *is asleep on a table, holding in one hand a Turkish pipe and in the other a bottle of rum.* BARDOLPH *is under table.* TOM *is asleep in a chair.* DAVID *is straddling a chair, his head resting on the back. A shawl hangs from a peg on the wall.* SOLOMON *appears at door, right, with* PISTOL.

SOLOMON: (*In low voice*) Quiet, Pistol. The illustrious Kean, pride of England, slowed down last night and decided to go to bed. We want to be sure he's not still asleep.

PISTOL: I won't make a sound, Mr. Solomon.

SOLOMON: I had enough trouble getting him to stay away from a dirty tavern last night. These nights of sound sleep are rare for him. (*Opens shutters and room is flooded with light. They look at the scene before them.*) I'm a simpleton as usual. He's done it again. This is the sixth time this month, and today is only the seventh. And look who's with him on his orgy. Those miserable hams who play the Lion, the Wall, and Moonlight in *Midsummer Night's Dream*. It would be shameful for Kean if anyone found them here. (*Nudges* TOM, *and calls in undertone.*) Tom!

TOM: (*Waking*) What?

SOLOMON: Shh—don't wake the others. You know, on our way here, I met John Ritter.

TOM: That ass!

SOLOMON: He was coming from your house, and since he couldn't find you, he asked if I knew where you were. I told him to go to Betsy's house, because I knew you go there sometimes.

TOM: Yes—but I don't want him going there!

SOLOMON: Well, if you want to get there first, you haven't a minute to lose.

TOM: (*Rushing out*) Thanks, old fossil.

SOLOMON: That's one! (*Goes to* DAVID.) David! David! (DAVID *gives a roar.*) He's dreaming that he's still playing the lion. Go on—roar! Bravo! Bravo!

(*Applauds.*)

DAVID: Who's applauding me?

SOLOMON: Don't worry—it's not the audience.

DAVID: So it's you, Father Time?

SOLOMON: In person. And glad to see you.

DAVID: Why?

SOLOMON: Quiet! You live on Regent Street, don't you?

DAVID: Number 20.

SOLOMON: That's right. Well, I wanted to go to your house this morning to tell you how well you acted last night.

DAVID: Really?

SOLOMON: Word of honor. That lion skin becomes you beautifully. When I got to the end of the street, by the fountain, a guard stopped me. "You can't pass," he says. "Why?" I asked. "Because of the fire," he said. "That doesn't matter," I said, "I'm going to see a friend at number 20." "Number 20?," he screams, "that's the house that's burning. Your friend has other things to do than see you."

DAVID: What! Number 20 is on fire? Why didn't you tell me right away, you old fool?

SOLOMON: Oh, you have time. The fire started in the cellar, and you live in the garret.

DAVID: (*Running out*) Vile traitor!

SOLOMON: Two! We're alone now. (*Hearing* BARDOLPH *grunt under table, looks.*) I'm wrong—here's another. This will be a hard one. When he sleeps, it's not for a little bit, it's for a long time—just like when he drinks. Bardolph! Bardolph! Have a glass of punch.

BARDOLPH: (*Half-awake*) Present!

SOLOMON: That was a good idea I had. Wait, I'll really wake you up.

(*Pours water from pitcher, hands him a glass.*)

BARDOLPH: To your health, old man. (*Drinks, makes a terrible face.*) What's that you're giving me, you old poisoner. Pouah!

SOLOMON: Pure water from the Thames. Haven't you ever tasted water before?

BARDOLPH: Water! What kind of joke is that? Pooh! Filthy stuff! (*Sees* KEAN *sleeping*) Let me wake up Kean.

SOLOMON: Already? Good heavens, you have plenty of time to fight.

BARDOLPH: What do you mean—fight?

BARDOLPH: You two were to fight this morning, you know very well. A duel!

BARDOLPH: Us?

SOLOMON: You're the one who was wrong. You know that very well.

BARDOLPH: Me?

SOLOMON: Yes, yes, you provoked him. I suppose the wine has made you forget everything that happened.

BARDOLPH: And we're going to fight?

SOLOMON: With swords.

BARDOLPH: Swords? With him? Give me a glass of water!

SOLOMON: That's what your two seconds, Tom and David, said. But you were too busy pouring down wine to listen. You're to be at Hyde Park at ten o'clock.

BARDOLPH: Solomon, old friend, couldn't you straighten this out?

SOLOMON: Impossible. There's an insult to be wiped out.

BARDOLPH: I'll be the one wiped out! Solomon, my old friend, my king of prompters—if perhaps Kean has forgotten this quarrel—

SOLOMON: You remember it, don't you?

BARDOLPH: Of course! I remember I was insulted—but you know, if Kean's memory isn't as good as mine, and if he's forgotten all about it—(*Starts out.*) Don't remind him of it!

(*He dashes out.*)

SOLOMON: Three! If I hadn't got rid of them, they would have drunk until tomorrow, because there's no performance tonight. This time I think we're really alone. (*Sees shawl and takes it off hook.*) Damn! There must be another one. One of the female variety. (*Looks around, then into next room.*) Nobody! That's a relief! Well, let's inspect the battlefield. (*Picks up bottles, arranging them in a group.*) Ten against four. It wasn't a fair fight. Look, Pistol, here is the noble, the illustrious, the sublime Kean, friend of the Prince of Wales, the king of tragedians, past, present, and future. See, he's holding the sceptre.

(*Tries to take the bottle which* KEAN *clutches.*)

KEAN: (*Awakening*) What the devil are you trying to do?

SOLOMON: I was trying to save that poor little bottle that you're strangling. Give it to me!

KEAN: It appears I forgot to go to bed.

SOLOMON: And you promised to stay in last night.

KEAN: Well, I'm not outside, am I? I even spent the night at home, if I'm not mistaken. That doesn't always happen.

SOLOMON: But not alone. And not sober.

KEAN: Don't scold me. I was with Moonlight who never sleeps, and the Wall, which never lies down, and the Lion, which you know is the thirstiest animal in the Zodiac.

SOLOMON: Don't you think such nights will bring back your tired spells?

KEAN: Bah! A few bottles of Bordeaux wine?

SOLOMON: (*Taking bottle from* KEAN *and holding it up*) Since when do bottles of Bordeaux have labels that say "Jamaica Rum"? Sir, you are going to finish by burning clear through to the buttons on your shirt.

KEAN: You're right, old friend, you're right. I'll kill myself with orgies. But what do you want me to do? I can't change. An actor must know all the passions in order to express them. I study them in myself, and I learn them by heart. (PISTOL *has been withdrawn by the door during all this, and unseen by* KEAN. *He makes a slight noise which causes* KEAN *to turn.*) Who is that?

SOLOMON: That's right—I had forgotten. It's a boy you probably won't remember: the son of old Bob—little Pistol, the acrobat.

KEAN: Me, forget my old friends? Come here, Pistol—come over here.

PISTOL: Shall I come over there on my hands?

KEAN: On your feet! You need your hands to shake mine.

PISTOL: (*Shaking his hand*) Oh, Mr. Kean, this is an honor.

KEAN: For me, boy. Tell me—how is the troupe?

PISTOL: It gets along.

KEAN: And Kitty?

PISTOL: She still loves you, poor girl. But that's not surprising—you were her first.

KEAN: And old Bob?

PISTOL: He still blows the trumpet like a madman. He could have been a bagpipe-major in a Scottish regiment, but he didn't want to.

KEAN: What about your brothers?

PISTOL: The three smallest are on the trapeze, the oldest ones do a tumbling trick, and the in-between ones walk the wire.

KEAN: And Mrs. Bob?

PISTOL: She just had her thirteenth. Mama and the new one are doing fine, thanks.

KEAN: Tell me about yourself.

PISTOL: I replaced you. I inherited your costume and your poles. But I'm not as good as you were.

KEAN: So you came for some lessons, is that it?

PISTOL: Oh, no. . . . But I could use them. Especially in the egg dance. I've never learned to do it right. I always break two or three eggs. But now I make them hard-boiled, and that way they aren't wasted—I eat them. But I didn't come about that. When the thirteenth baby came, papa said that was an unlucky number, and on top of everything, the baby was born on Friday. "We'll have to choose a super godfather," papa said. "Who did you have in mind? The King or the Prince of Wales?" That's what mama answered, and then papa said, "Better than that— we'll have Mr. Kean." But they didn't think you'd come, that is, no one except Kitty. But she wouldn't go ask you because she said you had gone too high. So I said, "Just give me a step-ladder, and I'll go." You won't refuse us, will you, Mr. Kean?

KEAN: No! By the soul of Shakespeare, who started as an acrobat like us, I won't refuse you. We'll give your brother a royal christening, you can be sure of that.

PISTOL: It's a sister, but that doesn't make any difference. When will it be, Mr. Kean?

KEAN: Tonight, if you like.

PISTOL: But will you have time to find a godmother?

KEAN: She's found! Kitty the blonde! Do you think she'd refuse?

PISTOL: She, refuse? You don't know her. But I'll have to be careful when I tell her the news, or she'll faint dead away. Oh, Kitty will be happy.

(*He does a cartwheel.*)

SOLOMON: What are you doing?

PISTOL: Oh, Papa Solomon, I'm like a peacock—when I'm happy, I make a wheel. Good-bye, Mr. Kean.

KEAN: You're going already?

PISTOL: I want to tell all of them who said you won't come, that you will come.

(*Goes out.*)

KEAN: Solomon, send the boy home, and give him ten guineas for his mother to buy a layette.

PISTOL: (*Running back in*) You won't go back on your word, will you? There would be a flood of tears if a misfortune like that happened.

KEAN: I'll be there, Pistol, you can bet your life on it.

PISTOL: (*Starts out, turns back.*) I almost forgot—where will it be?

KEAN: At Peter Patt's tavern, the Coal Bin. Do you know where it is?

PISTOL: Yes, I know. On the wharf, ten steps from the Thames. Thank you, Mr. Kean. Good-bye.

(*He leaves with* SOLOMON.)

(KEAN *goes to window, watches them, smiling contentedly.* SOLOMON *re-enters.*)

SOLOMON: There's a lady to see you who says she wrote you yesterday.

KEAN: Anna Damby. Let her come in, and tell her to wait a moment. (*He goes into bedroom.* SOLOMON *ushers in* ANNA *and then leaves.* KEAN *appears, wearing a coat.*) Good morning. You did me the honor of writing to me. How can I be useful to you?

ANNA: Please excuse my embarrassment. As modest as you seem to be, I can't forget your reputation, your talent, your genius.

KEAN: Miss—

ANNA: And that frightens me, even though your welcome reassured me. But they say you are as good as you are great. If you had been only great, I wouldn't have come.

(*Raises her veil. They sit.*)

KEAN: You've said that I can render you a service. I don't want to hurry you, but I'm curious to know how I can be of assistance to a girl like you.

ANNA: It's a question of my happiness, Mr. Kean—my future, even my life.

KEAN: Your happiness? Your face beams with happiness. Your future? Which of Macbeth's witches dared to predict an evil fate for you? Your life? Everywhere it shines, flowers will grow as under a warm sun.

ANNA: Half an hour ago I was asking myself if I ought to come to you or die.

KEAN: You frighten me, Miss.

ANNA: Half an hour ago I was still the fiancée of a man I detest. I was being forced to marry him—not by my mother or father— they're dead—but by my guardian, under whose authority my parents left me. Yesterday morning the marriage would have taken place if I hadn't left my guardian's home. Call it inspiration or folly, but I ran away. I asked where you live, and I came here.

KEAN: Who advised you to come to me for advice or defense, or whatever it is you want?

ANNA: No person—only your example which proves that one can accomplish glorious things.

KEAN: I see! Then you've been dreaming of the theatre.

ANNA: Yes, for a long time I've thought of nothing else. I want to be another Mrs. Siddons or a Fanny Kemble.

KEAN: Poor girl!

ANNA: You seem to pity me, but you don't answer me.

KEAN: You're so young, so naive—it would be a crime for someone as perverse as I—or as they say I am—not to tell you exactly what I think. May I speak to you like a father?

ANNA: Please. (*Rising*)

KEAN: Sit down—don't be afraid. You've seen only the gilded side of our existence, and it has dazzled you. I'm going to show you the reverse of the medallion—the thorns on the rosebush.

ANNA: I'm listening as if God were speaking.

KEAN: What I am going to say is not for Miss Anna Damby, the girl you have been, but for the artist you might be, who gives me her confidence and does me the honor of asking my advice. You are beautiful and that's a great deal, especially for the career you wish to embrace. But that's not enough. Nature has done her part, now art must do hers.

ANNA: But guided by you, I will study, I will make progress, I will acquire a name.

KEAN: In five or six years, possibly. Any talent you may have is naturally in the rough, and must be fashioned by experienced hands, just as an artist makes a statue from a block of marble. Let us say that you are one of the elect, and that in four or five years perhaps, you will have the fame you desire. I presume that glory is your only objective. You have wealth enough not to be interested in that.

ANNA: I abandoned all that when I ran away from my guardian.

KEAN: Then you have nothing?

ANNA: Nothing.

KEAN: Let us suppose you possess all the necessary talent. You still must study for six months before you can go on a stage.

ANNA: I will work in order to live during that time.

KEAN: Very well. At the end of six months, suppose you finally find a director who will offer you a hundred pounds a year.

ANNA: With my simple tastes, that's a fortune.

KEAN: It's only a quarter of what you'll have to spend for costumes alone. Silks and velvets are expensive, my dear. Are you disposed to sell your love in order to provide for your person?

ANNA: (*Rising*) Sir—!

KEAN: Let me tell you something! I will not speak another word, or I will tell you everything. When you leave this room, the conversation will be forgotten. What is your choice?

ANNA: Speak, sir.

KEAN: I'm sure you don't know the journalists of England. Oh, there are some who understand their mission, and who admire all that is beautiful and fine. They are the glory of the press. But there are others, Miss, who have been driven to criticism because they were powerless to produce anything themselves. They are jealous of everything. They blight whatever is great, and tarnish whatever is beautiful. One of these men—to your misfortune— will find you attractive. The next day he will attack your talent, the day after, your honor. Then, in complete innocence, you will wish to know the cause, and you will go to see him, as you have come to see me. You will ask the reason for his hatred, and what you can do for it to stop. He will say that you mistake his intentions, that he admires your talent, that he does not hate you, that on the contrary he loves you. You will start from your chair as you did a moment ago, and he will say: "Sit down—or tomorrow—!"

ANNA: Terrible!

KEAN: But supposing you escape that test, there are others—your rivals! In the theatre you will have neither friends nor competitors—only rivals. Your rivals will do to you what they have tried to do to me. There will be a thousand arms extended to prevent your going a step higher, and there will be a thousand mouths to spit mockery into your face, and to speak well of themselves while they lie about you. They will employ means that you despise in order to betray you. The credulous and ignorant public will take everything for truth. One day you will realize that study, talent, and genius are nothing—that baseness, hypocrisy, and ignorance are everything. You won't want to believe it, but you will end by cursing the day that you wished to seek a glory that costs so dear and brings so little.

ANNA: Oh, Kean, you must have suffered. How did you do it?

KEAN: Yes, I suffered—but I am a man, I can defend myself. My talent is at the mercy of the critics, to be sure. They step on it, they tear it to pieces, they chew it with their teeth. That is their right. But when these bar-room spiders try to crawl into my private life, the scene changes. I am the one who menaces, and they are the ones who tremble. But that doesn't happen often. They have seen my swordplay in Hamlet and they know better than to quarrel with me.

ANNA: But aren't all these things forgotten when you can say to the public: "I am king"?

KEAN: Yes, I am king, that's true—five times a week, king with a wooden sceptre, paste diamonds, and a cardboard crown. I have a kingdom of two hundred square feet. Oh, yes, I am a highly respected king, a powerful king, and especially, a happy king.

ANNA: But when the world applauds you and envies you, and admires you—?

KEAN: Sometimes I curse madly. I become jealous of the porter and his burden, of the laborer in the field, of the sailor on the sea.

ANNA: And if a young and rich woman who loved you came to you and said: "Kean, my fortune and my life are yours if you will leave this existence that is devouring you—leave the theatre."

KEAN: Leave the theatre? I? Oh, you don't know what this robe of Nessus is—that can be taken from your shoulders only by tearing your own flesh. Me, quit the theatre—renounce its emotions, its dazzle, its pain, and leave my place to others? No! And let everyone forget me in a year, in six months even? No! Remember that an actor leaves nothing after him. He lives only his life, and his memory goes with his own generation as he falls from the throne into nothingness. Once you put your foot into this fatal career, you must go on until the end—exhaust its joys and its sorrows, drink its honey and its lye. You must finish as you began—die like Molière, to the accompaniment of applause. But you, Miss Anna, haven't entered the gate, and you can turn back. Believe me, on my honor, believe me.

ANNA: Your advice is an order, Mr. Kean. But what must I do?

KEAN: Where did you go yesterday when you left your guardian?

ANNA: To my aunt's. She loves me like a daughter.

KEAN: Well, go back there and ask her protection.

ANNA: But Lord Melville is powerful, and if he finds where I am—

KEAN: The law protects the weak as well as the powerful—except of course we actors who are outside the law. Does your aunt live far from here?

ANNA: On Clary Street.

KEAN: I'll take you there. It's no more than a ten-minute walk.

SOLOMON: (*Entering*) His Royal Highness, the Prince of Wales is here.

ANNA: My God!

KEAN: Say that I can't see him. Tell him I'm sleeping.

SOLOMON: I'll add that you spent the night studying, sir.

KEAN: No—add that I spent the night drinking—there's more chance he'll believe it. Come, Miss—this way.

(*She takes his arm and they go out.*)

End of Act II

Act III

The Coal Bin, a river-front tavern frequented by sailors. At one side is door to street. A hallway leads to guest rooms. A door at rear, on the side, leads to private dining room and other parts of tavern. Some booths in rear are made of partitions which give privacy to drinkers even though they are in a common room. Tables further downstage.

JOHN COOK and drinkers in booth at rear. At right, at table, CON-STABLE is reading a paper.

FIRST DRINKER: So they carried him away senseless? Is that what you're trying to say?

JOHN: (*Belting a glass of beer*) As senseless as a hitching post.

SECOND DRINKER: Is it true you knocked out seven teeth?

JOHN: (*Holding out his glass.* PETER *enters with more beer.*) Seven! Three uppers—two lowers—I mean four lowers.

THIRD DRINKER: Then the Duke of Sutherland won. He was betting on you.

JOHN: I should say he won. And he gave me a guinea for each tooth. By Jove, I promised to drink his health. Here it is!

(*Empties his glass.*)

FIRST DRINKER: And do you mean that all you got was that black eye?

JOHN: That's all! And what's a black eye? A matter of seventy-two hours—today, black, tomorrow, purple, the next day, yellow, and then it's gone.

LORD MELVILLE: (*Entering*) Who is the host here?

PETER: I am, your honor.

MELVILLE: Listen, friend—and remember what I tell you.

PETER: I'm listening.

MELVILLE: A young girl will come this evening and will ask for a room. Give her the best in your inn, give her anything she wants. Watch her and be attentive to her, because this young girl is going to become one of the greatest ladies in England. Here's something in advance for your trouble.

PETER: Is that all you wish, my lord?

MELVILLE: No, there's something else. Do you know someone who will rent a boat for a week?

PETER: Just the man you want is right here. George! (FIRST DRINKER *comes from rear.*) Here's a gentleman who wants a good sloop for a week or ten days.

FIRST DRINKER: He can have it for ten years if the price is right.

MELVILLE: She must be a good traveler.

FIRST DRINKER: Say! Everyone knows my boat—she's the Queen Elizabeth. Ask anyone around here, and they'll tell you she makes eight knots an hour. She's lovely.

MELVILLE: Can you bring it up here?

FIRST DRINKER: I'll take her anywhere you want. She only draws three feet of water. Empty a barrel of beer and I'll sail her right in this room.

MELVILLE: May I see it? We'll discuss terms on the way.

FIRST DRINKER: Right enough! She's hitched just a quarter of a mile from here. First, my beer.

(*He goes back, gulps his beer, exits with* MELVILLE.)

PETER: (*Who has been at rear talking to the other drinkers.*) How long will the other fellow be laid up?

JOHN: For three months if he's lucky, I'd say. And he won't eat anything but soup in that time, I'll wager. That'll teach him to feel around with John Cook.

KEAN: (*Entering, dressed as a sailor.*) Mr. Peter Patt!

PETER: Here I am. Oh, it's you, governor.

KEAN: In person. Is everything ready for the supper?

PETER: They're preparing the tables in the big dining room. You see, there's nothing too good for you, governor.

KEAN: (*Sitting at table, opposite the* CONSTABLE) That's fine! Give me something to drink while I'm waiting.

PETER: Ale or porter?

KEAN: What do you think I am? Give me some champagne. The best!

(PETER *exits.*)

JOHN: Did you hear that fresh-water sailor? Beer isn't good enough for his gullet.

KEAN: (*To* PETER, *who has brought a bottle of wine*) Hasn't anyone arrived yet?

PETER: Not yet.

KEAN: Go give a glance at the supper. I think I smell it burning.

PETER: I'll see to it, governor.

(*He exits.*)

JOHN: I'm going to give that faker a working-over. Watch me if you want a good laugh.

SECOND DRINKER: What are you going to do?

JOHN: I'll tell you: if he drinks a drop from the bottle in front of him, my name's not John Cook. (*Approaches* KEAN *with a bantering air.*) It seems that the fishing wasn't too bad, Mr. Whaler. Lots of good blubber!

KEAN: What's that on your eye?

JOHN: And now you're swapping whale oil for champagne, eh? Very fancy!

KEAN: You ought to put a poultice on that eye. It doesn't look very pretty.

(*Pours a glass of champagne.*)

JOHN: (*Quickly picking up the glass.*) You got the best brand, didn't you? You're a real sport.

(*Drinks it down, puts glass on table as* KEAN *watches him steadily.*)

KEAN: At least you can get the other eye to match that one. It shouldn't be difficult, the way you're going on.

JOHN: You think so?

KEAN: (*Pouring another glass*) I'm sure of it.

JOHN: You'll pay me back, eh?

KEAN: Without charge. Interest free!

JOHN: (*Taking glass and drinking it down*) To your health!

KEAN: (*Taking off his coat*) Thanks, friend. But take care of your own health.

JOHN: You're going to keep your word, huh? 'Pon my soul!

KEAN: (*Taking off his vest*) Yes—and I want to save wear on my clothes.

JOHN: Ha! Ha! Ha! That's a good one! Thinking of your clothes, are you?

PETER: What are you going to do, John?

JOHN: You can see very well. I'm going to wait.

PETER: What are you doing, governor?

KEAN: You can see—I'm getting ready.

PETER: (*To* JOHN) Do you know who this man is?

JOHN: What difference does that make? He's nothing to me!

PETER: (*Runs to* CONSTABLE.) Constable!

CONSTABLE: (*Getting on chair*) Get out of my way, so I can see, will you, fool?

PETER: All right, all right, go on and fight if it will give you pleasure.

(*He goes out.*)

(KEAN *and* JOHN *box.* JOHN *is violent,* KEAN, *very cool.* JOHN *receives a blow on his other eye and falls into the arms of his friends who surround him.* KEAN *puts on his coat and vest and sits.*)

KEAN: Peter!

PETER: (*Entering*) Here I am!

KEAN: A clean glass.

PETER: Is it all over? That didn't take long.

CONSTABLE: (*Going to* KEAN's *table as waiter brings two glasses*) I want to offer my compliments, mister sailor.

KEAN: May I offer you some of my champagne?

CONSTABLE: You gave him a mighty punch, young man.

KEAN: You flatter me. Actually, it was a third-class blow. Very shabby. If I had tightened my elbow to my body, and given him an upper-cut, I would have split his head in two.

CONSTABLE: That's too bad! Maybe you'll have that pleasure some other time.

KEAN: Oh, I did what I set out to do. I promised him a black eye to match the one he had, and I'll warrant I gave it to him.

CONSTABLE: Oh—religiously! He can't complain of it. I really believe it's a better quality black eye than the one he had.

KEAN: I believe you enjoy a fight.

CONSTABLE: I've never missed a boxing match or a cock-fight in my district yet. I'm a great admirer of artists.

KEAN: Really? Well, Mr. Constable, if you want to be one of my guests, I'll let you meet an artist.

CONSTABLE: Are you giving a supper?

KEAN: I'm a godfather. Wait a minute—here's the godmother. Isn't she pretty?

(KITTY *and the other guests have walked in.*)

CONSTABLE: Charming! I'd better go tell my wife I won't be home until late.

KEAN: Better tell her you won't be home at all. It's safer. (CONSTABLE, *laughing, exits.* KEAN *goes to* KITTY, *kisses her.*) Kitty!

KITTY: Oh, Mr. Kean, then you haven't forgotten me altogether?

KEAN: And do you remember David, the poor tumbler, even though he's now called Edmund Kean?

KITTY: Of course I do.

KEAN: What have you been doing since I've seen you?

KITTY: Thinking of the time when I was happy.

KEAN: Well, Kitty, I hope that time comes again to you.

KITTY: (*Sadly*) Impossible, Mr. Kean.

KEAN: You love someone, I'll wager. Let's see.

(*Tries to look into her eyes.*)

KITTY: I don't love anyone!

KEAN: But if you ever should, Kitty, come to me and I'll take care of the dowry.

KITTY: (*Half-crying*) I'm never going to marry, Mr. Kean.

KEAN: Excuse me, Kitty. I'm an awful fool. (*To* PISTOL, *who has come in*) Well, Pistol, is old Bob coming?

PISTOL: Old Bob is in bed, Mr. Kean.

KITTY: In bed?

KEAN: What happened?

PISTOL: Terrible luck! You know, Mr. Kean, he was in the street, all ready to go. He looked so fine in his grey hat, his pistachio coat, and his big collar that cuts off his ears. We went about four steps, and he said, "Oh, I forgot my trumpet." "They know all your songs," I said, "and besides, you need your wind for other things." He got angry, and said, "Go get my trumpet, and don't argue." I told him to get it himself, and I started on. Out of the corner of my eye, I saw him swelling up to give me a big kick.

KEAN: Well, you got kicked. What of it?

PISTOL: That's the trouble—I jumped to the side.

KEAN: Then you didn't get kicked. What's the misfortune in that?

PISTOL: Well, he was expecting to find some sort of resistance at the end of his foot, poor old fellow. And when he didn't find it, he lost his balance and fell over backwards.

KITTY: Good heavens!

PISTOL: Don't say what you think, please. I would rather have been kicked twenty times where he was aiming, than to be the cause of all his misery.

KITTY: Is he hurt badly, Pistol?

PISTOL: (*Almost crying*) They think he's dislocated his shoulder. And all because he wanted to kick my ass.

KEAN: Did you send for a doctor?

PISTOL: Yes.

KEAN: What did he say?

PISTOL: He said he'll have to stay in bed six weeks, without budging. That means the troupe will starve. Papa's trumpet is like our sign-board. Tomorrow, if our sign is gone, people will think we've gone bankrupt, and they won't come.

KEAN: Is starvation the worst thing you expect?

PISTOL: Isn't that enough? Fasting six weeks when it isn't even Lent. Fasting makes you hungry.

KEAN: Peter! Peter Patt!

PETER: Here I am!

KEAN: A pen, ink, and paper!

KITTY: What are you going to do?

PETER: (*Bringing articles*) Here they are.

KEAN: (*Writing*) Have this letter sent to the director of Covent Garden. (*Finishes it, hands it to* PETER) I'm informing him that I will play the second act of Romeo, and the role of Falstaff tomorrow night for the benefit of one of my old comrades who has dislocated his shoulder.

KITTY: Oh, Mr. Kean.

PISTOL: (*Joining* KITTY *in embracing* KEAN) There's a real friend, Kitty.

PETER: (*Calling*) Philip!

(*A boy enters.*)

KEAN: Take that letter and wait for an answer. Well, is everyone ready?

PISTOL: Everyone!

KEAN: Let's go, then.

PISTOL: That's right. We mustn't keep the vicar waiting.

KEAN: I'm not thinking about the vicar. He can wait. But the dinner won't. Peter, we turn everything over to you. Kitty—take my arm. We go into the banquet hall.

(KEAN *and all the guests go into dining room.*)

PETER: I'll be there in a moment. (*Calling*) Wine boy! Wine boy!

WINE BOY: (*Entering*) Here I am, sir.

PETER: Be careful that there isn't a single drop of water in the wine you serve to Mr. Kean.

WINE BOY: What about the others?

PETER: Just the same as usual for the others. Fifty-fifty!

WINE BOY: Very good, sir.

(*He leaves.*)

ANNA: (*Entering*) Sir, I'd like to have a room.

PETER: It's ready.

ANNA: What?

PETER: Yes. Someone told me to prepare my best room for a lady who would be here this evening. You're the one, I suppose.

ANNA: Show it to me quickly. I'm afraid someone might come in.

PETER: Dolly! Dolly! (CHAMBERMAID *enters from hallway.*) This way, miss. Show the lady to number one, Dolly. Is there anything more you wish, miss?

ANNA: Thanks—nothing.

(*She follows* DOLLY *out.*)

SOLOMON: (*Entering*) Good evening, Peter.

PETER: Oh, Solomon, it's you. You're too late for the baptism, and too early for the supper. What can I offer you while you're waiting?

SOLOMON: Nothing, Peter, absolutely nothing. I came just to speak to our great and illustrious Kean—a theatrical matter—a trifle.

PETER: All the same, I'm going to bring you some beer. You can talk to it while you're waiting.

SOLOMON: Good! Time doesn't drag when you're with a friend. Tell our great tragedian that I am waiting, and that I want to speak to him alone as soon as the ceremony is finished.

PETER: (*Leaving*) Just as you say.

(SOLOMON *sits at table where the* CONSTABLE *had been. There are newspapers on the table.*)

SOLOMON: (*Picking up a newspaper*) Let's see what they said about our last Moor of Venice. (*A waiter brings him a beer.*) Thanks, my friend. (*Looking through paper*) Hm—hm—news of Russia—Austria—politics—who cares about that? (*Finding what he wants*) Here's all that interests me. (*Reads.*) "Drury-Lane, The Moor of Venice, with Mr. Kean—hm—hm—mediocrity of the actors." (*Aloud*) Only the best in the world—Miss O'Neill, Mrs. Siddons, and Kean. (*Reads.*) "Kean made Othello a savage." (*Aloud*) What should he be—a fop? No wonder, when I see who wrote the article. The devil take these critics who judge and condemn. (*Takes another paper.*) "Mr. Brixon was magnificent as Iago." (*Aloud*) He thinks Mr. Brixon is magnificent when he's *not* Iago. They sleep together. (*Reads.*) "Kean's Othello was a bit too mild." (*Aloud*) This one finds him mild—the other one, too strong. They're bloody idots. (*Throws down the paper.*) Thank God, I'm only a miserable prompter.

KEAN: (*Entering*) What's the pressing news, Solomon—and why didn't you come in to join us at supper?

SOLOMON: I didn't come to eat. I'm not hungry. Something has just happened.

KEAN: What is it?

SOLOMON: It's that villain, Samuel, the jeweler. He's got a warrant for your arrest—on account of the four hundred pounds you owe him. The sheriff and the bailiff are at your home.

KEAN: What does that matter, since I'm here at the tavern?

SOLOMON: But they said they'd wait until you come home.

KEAN: Well, my friend, do you know what I'll do?

SOLOMON: No.

KEAN: I won't go home.

SOLOMON: A pregnant idea!

KEAN: What's lacking here? We have good wine, good food, good friends, and inexhaustible credit. Let the sheriff and the bailiff bore themselves at my house—we'll enjoy ourselves here. And we'll see who is the first to give in.

ANNA: (*Appearing from hallway*) Mr. Kean! I thought I heard your voice.

KEAN: Miss Anna! What are you doing in a tavern like this? I thought I knew you, and I formed my opinions, but you will have to explain what you are doing in this black hole in the heart of London. (*To* SOLOMON) Solomon, old friend, go in and tell them to go on with the supper—and partake of it!

(SOLOMON *exits.*)

ANNA: Now that we're alone—explain yourself.

KEAN: But it's for you to explain. What brings you to a river-front tavern?

ANNA: Your letter.

KEAN: My letter? I wrote no letter.

ANNA: You didn't write that my liberty was compromised, and that I should leave my aunt's house and come here? I have your letter. Here it is.

KEAN: There's something rotten about all this. This is not my handwriting, although someone took great pains to imitate it.

ANNA: Read it just the same. It will explain my being here.

KEAN: (*Reading*) "Someone saw you entering and leaving my house. You were followed and your retreat has been discovered. They will obtain an order to take you away. There is one way to escape your tormentors. Come this evening to the Coal Bin, and you will be given a room. Wait for a man with a black mask. Follow him and trust him to take you to a place where you will be safe from those who mean to harm you. Edmund Kean."

ANNA: Read the postscript.

KEAN: (*Reading*) "They are spying on me, also. That is why I do not come in person to give you these instructions that can save you."

ANNA: Now you know why I am here. I thought the letter was from you. I trust you, so I came.

KEAN: I can only say that I thank the chance or the Providence that brought me here tonight. I swear I'll get to the bottom of this. But you must tell me everything. You must keep no secrets from me.

ANNA: I'm not afraid of anything when I'm near you.

KEAN: But it appears that you are trembling.

ANNA: It's not kind of you to question me when I can't tell you everything.

KEAN: How can a young heart like yours have things to hide? Speak to me as a friend.

ANNA: But how can I look you in the eyes?

KEAN: I am going to try to anticipate your words—raise the veil on your secret, so to speak. We actors are accustomed to reproduce human feelings. We must study to find these feelings. If I am not mistaken, I detect that your hatred for Lord Melville comes from a great love for someone else.

ANNA: You're not mistaken. But it's not my fault. I was carried by a strange fatality that no woman could resist. Oh, why didn't they let me die!

KEAN: Die? Why would you wish to die?

ANNA: I didn't wish it but I think God did. I fell into a profound melancholy. It seemed impossible for me to live. My guardian consulted the finest doctors in London, and each of them said my ailment had no cure. Only one of them made a suggestion—the theatre. I had never been allowed to go before. My guardian arranged for a box. My first impression was that I was suffocating. Then, when the lights went down, and the curtain went up, I felt that I could breathe again. I heard a voice! My whole body trembled. I had never heard such a melodious voice. The voice was speaking words of love that I had never known could be uttered by human lips. I was like a statue, watching, listening. They were playing *Romeo and Juliet*.

KEAN: Who was playing Romeo?

ANNA: The next night we saw *The Moor of Venice*. It was not the same voice, not the same love words, not even the same man, but it was the same delight, the same ecstasy. It was sublime.

KEAN: Who was playing Othello?

ANNA: The next day I asked to go to Drury Lane. It was the first time in a year I had expressed a desire for anything. I returned to the palace of enchantment. I wanted to see the sweet face of Romeo, or the burning, tanned countenance of Othello, but I saw instead the melancholy face of Hamlet. This time, my feelings that had been building up for three days, spilled over, flooded my heart. I wept with joy.

KEAN: And who was playing Hamlet, Anna?

ANNA: Romeo made me know love, Othello, jealousy, Hamlet, despair. This triple initiation completed my cure. My languor, my emptiness, were gone. The soul of the actor had passed into me. I began to live and breathe for the first time.

KEAN: But you have not told me the name of the man who gave you rebirth.

ANNA: I dare not speak his name. I could not look you in the eyes.

KEAN: Anna, is it true? Is it really true? Am I such a fool? Am I so unhappy?

ANNA: (*Frightened*) What are you saying?

KEAN: Something you couldn't understand, Anna, something I will reveal to you someday—later. But at this moment, let me think of you as a sister who needs my help.

ANNA: Oh, Kean—my brother—my friend.

KEAN: Let us go back to this letter, because—now that I know everything—there is not a moment to lose.

ANNA: But now it's your turn to tell me why you are here—and in that costume.

KEAN: I'm godfather to a child of some poor people I knew a long time ago. I thought this garb would make them feel easier with me. But back to you—has the masked man come yet?

ANNA: Not yet.

KEAN: But he'll be here.

ANNA: I'm sure.

KEAN: (*Calling*) Peter!

ANNA: What are you going to do?

(PETER *enters.*)

KEAN: Has the Constable returned?

PETER: Oh, yes. He's at supper with the other guests.

KEAN: Tell him to come in here.

ANNA: Kean, I'm beginning to be frightened.

KEAN: What are you afraid of?

ANNA: I'm afraid for you.

KEAN: Don't worry! (CONSTABLE *enters.*) Oh, Constable, come here. This is Miss Anna Damby, one of the richest heiresses of London. Someone wants to do her violence regarding the choice of a husband. I'm putting her in your care. Extend your strong arm to her, and save her.

CONSTABLE: What a change! Who are you to claim my aid with such authority?

KEAN: Never mind who claims the protection of the law, since the law is equal for all, and since Justice has her eyes covered. But if you want to know my name, I am Edmund Kean, the actor. You said you like artists. I promised to let you meet one. I'm keeping my word.

CONSTABLE: Edmund Kean! How could I be so stupid not to recognize you? Why, I've seen you play a hundred times. I have your autograph. (*Turning to* ANNA) So you want my protection, Miss?

ANNA: I beg for it.

CONSTABLE: You have it! But tell me, in what way—?

KEAN: Anna, go with the Constable to your room. You can explain everything to him. Meanwhile, I'll remain here and wait.

ANNA: Be careful, Kean.

KEAN: Go in, quickly—please. Constable, don't think this little interruption will ruin your evening. We'll dine joyously later, I promise you. (ANNA *and* CONSTABLE *go down hall.*) A thousand to one chance that I should be here! Now I understand how the story that I had abducted Anna spread so quickly. I am being used as a tool by a ruined lord who wants to rebuild his fortune. But Anna is protected, and I'm waiting. Here comes someone.

(*He extinguishes candle on table nearest door. The room is quite dark.*)

(LORD MELVILLE, *masked, enters, tries to pass* KEAN.)

MELVILLE: Pardon, friend, but I wish to pass.

KEAN: Pardon, my lord, but you shall not pass.

MELVILLE: And why, if you please?

KEAN: Because this is not the right time of year—not even the right
century—for wearing a mask.

MELVILLE: It so happens that it is necessary to hide my face.

KEAN: An honest man needs no mask! I already know your project,
and I'll soon know your face, because I swear before God that if
you don't take off that mask, I'll tear it off. Do you understand?

MELVILLE: Sir!

KEAN: Be quick about it! (MELVILLE *makes a movement to leave, but* KEAN
seizes his arm.) Oh, no—you don't leave! You still have an arm
free—use it to unmask yourself. And believe me, don't force me
to get my hand near your face.

MELVILLE: (*Trying to free himself*) I want to know who the drunkard is
that is insulting me like this.

KEAN: And I want to know who the coward is who wants to run away.
(*He tears off his mask, drags* MELVILLE *near dining room door and
calls in.*) Come in everyone, and bring some light so we can all
see who this is.

(*Everyone from dining room enters, some with candles.*)

MELVILLE: Kean!

KEAN: Lord Melville! I wasn't wrong!

MELVILLE: This is an ambush!

KEAN: Not at all—this is between us. You used my name to carry out
your evil designs. You will answer only to me, and everything
will be said.

MELVILLE: There's a small difficulty in that. I'm a lord, and a peer of
England, and I cannot fight with a buffoon and a clown.

KEAN: You are right! There's too much distance between us! Lord Melville is an honorable man from one of the first families of England—of rich and old nobility. If I'm not mistaken, iy is true that Lord Melville has eaten up the fortune of his fathers with cards and dice, and betting on cock-fights and horse races. It's true that his coat-of-arms is tarnished by his own debauched life, and that instead of going higher, he sinks lower. While the clown, Kean, born in poverty, abandoned in a public place, beginning without name or fortune, has made a name equal to the most noble, and if he wished, a fortune greater than that of the royal prince. But that doesn't prevent Lord Melville being an honorable man, and Kean a clown. It is true that Lord Melville wanted to regain a fortune at the expense of a young and defenseless girl, and with no concern that she was of lower class. He pursued her with his love, his pretensions, his influence. While the acrobat, Kean, received her like a brother and offered her protection—even though she was young and defenseless. Yet Melville is a lord, and Kean is an acrobat. It is true that Lord Melville, peer of England, makes and unmakes laws, has a coat-of-arms on his carriage, and has only to speak his name in order to open the door of the king's palace. But when Lord Melville deigns to descend among the people, he casts off his name, puts on a mask, and signs another's name to a letter—a criminal offense—no more, no less. But the actor Kean shows his face to the world, and speaks out his name, because his name does not come from his ancestors, but returns to them. The actor Kean tears off a mask in a theatre, or in a tavern when he demands satisfaction for an insult. But Lord Melville states that he cannot fight with a clown, an acrobat, an actor. On my honor, it was well said, because there is too much distance between us. But remember three things, my lord: first, that I could denounce you to the police; second, there are some insults which mark a man's forehead as with a hot iron, and I could insult you like that if I chose; third, right now you are in my power, and I could break you as I could break this glass—(*Picks up a glass, pretends he is going to smash it, then laughs.*)—if I didn't prefer to use it for a toast. Pour, Peter! (*Holds up glass.*) To the happiness of Miss Anna Damby, and to her free choice of a husband—and may this husband give her all the happiness she deserves.

ALL: Long live Mr. Kean!

KEAN: (*To* MELVILLE) Now, you are free to go, my lord! (*As* MELVILLE *is leaving,* JOHN, *who has been sulking in the background with his cronies, comes behind* KEAN *with a piece of wood, ready to hit him in the head.* KITTY *cries out just in time, and* KEAN *intercepts the blow and sends* JOHN *reeling.* JOHN's *friends begin badgering* KEAN *and it becomes a free-for-all, with* PISTOL *getting in some kicks and blows, and* SOLOMON *knocking out one of the drunks. The room is quiet at last.*) Solomon, I do believe you enjoy a fight.

SOLOMON: Only when I'm winning.

KEAN: Shall we go in and finish our delicious supper?

(*They all adjourn as curtain goes down.*)

End of Act III

Act IV

SCENE 1

KEAN's *dressing room. Door at one side to stage area, door on other side to corridor and exterior. There is an alcove with drapes, where* KEAN *can dress privately. There is a large wardrobe or cupboard filled with costumes. Inside must be a working secret door that enters into the room.*

PISTOL: Papa Solomon, if I'm not too curious, what are you doing?

SOLOMON: (*Who is adding sugar to a glass of water*) I'm preparing a glass of water and sugar for Mr. Kean.

PISTOL: Papa Bob is like Mr. Kean—he always has to gargle between acts. But he uses rum.

SOLOMON: If I didn't have sense enough for both of us, that would be happening here. But I'm very strict about it. Once in a while, I might allow him a glass of grog, nothing more.

PISTOL: You're right. (*Looking into wardrobe*) What's all this rubbish?

SOLOMON: What did you say, silly? You call that rubbish? Those are magnificent costumes.

PISTOL: With gold—real gold! Oh, excuse me. There must be a few shillings in all that.

SOLOMON: That wardrobe is worth two thousand pounds sterling, if a tuppence.

PISTOL: Even more valuable than the king's? Better than the diamonds in the crown? Say—there's a door in here.

SOLOMON: Shh—

PISTOL: But it's a real door.

SOLOMON: Shh—

PISTOL: Does Mr. Kean know about it? Someone could come through there to steal. But it looks like it won't open. (*He is working with the door in the wardrobe.*) It does open!

SOLOMON: You sneaky little devil! How did you do that?

PISTOL: With the point of my knife.

SOLOMON: Close it! Oh, if Mr. Kean knew what you just did!

PISTOL: Would he be angry? Then we won't tell him. We'll pretend that I didn't see anything. There's no door! Where is a door? Who said there was a door? I didn't. Did you, Mr. Solomon?

SOLOMON: No! Tell me, will there be a big crowd this evening?

PISTOL: What a crowd! There's a queue that goes three times around the theatre. I was walking for fifteen minutes along the queue.

SOLOMON: And what were you thinking about?

PISTOL: I was thinking that in every pocket I passed there was money that was going to be Papa Bob's. He's going to be so happy! I'll never be lucky enough to have a misfortune like his happen to me.

SOLOMON: Quiet—Mr. Kean is here!

PISTOL: I'll run.

(*He goes out stage side as* KEAN *enters other door.*)

KEAN: (*Rather drunk, throws down his hat.*) Solomon!

SOLOMON: Yes, master?

KEAN: Put my lion skin on the floor—or a bear skin—or a rug— anything you like.

SOLOMON: What are you going to do?

(*He gets lion skin from a chest and puts it on floor.*)

KEAN: Some handsprings.

SOLOMON: Handsprings?

KEAN: That's the way I started—in the square in Dublin. And I may be forced to take up my old trade. Shout to the four corners of London that the mountebank Kean will do some acrobatic routines in Regent Street and St. James, on condition that he will receive five guineas per window. In eight days I'll make a royal fortune, because everyone will want to see Hamlet walking on his hands, Othello doing cartwheels, and Romeo falling on his backside. In this cursed theatre, even with Shakespeare's help, it will take years, and the more years that pass, the more debts I'll have, trying to put aside enough to spend my last days in miserable honesty in some village in Devonshire, with a piece of dried beef and a pot of beer. Oh, fame! Oh, genius! Oh, art! Emaciated skeletons—vampires, dying of hunger! In whose honor we throw a golden mantle over our shoulders, so we can adore them as if they were gods! I can still be the victim, but I refuse to be the dupe.

SOLOMON: What's wrong with you, master?

KEAN: Only that my house is surrounded by bailiffs, and that I lived all day in my carriage, after having passed the night at that tavern. This puts me in a wonderful mood to be hissed this evening. And all for a miserable bill of four hundred pounds. Come now, tell me I'm the first actor of England, and that you wouldn't change my place for that of the Prince of Wales. Tell me, vile flatterer.

SOLOMON: But it's your own fault! If you would only put some order in your life.

KEAN: Order! And what would become of genius while I had order? In a life as full as mine, do I have the time to calculate minute by minute, or penny by penny, what I should spend, either in time or in money? If God had given me that honorable faculty, I should at this very moment be a linen merchant on Middlesex Street, and not a merchant of verse at Covent Garden and Drury Lane.

SOLOMON: But it seems to me that you could raise the four hundred pounds from tonight's receipts.

KEAN: Are the receipts mine? They are for my good and old friends. Do you want them to pay for the gift I'm making them? That was a lackey's advice, Solomon.

SOLOMON: But you didn't understand. In three or four days you could return it to them.

KEAN: So, that's it? I should borrow from my friends! How can you say that?

SOLOMON: Pardon me, Master, pardon me. I'm a silly fool.

KEAN: Very well. Look carefully over my lines for tonight. See that I don't miss a single word.

SOLOMON: Yes, sir.

KEAN: Otherwise, you'll have me to deal with! And you know what I'll do! (*Puts his arm on* SOLOMON's *shoulder.*) My good Solomon, my old comrade, my only friend!

SOLOMON: Well, it appears the storm is over. Is the storm over?

KEAN: And why not? Am I not Prospero the magician? When I wave my wand, can I not stir up a tempest, or calm one? Can I not evoke Caliban or Ariel? Go away, Caliban—I'm waiting for Ariel.

SOLOMON: Why didn't you say so at the very first? I'm going! I'm going! Caliban is going! (*Turns back.*) Don't forget we are playing six acts tonight—and I don't mean with Ariel.

(*He starts toward door that leads to stage.*)

KEAN: Good and excellent man! Friend for all time! Mirror of my vanity! You come to me only to be caressed, as a dog to its master, but you receive only rough words. But I'll engrave your name on my tombstone in golden letters. Everyone will know that I had two friends—my lion and you. (*Picks up one end of lion skin.*) Stretched out to receive my creditors. I should like to lie on you and sleep. But I hear someone. It must be she! On your way, Solomon! (SOLOMON *exits.*) (*He opens wardrobe, pushes costumes aside and opens secret door, after first locking the other door.*) Elena!

(ELENA *enters with her maid,* GIDSA.)

ELENA: Kean! (*Turns towards door.*) Wait for me, Gidsa. I'll just be a moment.

KEAN: (*Closing door and arranging costumes in front of door.*) Are you sure of that woman?

ELENA: As of myself. She's from Venice.

KEAN: So you came! I was waiting, but I didn't expect you.

ELENA: I have some thanks, and some reproaches to give you. How careless you were to bring that letter to my home.

KEAN: Do you want me to repent what I have done?

ELENA: Who asked you to repent?

KEAN: You came! Here you are! I can scarcely believe my happiness.

ELENA: Do you believe I love you now?

KEAN: Yes, I believe it.

ELENA: You men are always unjust. It's not enough that we confide our honor to you—we must risk losing it for you.

KEAN: Oh, no! Put yourself in the place of a poor outcast who feels chained to his place. He cannot come to you, so you must come to him.

ELENA: Since I can't come as often as I should like, I want you to have my portrait.

(*She takes out a miniature portrait meanwhile placing her fan on table.*)

KEAN: Your portrait? You had it made for me? (*Looks at it.*) But you are even more beautiful.

ELENA: Don't you want it?

KEAN: Of course—here—near my heart—always.

(*Puts portrait in a pocket.*)

ELENA: Then you love me?

KEAN: How can you ask?

ELENA: (*Taking his hand*) My Othello!

KEAN: Correct, Desdemona—because you know I am as jealous as the Moor of Venice.

ELENA: Jealous? Of whom?

KEAN: You know very well.

ELENA: I swear to you.

KEAN: Don't swear—I might not believe you at some later time. A woman has an instinct that tells her a man loves her, even before he says so.

ELENA: Many men try to court me.

KEAN: I know that—but it is only one man I fear.

ELENA: You fear someone?

KEAN: I fear his rank, his power.

ELENA: You mean the Prince of Wales, naturally.

KEAN: Yes! I'm not afraid that you love him, I'm only afraid that someone will tell me that you do.

ELENA: But what can I do? He does not say he comes to see me—he says it is my husband.

KEAN: I know that, and that is what torments me. At your home, at the theatre, everywhere—he is always at your side. How can one believe that the richest, the noblest prince in England after the king, can live without hope—when we know very well that is not his custom? When I see him near you, I go mad.

ELENA: Do you prefer that I don't come to the performance tonight?

KEAN: On the contrary—please come. If you did not come, and he by chance did not come, I would think you were together.

ELENA: You're foolish to have such fears.

KEAN: But aren't we always unhappy? Unhappy, if we are not loved, unhappy if we are? Elena—pardon me, please—pity me.

ELENA: Why should I pardon you, dreamer? Or pity you, jealous one?

KEAN: Pardon me for having passed these few minutes tormenting you and myself, instead of using them to say I love you, and to repeat it a thousand times.

ELENA: Someone is knocking.

KEAN: Who is there?

PRINCE: It's I!

ELENA: My God! The Prince!

(KEAN *goes to door.*)

KEAN: Who did you say was there?

PRINCE: (*Behind the door*) The Prince of Wales, goddamn it!

KOEFELD: (*Behind the door*) And Count Koefeld.

ELENA: My husband! I'm finished. What shall I do?

KEAN: Shh—leave quickly. (*Points towards secret door, then goes to door where* PRINCE *is.*) I'm having some difficulties. I'm being pursued for a miserable four hundred pounds that I owe.

PRINCE: I understand.

ELENA: How do I open this door?

KEAN: Wait! (*To* PRINCE) I must be careful that someone isn't using your name and imitating your voice. Will you be good enough to write your name and slip it under the door?

PRINCE: Then what?

KEAN: I'll open the door. (*Rushes to wardrobe, works with secret door.*) I love you, Elena—good-bye. We'll meet again soon. (*She goes out secret door,* KEAN *puts things in order, then goes to other door and picks up paper which has been pushed under the door.*) Four banknotes! Four hundred pounds! These are royal calling cards! Come in, your highness, come in.

(*He opens door to admit* PRINCE *and* KOEFELD.)

PRINCE: (*Looking all around*) There's only one thing to surmise, Count, and that is that fair Juliet has flown.

KOEFELD: Really?

KEAN: What an idea! Look for yourself. How could someone have left?

PRINCE: (*Laughs.*) Don't you know that an actor's dressing room is engineered like Anne Radcliffe's old castle? There are invisible doors that lead to subterranean chambers, sliding panels that open on unknown corridors, and—

KEAN: (*To Koefeld*) I'm honored that your excellency would visit the dressing room of a poor actor.

PRINCE: Oh, don't think it was to honor you, Mr. Conceit. It was curiosity. The Count, diplomat that he is, had never been in the wings of a theatre, and he wanted to see—

KEAN: An actor dressing himself? I must tell you that we have an etiquette more strict than yours. We must be ready on time, or we get hissed. And the moment is almost here. Will you permit me?

KOEFELD: Continue as if we weren't here. We won't disturb you.

SOLOMON: (*Entering*) Here I am, Master.

KEAN: Your highness, please take back these banknotes.

PRINCE: Not at all! That's the price of my box that I deliver to you personally.

KEAN: I accept. Here, Solomon, you know what to do with this money.

(*Hands him the notes, goes behind drapes.* SOLOMON *exits.*)

KOEFELD: (*To* PRINCE) Do you think he was with a woman?

PRINCE: I'm sure of it.

KOEFELD: Miss Anna, perhaps.

PRINCE: It's difficult to know.

KOEFELD: (*Suddenly sees* ELENA's *fan on a table, picks it up without the* PRINCE *paying attention.*) But I'll find out—I promise you.

(*He quickly puts the fan in his pocket.*)

PRINCE: How will you do it?

KOEFELD: It's a diplomatic secret.

KEAN: (*From behind drapes or screen*) Well, your highness—what news?

PRINCE: Nothing important. Oh, some ruffian insulted Lord Melville last night at a cheap tavern called the Coal Bin.

KOEFELD: Why?

KEAN: Because Lord Melville refused to fight with him, under pretext that he was an actor. I heard about it.

PRINCE: What do you think of Melville's excuse, Count?

KOEFELD: I don't know what your English customs are under such circumstances, but I know that we Danes would fight the whole world if we were insulted—except thieves of course—we leave them to the law.

KEAN: (*Appearing in tights and pointed shoes*) Well, your excellency, you have a courageous heart, and the Danes are courageous people. I promise to go to Copenhagen to get myself killed.

KOEFELD: You'll be well received. Meanwhile, I thank the prince for introducing me to this sanctuary.

KEAN: The high priest welcomes you as an initiate.

KOEFELD: Let us allow Mr. Kean to finish dressing.

KEAN: (*Low, to* PRINCE) I would like to speak to you.

PRINCE: Count, I'll join you in a moment in the box. (*Low to* COUNT) You'll tell me, won't you?

KOEFELD: Of course, your highness. (*To* KEAN) Good evening, Mr. Kean.

KEAN: Your excellency! (KOEFELD *leaves.*) I'm happy to be here alone with you.

PRINCE: Why?

KEAN: First, to thank you for your generosity, second, to make my excuses. You called at my home, and you were told I was not in.

PRINCE: But you were in?

KEAN: Yes! But I had important business.

PRINCE: Between friends—is someone bothering you?

KEAN: I want you to stop at those words: "between friends."

PRINCE: Do you think they compromise you?

KEAN: Certainly not! But I should like to know if his Royal Highness lets those words drop from his lips or from his heart.

PRINCE: What have I done that Mr. Kean should question me so precisely and so pointedly? Isn't my purse always at his service? Isn't my palace open to him at all hours? And do not the people of London see him riding at my side, in my carriage?

KEAN: I know all those things, and I am certain that people believe I have only to ask your highness to obtain anything I desire.

PRINCE: People believe that?

KEAN: Except Kean, your highness—except Kean, who is not deceived by superficial signs that simply puff his vanity, but on the other hand has doubts deep in his heart.

PRINCE: What doubts, if you please?

KEAN: For example, if I had to ask your highness—not for a favor that a prince accords his subject—but one of those sacrifices that are made from equal to equal.

PRINCE: Try it.

KEAN: If I said to you—we artists have strange love affairs that do not resemble those of other men because they seldom clear the obstacles. But these loves are no less full of jealousy. Sometimes an actor chooses a woman who has habitually attended his performances, one who inspires him, one to whom he can speak his lines with feeling. The two thousand spectators in the hall disappear from view, and he sees only her. It is only her applause that matters to him. It is not for reputation, or for fame that he acts, it is for a sight—for a look—for a tear of hers.

PRINCE: Well?

KEAN: Well, your highness, if this woman who exercised such influence over him, overlooked the great distance between them, and permitted him to hope and to dream—there would be jealousy, just as in any other sort of love, and the man who causes it should take pity on the unfortunate actor.

PRINCE: You mean that I'm your rival, don't you?

KEAN: That word implies equality, and you know I am far below you.

PRINCE: Hypocrite! And what can I do for the tranquility of your great love, Mr. Kean?

KEAN: Your highness, you are young, handsome, you are a prince. There is not a woman in England who would refuse you. You not only have London, you have the provinces, you have Scotland, you have Ireland—three kingdoms in fact. Very well—court all the women in your realms except—

PRINCE: Except Elena, is that it?

KEAN: You guessed it, your highness.

PRINCE: So, it's the beautiful Countess Koefeld—the lady of your secret thoughts? I suspected it when I saw you rashly enter her home to exonerate yourself. You are her lover.

KEAN: No, your highness. I have only that love I spoke about—the love an actor has for his greatest success. But this love has become my life. More than my life—my glory.

PRINCE: But if I withdraw, another will take my place.

KEAN: What does another matter? I can avenge myself on another—but not on you.

PRINCE: You are her lover!

KEAN: No! But if you have the least friendship for me—and if you do not wish to drag me into a scandal that I shall regret—don't go to her box—please. (*Knock at stage door.*) I am forgetting myself. They are ready to begin and I'm not finished dressing.

PRINCE: I'll leave.

KEAN: Do you promise?

PRINCE: Admit that you're her lover.

KEAN: I can't admit what isn't so.

PRINCE: Good-bye, Kean. I'll applaud you.

KEAN: From your own box?

PRINCE: If you give me half-confidences, Mr. Kean, I can give you only half-promises.

KEAN: I can't tell you what is—(*Resigned*) Act as you see fit, your highness.

PRINCE: Thank you for your permission.

(*He goes out laughing.*)

SOLOMON: (*Entering from stage door, doublet in hand*) Kean! Kean! Hurry!

KEAN: I'm ready! (*He puts on the doublet.*) Solomon, there is no friendship except between equals. The Prince of Wales is just as vain to have me next to him in his carriage, as I am foolish to sit there. (*A knock at secret door*) Someone is knocking at that door. Only Elena knows about it.

GIDSA: (*From behind door*) Open, Mr. Kean. It's Gidsa!

KEAN: (*Opening*) Gidsa! What do you want? What happened?

GIDSA: The Countess forgot her fan. I came to get it.

KEAN: Her fan? Have you seen it, Solomon?

SOLOMON: No, Mr. Kean.

KEAN: Look everywhere, Gidsa.

GIDSA: Oh heavens, how can this be? The Countess valued that fan. It was a present from the Prince of Wales.

KEAN: From the Prince of Wales? Then look in his carriage—perhaps she left it there.

GIDSA: That's possible.

KEAN: (*Hands her some money.*) If your mistress has lost her fan, you will at least have something.

GIDSA: Thank you, Mr. Kean.

(*She leaves by secret door, with help of* KEAN.)

KEAN: A fan from the Prince of Wales. I can understand how one wants to hold on to a royal present. (*Calling*) Darius! Where is that imbecile wigmaker?

DARIUS: (*Entering with wig*) Coming, sir.

(KEAN *sits.* DARIUS *puts on his wig and combs it.*)

STAGE MANAGER: (*At door*) May we sound the bell in the lobby, Mr. Kean?

KEAN: Yes, I'm ready.

STAGE MANAGER: Thank you.

(*He goes out.*)

KEAN: Solomon, while he's working on my wig, try to find that fan.

DARIUS: What fan?

KEAN: A fan that was lost here.

DARIUS: The reason I asked—I saw the gentleman who came to see you with the Prince of Wales holding a funny-looking fan.

KEAN: A fan with diamonds?

DARIUS: Something that sparkled—all over it. When I saw him looking at it, I said to myself: "If I found a fan like that, I wouldn't have to make any more wigs."

KEAN: You're certain that you saw that fan in the hands of Count Koefeld?

DARIUS: I don't know his name! All I know is he didn't look too happy about it. He put the fan in his pocket and gave a kind of growl.

KEAN: What is he going to think? He will suspect that Elena came here.

STAGE MANAGER: (*Entering*) Curtain going up, Mr. Kean.

KEAN: I'm not ready.

STAGE MANAGER: But you told me to warn the audience.

KEAN: Go to the devil!

STAGE MANAGER: (*Dashing out*) Don't raise the curtain! Hold the curtain!

KEAN: (*Rising*) How can I warn her? I can't go to her, and I can't send for her. This is maddening.

DARIUS: Can I finish your wig?

KEAN: Leave me alone.

(*There is loud noise from audience.*)

SOLOMON: Do you hear that? The audience is impatient.

KEAN: What difference does it make to me? What a cursed profession! No sensation is our own—neither our joy, nor our pain. If our heart is breaking, we have to play Falstaff—if we're full of joy, we must play Hamlet. Always a mask—never a face! Oh, yes, the audience is impatient, because it waits for me to amuse it, and it doesn't know that at this moment, my heart is heavy. What a torture! And if I go on stage with all the horrors of hell in my heart, I must smile when I'm supposed to smile, I must say every word as it should be said, or the audience will hiss— the audience that knows nothing, understands nothing, and guesses nothing of what goes on behind the curtain. They take us for machines, with no feelings but our roles. I will not go on tonight!

(PISTOL *has come to stage door.*)

SOLOMON: Master, what did you say?

KEAN: I will not play! That is what I said!

STAGE MANAGER: (*Who had come to door*) Mr. Kean, they will force you to play.

KEAN: Who will?

STAGE MANAGER: The Constable.

KEAN: Let him come!

SOLOMON: Name of heaven—he will put you in prison.

KEAN: Prison? Good! I still will not play!

SOLOMON: Nothing will change your mind?

KEAN: Nothing! I will not go on!

STAGE MANAGER: But the tickets are all sold.

KEAN: Refund the money!

STAGE MANAGER: Mr. Kean, you're failing in your duty.

KEAN: I won't go on! I won't go on! I won't go on!

(*He picks up a chair and throws it to floor.*)

STAGE MANAGER: Do as you like—I'm not a beneficiary.

(*Goes out.* KEAN *falls into a chair. There is more noise from audience, louder and louder.*)

PISTOL: Well, Mr. Kean—what about Papa Bob?

SOLOMON: These people cannot pay for tonight's expenses.

PISTOL: It's not our fault that someone has troubled you.

SOLOMON: Have pity on the unfortunate, master.

PISTOL: You gave us your word.

SOLOMON: And it would be the first time you've broken it.

KEAN: (*With the greatest dejection*) Enough! Where is Darius?

SOLOMON: He ran away.

DARIUS: (*Coming from behind drapes*) Here I am!

KEAN: Where is the stage manager?

SOLOMON: (*To* PISTOL) Go look for him.

KEAN: Where is my cape?

(SOLOMON *hands it to him.*)

PISTOL: (*Running in*) Here he is, Mr. Kean.

STAGE MANAGER: You called me?

KEAN: Yes, sir. My sword!

(*The* STAGE MANAGER *cringes.*)

SOLOMON: Your sword?

KEAN: Yes! My sword! Does that astonish you? With what am I going to kill Tybalt? (*To* STAGE MANAGER) I'm playing.

STAGE MANAGER: Thank you, Mr. Kean.

KEAN: But I want you to make an announcement. Say that I'm indisposed—that I'm sick—say whatever you like—that I'm dying.

STAGE MANAGER: Thank you, Mr. Kean.

(*He goes out.*)

SOLOMON: It's about time. The audience was beginning to tear the benches apart.

KEAN: They're right. I would like to see you in the audience, after buying a ticket at the door, being made to wait. What would you say?

SOLOMON: Damn! I don't know!

KEAN: What would you say? You would say that an actor's first duty is to his audience.

SOLOMON: Oh!

KEAN: And you would be right! Let's go, Kean, you old work-horse— now that you're all harnessed—go plough up your Shakespeare.

STAGE MANAGER: I'm ready, Mr. Kean. May I make the announcement now?

KEAN: Yes. Are there many heads?

STAGE MANAGER: Packed house—and more are fighting to get in.

KEAN: Let's go!

(*The curtain falls. The* STAGE MANAGER *comes in front, and goes center.*)

STAGE MANAGER: Ladies and gentlemen, Mr. Kean is ill this evening, and fearing that he will not be worthy of the attention you show him, he asks me to beg your indulgence.

AUDIENCE: Bravo! Bravo! Bravo!

(*The* STAGE MANAGER *bows and retires. Orchestra plays "God Save the King," then the curtain rises on the scene from* Romeo and Juliet.)

End of Scene 1

SCENE 2

The stage of the theater. The set is for Act III, Scene V of Romeo and Juliet. *On one side of stage, far down, in box, are* ELENA *and* COUNT KOEFELD. *On the other side in a box is* LORD MELVILLE.

JULIET:
"Wilt thou be gone? it is not yet near day:
It was the nightingale and not the lark,
That pierced the fearful hollow of thine ear;
Nightly she sings on yond pomegranate-tree:
Believe me love, it was the nightingale."

ROMEO: (*Kean*)
"It was the lark, the herald of the morn,
No nightingale: look, love, what envious streaks
Do lace the severing clouds in yonder east:
Night's candles are burnt out, and jocund day
Stands tiptoe on the misty mountain tops:
I must be gone and live, or stay and die."

JULIET:
"Yond light is not day-light, I know it, I:
It is some meteor that the sun exhales,
To be to thee this night a torch-bearer,
And light thee on thy way to Mantua:
Therefore stay yet, thou needst not to be gone."

ROMEO:
"Let me be ta'en, let me be put to death;
I am content, so thou wilt have it so.
I'll say yon grey is not the morning's eye,
'Tis but the pale reflex of Cynthia's brow;
Nor that is not the lark, whose notes do beat
The vaulty heaven so high above our heads:
I have more care to stay than will to go:

Come death, and welcome! Juliet wills it so.
How is't, my soul? let's talk: it is not day."

JULIET:
"It is, it is: hie hence, be gone, away!
It is the lark that sings so out of tune,
Straining harsh discords and unpleasing sharps.
Some say the lark makes sweet division;
This doth not so, for she divideth us:
Some say the lark and loathed toad change eyes;
O, now I would they had changed voices too!
Since arm from arm that voice doth us affray,
Hunting thee hence with hunts-up to the day.
O, now be gone; more light and light it grows."

ROMEO:
"More light and light: more dark and dark our woes!"

(NURSE *enters*.)

NURSE:
"Madam!"

JULIET:
"Nurse?"

NURSE:
"Your lady mother is coming to your chamber: The day is broke; be wary, look about."

(*She exits.*)

JULIET:
"Then, window, let day in, and let life out."

ROMEO:
"Farewell, farewell! One kiss, and I'll descend."

(*He kisses her and then has one leg over the balustrade, preparing to descend, when he sees the* PRINCE OF WALES *come into* ELENA's *box. Instead of disappearing out the window, he comes into the room, looks up at the box, and crosses his arms.*)

JULIET: (*Trying to guide him to window as she speaks*)
"Art thou gone so? my lord, my love, my friend!"

I must hear from thee every day in the hour,
For in a minute there are many days:
O, by this count I shall be much in years
Ere I again behold my Romeo!"

ROMEO:
"Farewell!
I will omit no opportunity
That may convey my greetings, love to thee."

(*He pulls away from* JULIET, *glares at* ELENA'S *box.*)

JULIET:
"O, Think'st thou we shall ever meet again?"

ROMEO: (*Mechanically, not looking at her*)
"I doubt it not; and all these woes shall serve
For sweet discourses in our time to come."

JULIET:
"O God! I have an ill-divining soul.
Methinks—"

ROMEO: (*Cutting her*)
"Dry sorrow drinks our blood. Adieu, adieu!"

(*Pulls away from her, crosses his arms again.*)

JULIET: (*Undertone, at his side*) What are you doing? You're missing your exit.

SOLOMON: (*Sticking head in from edge of stage*) Kean! Kean! (*Motions for him to go to window and out.*)

JULIET: (*Pulling him by the arm*) Adieu, my Romeo.

SOLOMON: (*Prompting loudly*) Adieu, Juliet!

KEAN: (*Wildly*) Ah! Ah! Ah!

SOLOMON: (*Prompting*) Adieu, Juliet!

JULIET: (*Both arms around his waist, tries to pull him to window.*) Romeo!

SOLOMON: (*Pointing to window*) Kean! Romeo!

KEAN: Who's calling me Romeo? Who believes I am playing the part of Romeo? It's a lie! "To be or not to be: that is the question: Whether 'tis nobler in the mind to suffer—to suffer—to suffer—"

SOLOMON: Kean, you've gone mad! Go out the window!

KEAN: I am not Romeo! I am Falstaff, companion in debauchery to the royal Prince of England. Come to me Peto, come to me Nym, come to me Bardolph, and you too, Mistress Quickly— pour, pour the glasses full so I may drink to the health of the Prince of Wales, the most dissolute, the most indiscreet, the most egotistical of us all. To the health of the Prince of Wales, who loves every female, from the girl who serves sailors in a tavern, to the lady-in-waiting who places the royal cloak on his mother's shoulders. To the Prince of Wales, who cannot look at a woman without seducing her with his look. To the Prince of Wales, whose friend I thought I was, but whose toy and clown I now know I am. Oh, Royal Prince, thank yourself that you are sacred, because—I swear to you—if you were not, you would have Falstaff to deal with.

MELVILLE: (*In his box*) Down with Falstaff, and down with the actor Kean!

KEAN: Falstaff? I am no more Falstaff than I was Romeo. I am Punch, the Falstaff of the street puppet shows. Who has a stick to beat Punch? And who has a stick for Lord Melville? Quickly—a stick for that miserable abductor of young girls, who carries a sword at his side, but refuses to fight with a man whose name he has stolen. And why will he not fight? Because he is a lord, and a peer! A stick for Lord Melville, and let us laugh while Punch suffers—suffers—suffers. Beat me! Beat me, I say! Oh, my God, make them beat me!

(*He tears off his wig, throws it on the floor and collapses in the arms of* JULIET *and* SOLOMON *who have come near him at the last lines. They drag* KEAN *through door and off.*)

STAGE MANAGER: (*Entering from other side*) Where is the theatre doctor?

DARIUS: (*Running in to pick up wig*) The doctor is with Mr. Kean.

STAGE MANAGER: Where?

DARIUS: (*Pointing in direction* KEAN *went*) There!

MERCUTIO: (*played by* DAVID) (*Enters with* CAPULET *both in costume.*) What happened?

CAPULET: (*Played by* TOM) I don't know! But it must have been while he was on stage.

STAGE MANAGER: (*Low to the actors*) Clear the stage! (*They go off as* SOLOMON *runs in, quickly whispers to* STAGE MANAGER *and goes off.*) Ladies and gentlemen, I regret to say the play cannot go on. The sun of England has been eclipsed—the celebrated Kean has been seized by an attack of madness.

(*There is a cry from* ELENA.)

End of Scene 2

Act V

Kean's home, Same scene as ACT II. BARDOLPH, TOM, DAVID, DARIUS, *and* PISTOL *are scattered around the room, listening to* SOLOMON.

SOLOMON: That's the way it was. Here is the visitor's list. Sign your names.

BARDOLPH: (*After writing*) How did he pass the night?

SOLOMON: Terribly.

TOM: Has he really gone mad?

SOLOMON: Fit to be tied!

DAVID: Is the doctor bleeding him?

SOLOMON: Bleeding him white.

BARDOLPH: But what sort of madness has he?

DARIUS: Yes, what is it?

SOLOMON: Paranoiac frenzy.

DAVID: Good God! What does he do in his attacks?

SOLOMON: He strikes out.

(*With a violent gesture*)

DARIUS: At what?

SOLOMON: At anything—anybody—but preferably people he knows.

DARIUS: What? He attacks his friends?

SOLOMON: My God—yes!

DARIUS: He would probably bite.

SOLOMON: I'm afraid so.

DARIUS: He's gone mad. I once dressed the hair of a crazy man. His madness came from writing tragedies that no one would play. But he still kept on writing them.

SOLOMON: Did he bite?

DARIUS: Yes—but no one was hurt—he had no teeth, poor man. His friends let him bite them—because he enjoyed it.

DAVID: Do you think there's any hope for Kean?

SOLOMON: I can only tell you it's serious. The doctor left a long list of instructions. (*Looks towards* KEAN's *room.*) Wait! I think I hear Kean. He may be coming.

DARIUS: I'm leaving!

SOLOMON: (*Peeking into* KEAN's *room*) He's not coming.

TOM: Good.

DARIUS: What did the doctor order?

SOLOMON: (*Caught off-guard, he quickly improvises.*) Oh—more bleedings, hot baths, poultices.

DAVID: Do you know what I think? The doctor's an ass.

TOM: My opinion too.

DARIUS: The doctor must be a fool.

SOLOMON: You think so?

DARIUS: I'm sure of it. Most doctors are.

TOM: I'd tie him up with some stout rope—that's what I'd do.

DAVID: If I were you, I would treat him my way.

SOLOMON: What would you give him? Let's hear.

DAVID: I would take a bottle of good Bordeaux wine, I would put it in a casserole with some lemon, cinnamon, and sugar and I would warm it for five or ten minutes, then I would give him a glass of it.

DARIUS: I wouldn't do a thing like that.

SOLOMON: What would you do?

DAVID: I tell you, a glass of—

DARIUS: No, listen, David, you play the lion very well, but when it comes to medicine, that's something else. If I were Solomon, I would make the wine hot.

DAVID: You see!

DARIUS: Wait! First I would shave his head as bald as his knees—that would refresh his brain. Then I would order a wig—a wig of the finest hair.

SOLOMON: And what about the hot wine?

DARIUS: I would drink it. (*Bell rings in* KEAN's *bedroom.*) Solomon—someone is ringing.

SOLOMON: Another attack!

DARIUS: An attack? I'm leaving!

(SOLOMON *grabs his arm to stop him.*)

DAVID: Let's go!

DARIUS: No foolishness, Solomon—please!

(*Another ring*)

TOM and BARDOLPH: Every man for himself!

(*They exit.*)

SOLOMON: Darius, my friend, you're braver than the rest. Stay with me.

DARIUS: Papa Solomon, if you don't let go of me, I'll make a complaint, I'll denounce you, I'll never powder a wig for you, I'll stick pins in your legs, and I'll bite your nose.

(SOLOMON *releases him, he leaves.*)

SOLOMON: If that's the way you feel! Get ye to a nunnery! (*Laughs.*) They're all gone! Now they'll spread the news, and that's what I want.

PISTOL: (*From a corner where he has been sitting*) Mr. Solomon.

SOLOMON: Are you still here? Why didn't you leave with the others?

PISTOL: Because you said you needed someone.

SOLOMON: You're a brave lad. You can go.

PISTOL: I don't want to go.

SOLOMON: Will you promise me to keep a secret?

PISTOL: Of course. (SOLOMON *whispers in his ear.*) Really?

SOLOMON: Not a word of this to anyone.

PISTOL: They could cut my throat first. I'm so happy, I'm so happy! Oh, Mr. Kean! Oh, Mr. Solomon!

(*He embraces* SOLOMON, *then runs out.*)

KEAN: (*Entering from bedroom*) With whom were you speaking?

SOLOMON: Friends from the theatre—the idiot Darius—little Pistol.

KEAN: What did you tell them?

SOLOMON: That you're ready for a strait-jacket, a raving madman.

KEAN: You did wrong.

SOLOMON: Why was I wrong? What if people learn that your madness was only faked?

KEAN: What if they do?

SOLOMON: And that you insulted the Prince of Wales and Lord Melville.

KEAN: And so?

SOLOMON: You'd be severely punished.

KEAN: What does that matter? What can they do to me? Put me in prison? Well, I'll go.

SOLOMON: Yes, but I won't go! If only you would pretend to be mad for a week. You're wonderful as King Lear.

KEAN: Solomon, I act from eight in the evening until midnight, but not during the day.

SOLOMON: Just one week—that's only seven days.

KEAN: Enough on that subject. Give me the list of people who came to see me.

SOLOMON: There are two lists. The porter downstairs has one. This is the list of intimate friends.

KEAN: Good! She wouldn't have dared come in, but she might have called downstairs, or sent someone. I'll discover by some sign or other that she thinks about me—after suffering so much for her.

SOLOMON: (*Gives him list.*) There are some names here that would be surprised to be found on the same list.

KEAN: I'm sure of it—the rich, the noble, the powerful, artists, workers, porters, everyone from the Duke of Sutherland to William the coachman. Every name is here but the one I am looking for. But she'll find a way to see me. Solomon, admit no one else except—

SOLOMON: Except Ariel?

KEAN: Yes, Ariel. If she comes, admit her instantly, without even asking her name, because she is a fine lady, you see.

SOLOMON: But how shall I recognize her?

KEAN: She's the only one I'm expecting.

SOLOMON: Depend on me.

(*He goes out.*)

KEAN: Solomon! (SOLOMON *comes in.*) I've changed my mind! Put my horses to the carriage. I'm leaving!

SOLOMON: You're leaving?

KEAN: Yes! I can't suffer a moment longer. Can't you see I'm burning with fever? I'll lower the blinds in the carriage. All I want to do is pass under her windows. (SOLOMON *stands there.*) Well, are you going to do what I asked?

SOLOMON: Yes, I'm going—I'm going. (*Knock at door in vestibule*) Someone knocked!

KEAN: Well, go open the door.

SOLOMON: If it's she, you'll stay, won't you?

KEAN: (*Laughing*) Imbecile!

SOLOMON: I'll run! (*He leaves.*)

KEAN: (*Leaning on back of chair*) What a child I am! God help me, but my heart is beating as if I were eighteen. I'm really mad—I don't have to fake it.

SOLOMON: (*Appearing*) It's she, master, it's she!

KEAN: Elena! Elena! It's you!

(ANNA *appears with hooded cape.* SOLOMON *goes out.*)

ANNA: (*Taking off the hood*) No, Mr. Kean—it's Anna.

KEAN: (*Falling into chair*) Oh!

ANNA: Pardon me for intruding like this, but this morning a frightful story was circulating—that last night you had an attack. I said to myself: "He has no mother, no sister. I must go to him."

KEAN: Anna, I know how devoted you are. You have a good and loyal heart. You didn't worry what people would say about you if they saw you come here. You didn't care if they said you were my mistress. You listened only to your heart.

ANNA: It's not true—what they say?

KEAN: I wasn't fortunate enough to go mad. It would be so pleasant to be mad—to laugh—to sing—to remember nothing.

ANNA: Now that I know you are not ill, I can make my journey without fear.

KEAN: Are you leaving London?

ANNA: That's not far enough, Kean. I am leaving England.

KEAN: But are you free to do so? What about your guardian?

ANNA: I attained my majority this morning, and the first thing I did was to sign an engagement with an agent from a theatre in New York.

KEAN: Nothing will change your mind? Not even the picture I gave you of that career?

ANNA: You painted a picture for a poor girl without funds, not for a rich heiress. Even if silks and velvets are costly, I think twenty thousand pounds a year will pay for my costumes.

KEAN: But with so much money and such beauty!

ANNA: Those things—and I add my talent—are not enough to make me love anyone—in America.

KEAN: Poor child!

ANNA: Will you remember the poor exile who left with but one aim—one hope?

KEAN: Dear Anna.

ANNA: May I write to you, to tell you about my work, and my troubles, and my progress—because I shall make progress—especially if you give me counsel from across the sea.

KEAN: I shall do everything possible for my best friend. When do you leave?

ANNA: In two hours.

KEAN: And how?

ANNA: I have booked passage on a ship called the Washington.

SOLOMON: (*Enters uneasily.*) Master, she's here. I asked her name. It's Elena.

KEAN: My God! What can I do?

ANNA: Let me see her, Kean.

KEAN: That can't be!

ANNA: Don't be afraid. All I want to say to her is: "Make him happy, because he loves you."

KEAN: No, Anna, that's impossible. She would never believe the innocence of our relations. What would she think seeing you so young and beautiful? Go in my bedroom, quickly—please—and forgive me.

(*Ushers her into his bedroom.*)

SOLOMON: (*Goes out, we hear him at vestibule door.*) Come in, come in.

(*Opens door for* ELENA.)

KEAN: Elena! You came! No matter what the risk! If you only knew how I had been hoping you would come.

ELENA: I hesitated a long time, but in view of our common danger, I—

KEAN: Our danger?

ELENA: You can be arrested at any moment.

KEAN: Arrested?

ELENA: Yes. Because the story has gone about that it was not madness but anger that prompted you to insult the Prince and Lord Melville. And Melville has obtained a warrant against you. You must leave London—leave England if possible. You must go to France or to Belgium—and at once.

KEAN: I? Leave London? Leave England? Like a trembling coward? You don't know me, Elena.

ELENA: You forget that another name will be brought up. They will look for the cause of your outcries against the Prince of Wales and they will find it.

KEAN: Yes, you are right, and that is perhaps a blessing. Do you love me, Elena?

ELENA: Can you ask?

KEAN: Listen to me—you too are compromised.

ELENA: I know it.

KEAN: No, you don't know everything. You left a fan in my dressing room yesterday.

ELENA: Well?

KEAN: It was found.

ELENA: By whom?

KEAN: By your husband!

ELENA: Good God!

KEAN: He knows the fan, doesn't he?

ELENA: Of course.

KEAN: Well?

ELENA: Well?

KEAN: You were advising me to leave the country, and I am ready. Do I go alone?

ELENA: Oh, you are mad, Kean! What you suggest is impossible. Our love was a moment of abandon, of foolishness, of error. We must not think of it again. We must forget it ourselves so that others will forget.

KEAN: Forget it? But if I exiled myself, would I not always have your image before my eyes? Why, I even have your portrait.

ELENA: I came to ask you to return it to me.

KEAN: Return your portrait—given to me yesterday? You came today to ask me to return it?

ELENA: Be reasonable! Kean, you love me, I am sure of it, but how long would that love endure if we were apart? With your talent, and your fame, opportunities will always be waiting for you. You will love another woman, and my portrait will become nothing but a victory trophy.

KEAN: Here it is, Countess. (*He holds up the portrait, but does not give it to her.*) Such a suspicion allows no refusal. In love, a doubt is an accusation.

ELENA: Kean!

KEAN: Here it is! I didn't keep it long, and no one has seen it. So if you have promised one to another man, you need not have it made—give him this one.

ELENA: Promised to whom?

KEAN: How do I know? In exchange for some fan, perhaps.

ELENA: Oh, Kean! Kean! After what I have done for you! After the sacrifices I have made for you!

KEAN: What have you sacrificed but your pride? It's true that the Countess condescended to love an actor, but you are right: that love was a moment of abandon, of foolishness, of error. But rest easy, Countess, the error was mine alone, the foolishness was mine alone. Yes, I was a fool to believe in the devotion of a woman, a fool to risk my future and my liberty for her—and all on a jealous suspicion—because I was so in love. I was wrong, I was wrong! To think that I have been waiting here since last night, my heart beating as if it wanted to break through my chest, every time someone knocked, just to hear such words come from your mouth. Oh, I was acquainted with affairs like this, and I know their depth and their duration, yet I was taken in. Here is your portrait, Countess Koefeld. (*He hands it to her.*)

ELENA: Kean, don't be angry with me just because I am more reasonable than you.

KEAN: More reasonable? More than that—you have just made a miraculous cure. I was delirious, I had something like a brain fever—you applied ice to my head and to my heart, and I am cured. Countess, if you remain here any longer it will only increase the suspicions of your husband, if by chance the fan has given him any. And besides, the Constable will probably soon be here to arrest me.

ELENA: Kean, I would rather endure your anger than your sarcasm. Is this the way you want me to leave?

KEAN: (*Stiffly*) Will the Countess permit the actor Kean to kiss her fingertips?

(*He starts to take her hand, when a voice is heard at the vestibule door.*)

KOEFELD: I tell you I want to go in!

SOLOMON: But I tell you that you can't go in!

ELENA: My husband!

KEAN: Hide, Elena. (*She goes to bedroom door.*) No! Not there! (*Indicates door upstage.*) Here! Here! Rather close quarters, but there's a window that looks out on the river.

ELENA: (*Turning at door*) My husband will demand satisfaction. Kean, please—

KEAN: Rest easy. Yesterday I would have given years of my life to fight him, but today, I do not hate him at all. The Count will be sacred to me.

KOEFELD: I tell you I must see him!

KEAN: (*Opening door*) You heard the Count, Solomon—why don't you admit him?

(SOLOMON *opens vestibule door and the* COUNT *enters the room.*)

SOLOMON: But you said—

KEAN: That I wished to see no one? That's true, but I was far from expecting the honor of a visit from His Excellency.

KOEFELD: It seems to me rather that you were seeing no one because you expected my visit.

KEAN: But why should I?

KOEFELD: Because of what I said in your dressing room—that Danes fight when they are insulted. Now, I am offended, and I come to fight. You are aware of the reason, but it must remain unknown. That is why I did not send word by seconds. We shall choose a place and we shall give some dispute about politics as the reason for our quarrel.

KEAN: But Count, you may have a motive sufficient for you, but not for me. I cannot fight when there has been no offense—and I certainly know of none.

KOEFELD: I understand your delicacy, and perhaps that is only a new insult. If you do not fight when you have offended someone, do you fight when someone has offended you?

KEAN: That depends. If someone offends me without reason, I attribute it to foolishness, and I pity the one who insults me, that's all.

KOEFELD: Mr. Kean, must I believe that your reputation for courage is counterfeit?

KEAN: Oh, no—I have proof of it.

KOEFELD: Take care—I will say you are a coward.

KEAN: No one will believe you.

KOEFELD: I will say I raised my hand—

KEAN: And I will add that I stopped it in order to spare one of us a mortal grief.

KOEFELD: Very well—if you won't fight, I can't force you. But I must give vent to my anger—and if it is not on you, it will be on your accomplice.

KEAN: I swear to you that you are in the deepest error. I swear to you that you have no reason to suspect me or anyone else.

KOEFELD: I wanted only your blood to satisfy my hate. Now you fear my vengeance, and you wish it upon a woman.

KEAN: Count Koefeld, there is something more cowardly than refusing to fight, and that is attacking a woman who cannot answer for herself.

KOEFELD: Vengeance is permitted when one knows the guilty.

KEAN: And I tell you that the Countess is innocent—I tell you she has the right to your respect. And I shall add, that if you say a word to compromise her, if you so much as touch a hair of her head in anger, there are men in London who will punish such an action—and count me among the first—I, who have seen her only once—I who hardly know her.

KOEFELD: Always the actor, Mr. Kean—but you just betrayed yourself. Now, speak honestly. Look me in the eyes, and tell me—do you recognize this fan?

(*Takes fan from pocket.*)

KEAN: This fan?

KOEFELD: It belongs to the Countess.

KEAN: Well?

KOEFELD: Well, yesterday I found this fan in—

SOLOMON: (*Entering, interrupts* COUNT.) An urgent letter from the Prince of Wales.

KEAN: Later.

SOLOMON: No, the messenger said you must read it at once.

KEAN: Will you permit me, Count?

KOEFELD: Of course. I won't stray away.

KEAN: (*After having quickly read letter*) Do you know the handwriting of the Prince of Wales, Count?

KOEFELD: Of course. But how can that matter now?

KEAN: Read this—please—aloud.

KOEFELD: (*Reading*) "My dear Kean, please look carefully in your dressing room. I believe I left Countess Koefeld's fan there, which I had borrowed from her so that I could have another like it made for someone else. Also, I'm going to pay you a visit so we can discuss that ridiculous outburst in the theatre last night—and all on account of a little ballet dancer. I can't believe a friendship like ours can be disturbed by such trifles. Affectionately, George."

KEAN: That letter replies much better than I could to the suspicions you had—and which I am just beginning to comprehend. And you can easily understand that my modesty did not allow me to think I was the object of them.

KOEFELD: Mr. Kean, there is talk of arresting you. Don't forget that embassies are sanctuaries, and that the Danish embassy is open to you.

KEAN: Thank you, Count.

KOEFELD: Good-bye, Mr. Kean.

(KEAN *walks with him to door,* COUNT *exits.*)

KEAN: She is saved! By that excellent Prince! It was a miracle that he learned of it in time. Now she must leave, in order to arrive before her husband. (*Hears* SOLOMON *admitting someone. Door opens.*) Solomon, are you going to admit everyone on earth?

CONSTABLE: (*Entering*) A thousand pardons—it's me! And it's unfortunate business that brings me here. But duty comes first. I have to arrest you.

KEAN: Of what am I accused?

CONSTABLE: Injurious remarks in a public place against the Prince Royal, and against a member of Parliament.

KEAN: What must I do?

CONSTABLE: Follow me and my men, that's all.

KEAN: And abandon my house?

CONSTABLE: I'll have my men close the shutters, and the house will be sealed. When you come back, you'll find everything just as you left it.

KEAN: Constable, there are a few things I can't do without during my absence. I know you must follow the law, but do you need to be so strict?

CONSTABLE: No—I can do something for an artist I admire.

KEAN: You have an order to arrest me, but not others who are found here—is that right?

CONSTABLE: The order is for you alone.

KEAN: Well, there's a young girl in there. (*Points to bedroom*) You know her. She would like to leave.

CONSTABLE: Before, I seal the house, of course.

KEAN: And without being recognized by your men.

CONSTABLE: And you say I know this young lady?

KEAN: Unless you've already forgotten the name of Anna Damby.

CONSTABLE: Miss Anna Damby?

KEAN: She leaves for New York in one hour on the Washington.

CONSTABLE: I know that. I accompanied her to the theatrical agent and I booked her passage for her.

KEAN: You understand of course that she has some personal matters to discuss with me before she leaves.

CONSTABLE: You promise that you won't try to escape?

KEAN: Word of honor! (*To bedroom door*) Anna!

ANNA: (*Appearing*) What did I hear? They're arresting you? Then I won't leave for America. I'll stay here.

KEAN: Anna, the Constable is kindly allowing me a few minutes to speak to you before you leave. Constable, you will recognize Miss Damby by this hooded cape and veil. I hold you to your promise to allow her to pass undisturbed.

CONSTABLE: I wouldn't break my word to an artist like you.

(*He goes out.*)

KEAN: Anna, I must make a strange request that you could refuse, but you won't refuse. You know another woman is here—a woman who would be ruined if her face were recognized—because she is married. Anna, in the name of what is most dear and sacred to you, take pity on her.

ANNA: (*Detaching her veil and her cape*) Take them, Kean.

KEAN: You are an angel! (*Runs to room upstage.*) Elena! Elena! You're saved! (*Opens door, utters a mournful cry.*) Oh, God!

ANNA: What is it?

KEAN: Elena! There's no one here! And the window over the river is open. Oh, she heard her husband's voice, and his threats. I'm her murderer, her assassin—I killed her! I'm damned forever.

(*Rushes to window, looks out, in utter dejection.*)

PRINCE: (*Entering, speaks in rather low voice.*) Saved!

KEAN: (*Wheeling around*) Elena?

PRINCE Yes.

KEAN: How?

PRINCE: By a friend who has had your house under surveillance since last night. There was a boat under your window, and a carriage by your door, just in case you or someone else needed to make a quick departure. Elena boarded the boat by means of a ladder. She wasn't even ruffled.

KEAN: Where is she?

PRINCE: At home, where she arrived well before her husband. I had one of my confidants accompany her while I was writing to you. Did you get my letter?

KEAN: Yes, my Prince, and you have saved me twice. How can I make up for all the wrongs against you? I will go to prison happily.

PRINCE: Not at all! You will not go!

KEAN: How is that?

PRINCE: I obtained from my brother—and with great difficulty—that is why my boat was under your window, and my carriage at your door—

KEAN: What?

PRINCE: I obtained an order changing your six months in prison— and that's the least you would have received—to one year in exile.

KEAN: You send me in exile, while Elena is—

PRINCE: Returning to Denmark, where her husband is going on orders of his king. Are you satisfied?

KEAN: Has the place of exile been indicated?

PRINCE: Wherever you wish, provided you leave England.

KEAN: I shall go to New York.

ANNA: What did he say?

KEAN: Must I leave at a certain time?

PRINCE: You have a week to arrange your affairs.

KEAN: I leave in one hour.

ANNA: Oh, Kean.

(*She moves to him.*)

KEAN: Has the ship on which I must leave been designated?

PRINCE: Whatever ship you choose.

KEAN: I choose the Washington.

ANNA: Kean!

PRINCE: I hope the American air will clear your brain, and make you more sensible.

KEAN: I intend to get married there.

ANNA: Ah!

PRINCE: Who is this young girl?

KEAN: Miss Anna Damby—engaged today to play leading roles in a New York theatre.

PRINCE: Miss Anna Damby—of course! (*Bowing*) Miss!

ANNA: (*Making curtsy*) Your Highness!

SOLOMON: (*Enters with valise and package.*) I'm ready!

KEAN: What?

SOLOMON: Aren't you going to New York?

KEAN: Yes.

SOLOMON: To give performances?

KEAN: Naturally.

SOLOMON: Well, you'll need a prompter. I'm your prompter.

KEAN: (*Embracing* ANNA *and* SOLOMON) You are my only friends—my real friends!

PRINCE: Kean—do you know that you are an ungrateful wretch?

KEAN: Your Highness was included, of course! But a Prince deserves a special embrace.

(*He embraces the* PRINCE.)

PRINCE: I'm only too happy to share an embrace.

(He puts his arm around ANNA *who puts her arm around* KEAN *who puts his arm around* SOLOMON.*)*

KEAN: What a happy ending this would make for *Romeo and Juliet.*

The End

Young King Louis

ABOUT THE PLAY

In 1853, Dumas père, who had voluntarily exiled himself in Brussels in opposition to the rule of Napoleon III, returned to Paris in order to inform Arsène Houssaye, manager of the Comédie-Française, that he had a great play based on Louis XIV at age twenty. Houssaye liked the suggestion, and gave Dumas 10,000 francs advance royalty, whereupon Dumas confessed the play was still only in his head. But one week later, Dumas had completed his play, *La jeunesse de Louis XIV,* and it was accepted unanimously by the committee. The role of Georgette was written especially for the actress Emilie Dubois.

Unfortunately, someone in the theater circle informed the Ministry of State, and the play was promptly banned by the censor. Napoleon's government did not approve of French kings being portrayed on the stage. Dumas returned the advance and went back to Brussels, where the play was successfully performed in 1854. In 1874, four years after the death of Dumas, the play was performed at the Odéon in Paris, but with a revised script reworked by Dumas fils. He cut several scenes, changed the order of some, and added one fine scene between the king and his mother. The play was performed again in 1897, and had a revival in 1917.

This translation follows Dumas père whenever possible, but uses the son's cuts and changes when they seem to improve the continuity of the play. This is the only play in existence which contains the work of both Dumas père and Dumas fils.

HISTORICAL BACKGROUND

Louis XIV was born in 1638, and became king at the age of five upon the death of his father, Louis XIII. His mother, Anne of Austria, was appointed regent, and Cardinal Mazarin, chief minister. During the civil war of the Fronde, it became necessary for the queen and her family to take refuge in the chateau of Saint-Germain, where they came close to starvation. The Prince de Condé conducted the royal family back to Paris in 1650, but the great warrior soon turned against Mazarin and allied himself with the Spanish against France.

The king was completely subjugated by his mother and Mazarin, although he struggled to assert himself. On one occasion, he appeared alone before the French Parlement, dressed in a red hunting costume, and forced that body to register some edicts that had been issued in his name. His love affairs were his only royal prerogative. He had an affair with Mazarin's niece, Olympe, and later with Mademoiselle de la Motte. Unfortunately, La Motte already had a lover, Chamarante, the king's valet. The break with this girl caused the king much distress, and the cardinal supplied a distraction in the person of a gardener's daughter. The girl became pregnant, and was married off to a willing gentleman near the court. Louis next turned his attention to Marie de Mancini, another niece of the cardinal. He was very much in love with the girl and wanted to marry her, but was dissuaded by Mazarin and his mother. If Mazarin had any real desire to see his niece become Queen of France, he was too shrewd to allow it to hinder his political aims. He urged a marriage with Maria Theresa of Spain, feeling that it would bring peace between Spain and France.

The king reluctantly gave up Marie, and married Maria Theresa. Condé was pardoned, and became a loyal subject of the king once more. A few months later, Mazarin died, and Louis became the real head and master of the state, the grand monarch who ruled for seventy-two years. Mazarin's will bequeathed two pieces of furniture to the king. Eighteen large diamonds were left to the crown, and the bulk of his estate went to his nieces.

Charles II of England, cousin of Louis XIV, was successful in gaining the support of General Monk, and was restored to his throne in 1660, only to earn the historical distinction of being England's most dissolute monarch. His sister, Henrietta, married the Duke d'Anjou.

Molière presented his first play before the king in 1658, in a theatre adjoining the Louvre. It was here, a year later, that he gave the world his famous "Les précieuses ridicules."

MAZARIN

Born in Piscina, Italy, he was the son of a fisherman. His imperfect French was the subject of endless ridicule. Mean and miserly, he overwhelmed the people with taxes, a large portion of which he kept for himself. His talents were ordinary, but he was proficient in intrigue and diplomatic cunning. It was believed that he was privately married to Anne of Austria, whom he treated without respect. Below middle height, he was well built and rather handsome. His complexion was clear, his eyes were brilliant, his nose prominent and well proportioned, his forehead broad, his hair a chestnut color and curly, his beard darker than his hair. He was very unjust to young King Louis, whom he tried to keep in profound ignorance and without money. But with his usual insight into character, he remarked: "There is stuff enough in that young man for four kings."

LOUIS XIV

Louis was endowed with all the gifts that make the perfect gentleman. He was not particularly handsome, but his face had a kindly aspect. His eyes were brilliant, and of azure blue. He had a certain oriental look, probably from his Spanish ancestors of Moorish and Jewish blood. He was of medium height, had an excellent figure, perfect legs, feet, and hands. He had a noble look and extraordinary grace. He never made a meaningless gesture, so that he appeared to some as a deity or an actor always on the stage. He was extremely gallant, but diffident in his relations with women. His vanity was excessive, he was easily excited and easily brought to tears. He had a mellow, ringing voice, which gave expression to all he uttered. When he appeared in public, he scorned familiarity, possessing always an attitude of unbending pride that seemed to say "I am the King."

DUKE D'ANJOU

Two years younger than Louis, he was physically almost a caricature of his brother. He was shorter, very oriental looking, with swarthy skin and dark brown eyes. Louis was devoted to him although he regarded him as a sort of joke. In spite of being one of history's most famous homosexuals, d'Anjou had two wives, a mistress, and eleven legitimate children. All the kings of France after Louis XIV, as well as Marie Antoinette and the son of Napoleon, descend from him. Carefully brought up by Mazarin in complete ignorance of public affairs, so that he would not embarrass his brother, he found his major interests in jewels, parties, clothes, objects of art, and boys. After the birth of the king's first son, he became the Duke d'Orléans.

MARIE DE MANCINI

Born in Rome, she was rather tall, had large dark eyes, dark hair, fine teeth. She was brought to court with her sister Hortense. Mazarin sent both nieces away from the court prior to the king's marriage.

HENRIETTA

Daughter of Charles I of England and Queen Henrietta, who was the daughter of Henri IV of France. She was rather tall, had delicate skin, small but appealing eyes, lovely nose and lips, and teeth like pearls. She was most gracious, but had a melancholy air that detracted from her beauty. She married Philippe, Duke d'Anjou, in 1661.

MADEMOISELLE DE LA MOTTE

Though not a striking beauty, she was amiable and gracious and possessed of extraordinary spirit. She had blue eyes and blonde hair. Dark eyebrows and skin gave her a striking appearance. She had a lovely figure, and a charming manner of speaking.

Characters

LOUIS XIV, 20, King of France
CARDINAL MAZARIN, 56, first minister to Louis XIV
JEAN-BAPTISTE POQUELIN (MOLIÈRE), *36, an actor*
ANNE OF AUSTRIA, 57, *mother of the King*
BERINGHEN, *attendant to the Queen*
DUKE D'ANJOU, *18, brother of the King*
LE TELLIER, *King's councillor*
FOUQUET, *Superintendent of Finance*
DUKE DE GRAMMONT, *King's councillor*
DUKE DE VILLEROI, *King's councillor*
COUNT DE DANGEAU, *King's councillor and historian*
MARQUIS DE MONTGLAT, *King's Master of Ceremonies*
GUITAUT, *Captain of Musketeers*
GEORGETTE, *the gardener's daughter*
BOUCHEVANNES, *Lieutenant of Musketeers*
MARIE DE MANCINI, *niece of Mazarin*
COUNT ARMAND DE GUICHE, *young man of the court*
HENRIETTA, *18, an English Princess, cousin of the King of France*
MADEMOISELLE DE LA MOTTE, *the Queen's maid of honor*
BERNOUIN, *Mazarin's valet*
CHARLOTTE, *maid to Princess Marguerite of Savoy*
CHARLES II, *28, deposed King of England*
PIMENTEL, *Ambassador from Spain*
Musketeers, servants, hunters

Time: Sept. 25 and 26, 1658
Place: The chateau of Vincennes
Act I: *The Council Room*
Act II, Scene 1: *The forest of Vincennes*
Act II, Scene 2: *The Council Room*
Act III, Scene 1: *The courtyard of the chateau*
Act III, Scene 2: *The King's reception room*

Act I

The Chateau of Vincennes, which has been occupied for the hunting season and is only sparsely furnished. The scene is the Council Room. Double door at rear leads to courtyard and corridor. Long, narrow windows at each side of door, set in thick walls. At times a musketeer on guard can be seen through the windows. Down left is a door leading to Mazarin's quarters. Down right a door to others of the Court. Two upholstered chairs and a round table covered with green cloth. No other furniture.

MAZARIN comes in rear door, followed by MOLIÈRE, who has notebook and papers in his hand. MAZARIN speaks with an Italian accent.

MAZARIN: This way, Monsieur Poquelin, this way. So your father is ill?

MOLIÈRE: Yes, Your Eminence. He requested me to present his bill to you. You will note that he has figured the rooms for the maids of honor at two thousand francs.

MAZARIN: It's the total I'm waiting for—the total. It will probably be too much.

MOLIÈRE: Your Eminence is far too just to haggle over my poor father's account. He makes very little profit from his work.

MAZARIN: They all say that, so why shouldn't the Royal Upholsterer?

MOLIÈRE: But I would like to read you one short paragraph in the letter he received from Bernouin, your valet.

MAZARIN: One paragraph?

MOLIÈRE: Yes. (*Reading*) "Dear Monsieur Poquelin, His Majesty has decided to spend the hunting season at his chateau in Vincennes. You are requested to proceed at once with all your workmen to said chateau so that the residence may be made ready for the 25th of next month."

MAZARIN: I know, I know! What about it?

MOLIÈRE: Here is the important part. (*Reading*) "The King desires that you spare no expense in this matter."

MAZARIN: Well?

MOLIÈRE: It's clear—"the King wishes to spare no expense."

MAZARIN: The King—yes. But it doesn't say "the Cardinal." Since I handle the purse strings, it's with me that you must deal. Let me see the total, Monsieur Poquelin, or we shall never finish.

MOLIÈRE: Here's the total, Your Eminence.

(*Holds up a sheet of paper*)

MAZARIN: I prefer to total it myself. (*He looks about.*) What sort of Council room has your father improvised here? There is neither paper, nor ink, nor pens.

MOLIÈRE: I shall call for what Your Eminence wishes.

MAZARIN: No, no—that would waste time. I always have some scraps of paper in my pocket. (*Digs into pocket, finds scrap of paper.*) This will do very well. Now, will you lend me your pencil? (*Takes pencil, sits.*) This chair your father made is devilishly uncomfortable, Monsieur Poquelin. Now, tell me the amounts.

MOLIÈRE: (*Referring to his list.*) For the dining room, two thousand francs.

MAZARIN: (*Writing*) Two thousand francs.

MOLIÈRE: Bedrooms of the King, the Queen mother, and the Duke d'Anjou—four thousand.

MAZARIN: Four thousand! If it were not for the King—but it is for the King. (*Writes.*) Four thousand.

MOLIÈRE: Bedroom for Princess Henrietta of England, two thousand.

MAZARIN: Since Henrietta is the King's cousin, I approve. Go on.

MOLIÈRE: Bedroom for His Eminence, Cardinal Mazarin, and room for Bernouin, his valet—eight thousand.

MAZARIN: (*Writing*) Very good! Go on!

MOLIÈRE: Bedroom for Mademoiselle de Mancini, your Eminence's niece—three thousand.

MAZARIN: That much for the young girl's bedroom?

MOLIÈRE: My father received a particular request on that item.

MAZARIN: From whom?

MOLIÈRE: From the King's valet. He requested that nothing be spared to make Mademoiselle de Mancini's bedroom attractive.

MAZARIN: Ah, ha! The King wishes to spare no expense on my niece's apartment. Very well, Poquelin, we'll allow that to pass, but we must quibble about the remainder, I warn you. Read on.

MOLIÈRE: Rooms for the maids of honor, two thousand.

MAZARIN: Two thousand for them?

MOLIÈRE: There are six of them.

MAZARIN: Can't they sleep in one room? You are going to ruin me.

MOLIÈRE: For the Council Hall—fourteen hundred. Total, twenty-two thousand, four hundred.

MAZARIN: Luckily for you, I'm in a hurry—we'll just make it a round twenty thousand.

MOLIÈRE: But, Your Eminence—that is impossible. My father assured me the figures are very low.

MAZARIN: Mine are more accurate. It's settled! Your father may come for his payment in eight days.

MOLIÈRE: Your Eminence, since you have a pencil in your hand, I would be grateful if you would give me an order for payment now. If so, I would consent to the reduction Your Eminence has imposed.

MAZARIN: Now? But what would I use for an order? I have no writing material.

MOLIÈRE: The piece of paper you have there would do very well. All you have to write is "good for twenty thousand francs—Mazarin." If you write "one million", I shall accept it gladly.

MAZARIN: I know what to write! One million! Where would I get one million? I would have to sell everything down to my biretta. (*Writes*) There you are—signed and official. You see, I have a weakness for you.

(*Hands him the paper*)

MOLIÈRE: Oh, Your Eminence!

MAZARIN: What is it now?

MOLIÈRE: You indicated payment for September 25, 1659, but this is 1658.

MAZARIN: Did I put it off one year? I made a slight mistake—I meant to put it off for two years. Let me have the paper.

MOLIÈRE: It's a triviality! I'll be happy to wait a year if His Eminence will grant me one favor. (MAZARIN *makes a movement*.) A favor that will not cost him a sou.

MAZARIN: What is it?

MOLIÈRE: You know that I am an actor.

MAZARIN: Yes, I know all about you. You call yourself Molière, and you believe you are a poet. But your father believes you are mad, and wants you to assist him in making furniture.

MOLIÈRE: Quite right, Your Eminence.

MAZARIN: Well?

MOLIÈRE: Well, Your Eminence. I have been barnstorming in the provinces for thirteen years with my troupe. All of us would like to remain in Paris, and we would be grateful to have a charter for a theatre at court.

MAZARIN: Really, my friend? Is that why you came here in your father's place?

MOLIÈRE: Not at all, Your Eminence. My father's work and mine are world's apart. I have spoken for him, now I speak for myself.

MOLIÈRE: Theatre privileges are state matters and consequently they concern the King. Address yourself to the King.

MOLIÈRE: But when shall I be able to see the King?

MAZARIN: I suggest that you ask his brother, the Duke d'Anjou, to arrange an interview. The Duke is fond of theatre, and all that sort of nonsense.

MOLIÈRE: Thank you, Your Eminence. Someday I hope to use you as a model for a character in one of my plays.

MAZARIN: I'm honored.

MOLIÈRE: (*Throwing line aside*) I'll call it "The Miser."

MAZARIN: What did you say?

MOLIÈRE: I said "No man could be wiser." Your Eminence has been most accommodating, and I thank you.

MAZARIN: You may go now, Monsieur Molière Poquelin—or Monsieur Poquelin Molière, as you prefer.

(*He bows, turns to go, sees* ANNE OF AUSTRIA *entering.*)

MOLIÈRE: Your Majesty!

(*He bows and exits.*)

ANNE: Are we alone, Cardinal?

MAZARIN: Yes, we are. Is it a secret?

ANNE: Yes—a family secret. But it can easily become a state secret.

MAZARIN: Well, I am a small part of your family.

ANNE: And a large part of the state. I'll go directly to the point. Have you by chance given some thought to the fact that the King is at an age for marriage?

MAZARIN: Peccato! Have I thought about it? I think of nothing else. A while ago, I was saying to myself: "The King is at an age for marriage."

ANNE: Really? And what ideas do you have?

MAZARIN: None! You know very well we've discussed every princess in existence, but for one reason or another, not one of them seemed suitable to be the Queen of France.

ANNE: Except the Infanta of Spain—Maria Theresa. She would be suitable on all points, except—

MAZARIN: Except—yes, I know—she is an only child, and she is therefore heir to the Spanish throne. That makes her as unsuitable as the others.

ANNE: Unless the Queen of Spain gives birth to a son, we cannot think of Maria Theresa.

MAZARIN: Unfortunately—no.

ANNE: But the King is growing up. He is twenty now. His romances, up to now, have been only passing affairs, but one day he will fall in love seriously.

MAZARIN: Really? With whom?

ANNE: How should I know? Some girl more ambitious, cleverer or craftier than the others. Someday one will lead him into something foolish.

MAZARIN: You fear that?

ANNE: Yes, and I must take precautions. Because Louis has always feared you, and loved me, we have held control of him during his younger years. But now he is ready to revolt.

MAZARIN: Revolt?

ANNE: Exactly. And if there is to be a struggle, he will win. I know his proud and haughty character. He would bend us to his will along with the others.

MAZARIN: What do you propose to do?

ANNE: I've written to my sister-in-law, the Duchess of Savoy, to come and spend a few days here, and to bring her daughter, Princess Marguerite.

MAZARIN: Marguerite? Do you think she will attract the King?

ANNE: It's possible. Marguerite is a most charming girl, and I think the King will be attracted—but, only if he does not suspect that the meeting was arranged. Marguerite would make a good match for Louis—at least that is my opinion.

MAZARIN: I think you are quite right.

ANNE: The Duchess and Princess Marguerite will be here this evening or tomorrow.

MAZARIN: Good.

ANNE: Meanwhile I told Beringhen to have the King join me here.

MAZARIN: Are you going to tell Louis that you are expecting these guests?

ANNE: Certainly not! He must believe that Marguerite is here simply by chance. If he grows interested in her, it must be by his own desire—he must make up his own mind.

MAZARIN: Or at least think he is doing so.

ANNE: Yes. (BERINGHEN *enters.*) Well, Beringhen?

BERINGHEN: Madame, the King has not yet returned—or at least, no one has seen him at Vincennes.

ANNE: Really? And is Mademoiselle de Mancini here?

BERINGHEN: Yes, Madame, because I just saw her at her window.

ANNE: The King's absence worries me. Monsieur de Mazarin, go and see what you can find out. There must be someone who knows where the King is. Go see with your own eyes.

MAZARIN: I'm going, Madame, I'm going.

(*He exits.*)

ANNE: Beringhen, you haven't told me everything, I'm sure. Where is the King?

BERINGHEN: When I last saw him, he was riding his horse, and he was in hunting costume.

ANNE: Of course, there's to be a hunt today. But was he occupied with anyone in particular?

BERINGHEN: Yes, Madame. For a time he accompanied Mademoiselle de Mancini, then he took leave of her and galloped off towards Paris with Monsieur de Guiche.

ANNE: To Paris? Beringhen, go to the courtyard and wait. As soon as the King arrives, tell me where he comes from and where he goes.

BERINGHEN: Yes, Madame. (*As he starts to leave he meets the* DUKE D'ANJOU *entering. He bows.*) Your Highness.

ANJOU: Good morning, Beringhen. (BERINGHEN *exits.*) Good morning, Madame.

ANNE: Philippe, we're alone—you may call me "mother."

ANJOU: That's much nicer, mother, because I have a favor to ask of you.

(*He kisses her.*)

ANNE: What?

ANJOU: First, tell me how I look this morning, little mother.

ANNE: Much too pretty for a man.

ANJOU: You, too? It's annoying. Do you know what Jacques gave me? Some pomade for my lips. Look at my lips. Aren't they luscious? Do you like them?

ANNE: They look adorably fresh.

ANJOU: And De Guiche gave me some whitener for my teeth.

ANNE: Your teeth are so pretty, they don't need a whitener.

ANJOU: Little mother, there is nothing so beautiful that it can't be embellished.

ANNE: Why do you want to be so handsome?

ANJOU: Why—why—to please you, that's all.

ANNE: Look at your brother the King—does he spend all his time in front of his mirror?

ANJOU: The King is the King—he can command—therefore, he doesn't have to please anyone.

ANNE: When you came in, you spoke of a favor.

ANJOU: Oh, yes. It's something very important to me, I warn you, little mother. (*Suddenly distracted by the gloves he is wearing*) By the way, did you see my new gloves? They're made of Spanish leather.

ANNE: Yes, I see them.

ANJOU: Manicamps gave them to me. He had them made especially. They smell divine. (*He holds the gloves to his nose.*) You adore perfumes—they should please you.

(*Holds them to her nose.*)

ANNE: Be careful. If you force me to like them, you might make me hate them.

ANJOU: No danger of that. (*Imitating* MAZARIN's *accent*) With perfumes and fine linens, Anne of Austria could be led to hell.

ANNE: What's that you're saying?

ANJOU: I didn't say it—it was Cardinal Mazarin.

ANNE: (*Annoyed*) And the favor that you spoke of—what was it?

ANJOU: Oh, yes. You know of course that the Prince de Conti was brought up with the Jesuits at Clermont.

ANNE: Yes, I knew.

ANJOU: Perhaps you didn't know that his closest friend was the son of our upholsterer, Poquelin. Speaking of upholsterers, these chairs are atrocious. And the room is practically bare.

ANNE: You know how economical Mazarin is. But go on with your story.

ANJOU: Well, our upholsterer's son calls himself Molière, and he seems to be a young man of great talent. Conti offered him a place as his secretary, but he refused. Of course you know that Conti is a bit violent. They say he killed his last secretary with a pair of tongs, and that isn't a very appetizing thought for his next secretary, you will agree. But Molière wasn't thinking of that. He's mad about the theatre, and all that rubbish. He writes plays, and acts in them himself. Well, Molière would like to have a charter for a theatre.

ANNE: A theatre charter? That is a matter for the King.

ANJOU: The King?

ANNE: Yes, it's a state affair.

ANJOU: Oh! Then the King is concerned with state affairs?

ANNE: Naturally, since he's the King.

ANJOU: But isn't war a state affair? And peace—that is certainly a state affair. And finances—wouldn't you call that a state affair? And treaties with foreign countries—are they state affairs?

ANNE: What are you trying to say?

ANJOU: Simply that you and Cardinal Mazarin take care of all those things. Do you want me to tell you something? I'm afraid that my poor brother, Louis XIV, is beginning to resemble my dear father, Louis XIII, whom Cardinal Richelieu allowed no duties except that of going to the bathroom, and even that royal function was subject to the Cardinal's detailed instructions.

ANNE: Don't talk like that, you naughty child.

ANJOU: Well, little mother, I know that I'm no great politician like Her Majesty Anne of Austria, and especially not like Cardinal Mazarin. But if I were in their place, I give you my word, I would leave something for poor Louis to do, for fear that some-day—

ANNE: What?

ANJOU: For fear that someday—since he is in charge of nothing—poor Louis will take charge of everything—war, peace, finances, alliances, and marriage. There! I've said it! In the meantime, Monsieur Molière must get his theatre. Since you have assured me that is in the King's domain—probably the only matter reserved for the King—or perhaps the King is reserved for it—I'm going to arrange an interview for Molière with Louis. God knows that's all I can do in this matter. I'm certainly not going to uncurl my wig for him. (*Goes to window and peeks out.*) Here come the great councillors of the crown. The Cardinal is leading, and there's the Superintendent of Finance, and all the others. We're going to be royally bored. Mother, where is Louis? I don't think they should have the right to bore us without the King being here.

(MAZARIN *enters, followed by* LE TELLIER, DANGEAU, FOUQUET, DUKE DE GRAMMONT, DUKE DE VILLEROI, MARQUIS DE MONTGLAT, *and* GUITAUT, *Captain of Musketeers. They all bow to the* QUEEN.)

MAZARIN: Be seated, gentlemen. (*To* ANNE) No one knows where the King is—and I know even less than the others.

ANNE: Then proceed with your affairs.

MAZARIN: (*To* COUNCILLORS, *who have seated at table*) Gentlemen, you know why you have been assembled. The Superintendent of Finance has issued several edicts which have been signed by the King. These edicts are necessary to raise funds for the state. The Parlement has refused to register them. I should like your opinions on the action we should take.

GUITAUT: I say arrest every member of the court and throw them in the Bastille.

MAZARIN: That is your opinion, Monsieur Guitaut?

GUITAUT: Give me the order and it will be done.

MAZARIN: What do you think of Guitaut's plan?

LE TELLIER: Since Monsieur Guitaut is a Captain of Musketeers, his suggestion is of course understandable. But the rest of us are not policemen. The Parlement is a body we must live with. It is a vital part of our government—our judiciary court.

VILLEROI: I believe that the Parlement has the right to disagree.

FOUQUET: But I deny that it has the right of refusal.

GRAMMONT: I agree with Monsieur Fouquet, and here is what I propose.

MAZARIN: Listen to the Duke de Grammont—he is a man of wisdom.

GRAMMONT: Thank you for the compliment. Here is what I propose—

(*There is noise and fanfare in the hallway.*)

BERINGHEN: His Majesty the King!

(*Door opens,* KING *appears in red riding costume, felt hat, high boots, whip in hand. Behind him are men of the court, including* DE GUICHE.)

KING: I salute you, gentlemen. It appears the Council is having an emergency meeting.

MAZARIN: Your Majesty, we are consulting on ways and means of persuading the Parlement to register your edicts. It is very important.

KING: Useless, gentlemen—the edicts have been registered.

MAZARIN: But how? Who accomplished this miracle?

KING: I did.

MAZARIN: But how did your Majesty—?

KING: I simply appeared before the Parlement.

MAZARIN: You must have delivered an eloquent oration.

KING: I merely said: "I wish it!"

MAZARIN: Diavolo! You appeared in your hunting costume?

KING: Am I any less the King in this costume?

MONTGLAT: (*Aside to* GUITAUT) The King has decided to be King.

GUITAUT: For me, he won't be King until he tells me to arrest someone.

KING: Gentlemen, it is eleven o'clock. The hunting party leaves at twelve. Put on your hunting clothes. We leave precisely at noon. (*There is a general exit.*) Mother—and Monsieur the Cardinal—I hope you will do us the honor of joining the hunt.

ANNE: Yes, my son.

(*She leaves the room.*)

MAZARIN: Yes, Your Majesty.

(*He leaves.*)

ANJOU: Don't rush away, Louis. I have a protégé who is coming to ask a favor of you.

KING: His name?

ANJOU: Molière, the son of Poquelin, our upholsterer.

KING: I have heard of him from his father. Very well, I shall see him. But you must go dress—and try not to be too long about it—if it's possible.

ANJOU: I'll be quick—I've already put on my face. But before I go, let me say bravo for what you did before the Parlement. You are a King at last. Who knows, perhaps what Cardinal Mazarin said about you is true.

KING: What did he say?

ANJOU: That there is enough stuff in you to make four kings. (*He laughs and hurries out.*) I won't be a minute.

KING: (*Sits, deep in thought.*) She was waiting by her window. But was she waiting for me?

(*He taps on table.*)

GEORGETTE: (*Crawling out from under the table*) Don't tap so loud, Sire.

KING: Who are you? What are you doing there, my child?

GEORGETTE: I'm no assassin—don't be frightened. Besides you should recognize me.

KING: But, of course—of course—you're Dupré's daughter.

GEORGETTE: Yes, Sire.

KING: He was second gardener at Saint-Germain.

GEORGETTE: And he's now the head gardener here at Vincennes. Oh, yes—you know me.

KING: We played together a hundred times in the flower beds of the new chateau, and in the towers of the old chateau. Remember the watch tower? You called it the "stairway to heaven". Your name is Georgette—how could I forget?

GEORGETTE: Yes, Georgette, the curious, because I was always hidden somewhere, behind a curtain, or under a table—looking and listening.

KING: (*Laughing*) Well, Georgette, it seems you have grown up and become very pretty, but you haven't changed your name or your habits—right?

GEORGETTE: Does the King think I was under the table because of curiosity?

KING: Well, it appears so.

GEORGETTE: Then the King is mistaken.

KING: Why were you there?

GEORGETTE: Because I was afraid.

KING: Afraid of what?

GEORGETTE: Of Cardinal Mazarin.

KING: For what reason?

GEORGETTE: I don't dare tell Your Majesty.

KING: Come now—you won't be telling your secret to the King—but to your old playmate, Louis.

GEORGETTE: In that case—

KING: I'm waiting.

GEORGETTE: Well, I must tell you there's been a great hubbub here at Vincennes for a week.

KING: I imagine so.

GEORGETTE: Everybody running around like mad, yelling "The King is coming! They're refurnishing the chateau! There will be balls and festivals."

KING: And what did you say when you learned all that?

GEORGETTE: I said, "I'm glad, I'm glad!"

(*She claps her hands.*)

KING: Why did you say you were glad?

GEORGETTE: That's the same thing my father asked me.

KING: How did you reply to him?

GEORGETTE: I replied, "I'm glad because the King is one of my good friends, and we'll play together in the garden just like we used to do."

KING: You know, Georgette, you're adorable.

GEORGETTE: Me? Oh, that's silly, what you just said.

KING: (*Taking her hand*) So you answered your father. What a very nice little hand.

GEORGETTE: No! My father answered me. He said, "The King is no longer the little boy you played with at Saint-Germain. He is a fine young man, a great prince, and a poet has even said that he is a god."

KING: Really? A very poor god, believe me, Georgette. A god without a Mount Olympus—a god whose only thunder is a rattle.

GEORGETTE: But father said you were a god, and that made me more curious than ever, because I've never seen a god except the marble ones in the gardens. So I said to myself, "I want to see a real flesh-and-bones god." So this morning, I crawled through this window because I thought the room wasn't being used. I waited by the window, thinking I would see you in the courtyard. I saw many people, but not one god. Then I saw Cardinal Mazarin and Monsieur Molière—and they were coming in here. Do you remember how Cardinal Mazarin used to frighten us?

KING: He still frightens me—sometimes.

GEORGETTE: You see! That proves that you would have done what I did if you had been in my place.

KING: What is that?

GEORGETTE: I crawled under the table. I thought they would leave when they finished talking about furniture.

KING: But they didn't leave?

GEORGETTE: Molière left, but the Queen came in and began talking of state affairs with the Cardinal.

KING: That must have amused you.

GEORGETTE: It was very boring. But when they spoke about your marriage, I listened very carefully.

KING: What? My marriage?

GEORGETTE: Yes—it seems you're going to be married. (*She puts her hand on her mouth.*) Oh! You're not supposed to know!

KING: I'm not to know?

GEORGETTE: No! It's a big secret. Nobody in the world knows about it but the Queen, the Cardinal, and— (*She grins.*) And me!

KING: Really?

GEORGETTE: Yes. But this morning, even the Cardinal and I knew nothing about it. It was the Queen who told us.

KING: So they want me to marry without my knowing about it?

GEORGETTE: I believe that is their intention.

KING: And whom am I supposed to marry?

GEORGETTE: Princess Marguerite of Savoy.

KING: My cousin?

GEORGETTE: Is she your cousin?

KING: All the princesses are my cousins. So, I'm to marry Marguerite?

GEORGETTE: Yes. She will arrive tonight or tomorrow with her mother. But you are to think they are coming for an ordinary visit, nothing else.

KING: Yes, of course.

GEORGETTE: But since the Princess is very pretty and very charming, she will make you forget your love.

KING: My love for whom?

GEORGETTE: I don't know. Your love for somebody, that's all.

KING: Oh! It's good to know these things, my dear Georgette. Is that all you heard?

GEORGETTE: That's all. But isn't that enough, Sire?

KING: Oh, yes. You did very well to hide under the table, Georgette.

GEORGETTE: Really? I'm so happy! I'll keep on hiding, Sire.

KING: And will you tell me everything you hear?

GEORGETTE: Everything.

KING: Are you sure you didn't hear anything more?

GEORGETTE: From the Queen and the Cardinal? No. But Monsieur Molière asked the Cardinal for a theatre, and the Cardinal said, "That concerns the King". And Monsieur the Duke d'Anjou asked the Queen for a theatre for Molière, but the Queen said, "That concerns the King."

KING: It's generous of them to allow the King to concern himself with something.

GEORGETTE: The reason the Duke asked you to wait for Molière is because Molière is coming to ask for the theatre himself.

KING: Everyone has a request. Do you have a request, Georgette?

GEORGETTE: Me? Heavens, no!

KING: Please, make a request. Everyone does.

GEORGETTE: Well, I would like to request—after you have given Monsieur Molière his theatre—

KING: You think that I will grant it?

GEORGETTE: I'm sure of it. Your Majesty loves the theatre.

KING: Well, what is your request?

GEORGETTE: I would like your Majesty to persuade Monsieur Molière to let me join his troupe.

KING: You want to be an actress?

GEORGETTE: Don't you think I have the qualifications?

KING: Yes—a sharp ear, a prompt answer, beauty, spirit, and—

GEORGETTE: And?

KING: (*Laughing*) Curiosity.

GEORGETTE: Then you promise?

KING: To interest Molière in you.

GEORGETTE: Oh, thank you, Sire! I'll be an actress!

KING: But, on one condition.

GEORGETTE: What is it? I accept!

(*She comes close to him, her face close to his.*)

KING: Whatever it is?

GEORGETTE: (*Wistfully*) Yes.

KING: Well, on condition that you continue to have alert eyes and sharp ears, and that whatever you see or hear that might be of interest to me, you will come and tell me.

GEORGETTE: (*She withdraws slightly from him.*) Is that all? Agreed! (*The* KING *goes to door and looks out.*) Is there something you want?

KING: Yes, Georgette the curious, I should like to speak to the Captain of Musketeers. (*Calling*) Captain Guitaut!

(GUITAUT *enters.*)

GUITAUT: Yes, your Majesty.

KING: Monsieur Guitaut, I should like you to take a careful description of this young lady here. Pass it on to all your men, so that she may come and go as she pleases. Her name will be her password. It's Georgette.

GUITAUT: The King will be obeyed.

KING: That will be all, Guitaut. Will you please send in Lieutenant Bouchevannes. (GUITAUT *salutes, goes out.* KING *speaks to* GEORGETTE.) You needn't run off. You already know most of what Bouchevannes can tell me. (BOUCHEVANNES *enters.*) Bouchevannes, you just returned from a leave in Savoy, did you not?

BOUCHEVANNES: Yes, Sire, eight days ago. I had the honor of serving the Duchess of Savoy.

KING: Come here, Bouchevannes. (BOUCHEVANNES *places his pike by door and comes to* KING.) You must know the Princess Marguerite.

BOUCHEVANNES: I had the honor of seeing her every day.

KING: What is she like?

BOUCHEVANNES: Do you mean physically or morally?

KING: Both.

GEORGETTE: (*Taking pike, which is by door, she bars the door to* MOLIÈRE, *who opens it and starts to come in.*) You can't come in!

KING: Very good, Georgette—guard the door for Monsieur Bouchevannes. (*He looks to see who is at the door.*) Oh, it's you, Monsieur Molière. I shall see you in a moment.

GEORGETTE: Molière! I didn't know it was you!

KING: (*To* BOUCHEVANNES) Back to my question.

BOUCHEVANNES: I can only state how Princess Marguerite appeared to me.

KING: That's all I wish to know.

BOUCHEVANNES: Well, Sire, the Princess is pious and gentle. She has black hair, large, sad eyes, a straight nose, skin slightly more olive than white, beautiful teeth, and a very graceful figure. If the King wishes more intimate details—

KING: Well?

BOUCHEVANNES: I had the good fortune of knowing Princess Marguerite's maid of honor very well. I can get any information you wish from her.

KING: You've told me all I need to know. You may go now. Send in Monsieur Molière.

GEORGETTE: Yes, send in Monsieur Molière! (*Realizing her boldness.*) Oh, Sire!

KING: (*Laughing*) Don't distress yourself. Now, Georgette, you must leave me with Monsieur Molière. You already know what he's going to tell me. Perhaps you'll learn something more important elsewhere.

GEORGETTE: I'll try.

KING: Come in any time—by the door or by the window. And many thanks to you.

GEORGETTE: (*To* BOUCHEVANNES, *who has ushered in* MOLIÈRE.) The King thanked me, Monsieur Musketeer—the King is obligated to me, so don't forget it. (*To* KING) Good-bye, Sire. (*To* MOLIÈRE) Don't be afraid, Monsieur Molière—I've spoken for you. (*She goes out proudly,* BOUCHEVANNES *following her, closing door behind him.*)

MOLIÈRE: I trust the King will excuse my boldness, but the Duke d'Anjou assured me that you had been advised of the subject of my visit.

KING: I have been told the object of your visit, but not by the Duke d'Anjou. My information comes to me in many ways.

MOLIÈRE: If my visit annoys you, you need only make a sign and I shall withdraw.

KING: No, Molière—I am a man of first impressions, and my first impression of you pleases me. Now, I understand that your family has been tormenting you, and making you unhappy.

MOLIÈRE: Sire, I cannot honestly have ill feelings toward my parents because of their attitude. I am certain that they are genuinely convinced that my pursuit of the theatre will cost me my body in this world, and my soul in the next one.

KING: But that is not your opinion?

MOLIÈRE: My opinion is that one can live honorably in any occupation. I believe God is too merciful to put a special curse on actors.

KING: Monsieur de Conti was your classmate, was he not?

MOLIÈRE: We studied together at the Jesuit college in Clermont.

KING: Monsieur de Conti has praised you highly. He stated that if he were king, he would consult you on all state matters. He says you are well versed in rhetoric, philosophy and poetry.

MOLIÈRE: Sire, Monsieur de Conti is too indulgent. It's true that I learned rhetoric and philosophy, but as for poetry—

KING: As for poetry—?

MOLIÈRE: I don't believe one learns poetry. A man is either born a poet or he does not become one.

KING: Really? Well, tell me Monsieur Molière—what is a poet?

MOLIÈRE: Has your Majesty read the story of Aristaeus and Proteus in Virgil?

KING: Yes, I have.

MOLIÈRE: You remember that this Proteus could change himself in a moment into a lion or a serpent or a flame or a cloud—always escaping the chain that sought to bind him, or the hand that tried to seize him. Sire, that is a poet. How can I give a definition of such a person?

KING: But you are a poet—you can try. The words you speak are so different from the language of the world that I inhabit, that it seems to me I am hearing a man speak for the first time. What is a poet?

MOLIÈRE: A poet, Sire, is a man born between Nature's sad smile and her burst of laughter. He is made of joys and tears—a bit of a woman sometimes—a child always. He leaves reality in pursuit of a dream. He cherishes a cloud above all the riches of the earth—the cloud that changes form twenty times in a minute, while drifting through the sky. Sometimes he is the poor cricket, singing under a leaf; sometimes he is king of a world of poppies and daffodils, which he prefers even to your kingdom. Sometimes he is the proud eagle, gliding above the clouds—emperor of space, shining like gold in the sun, uttering wild and raucous cries because he cannot go higher into the beyond. And finally, he is this man that Conti has said your Majesty should make his counsellor—a man on whom you could heap all the favors of fortune with a word—a man who asks for only a few boards enclosed by three walls—a space which he can enter and leave at will, and in which he can speak, and cry, and laugh, and suffer with the people of his imagination, people who exist only in his fantasy, but who are his only friends, his only family, his only world. That is the poet, Sire. And now it remains only to say how such a strange being has dared present himself before the greatest, the noblest, the most powerful King in all the universe—the King of France.

KING: The King of France! Ah, Monsieur Molière, you have given me such an excellent definition of a poet, that I should like you to tell me what a king is. That shouldn't be difficult.

MOLIÈRE: Sire, a king is a man that posterity curses—(*The* KING *starts, almost in anger.*)—when he is called Nero, and blesses when he is called Charlemagne.

KING: In your opinion—if a king could ask God for one gift, what gift should that be?

MOLIÈRE: Solomon asked for wisdom.

KING: I do not wish to do what others have done—even King Solomon.

MOLIÈRE: Well, Sire, the most precious gift for a king would be truth. Truth arrives with difficulty to the ears of kings.

KING: But how can a king know truth?

MOLIÈRE: Sire, sometimes he must pretend to know the truth.

KING: Explain yourself.

MOLIÈRE: Unfortunately, I am merely a poor comic poet, and therefore I can offer you only a method from comedy.

KING: Offer it, nevertheless.

MOLIÈRE: Well, Sire, suppose that Chance has suddenly given you possession of a secret.

KING: Chance has done better than that, Molière. Today it has brought me two very important secrets.

MOLIÈRE: Then Chance is treating you like a spoiled child, and that proves its intelligence. Well, your Majesty has only to spread the word that a secret agent brings you news of everything that is said and done at court. When you know what people are doing and saying, it's not difficult to guess what they are thinking.

KING: But how do I start?

MOLIÈRE: You say you know two secrets. Begin by whispering these secrets in the ears of two persons who think they are the only ones who know. Have no fear, these persons will tell the secrets to someone else. I know the men and women of the court. Each one will rush to tell you his neighbor's secret, and perhaps his own, for fear that your secret agent might tell you first.

KING: That's a very pleasant idea, and I am going to adopt it.

MOLIÈRE: Sire, that is a great honor for this poor poet. But to prove to your Majesty the merit of the method, I shall be the first to betray my neighbor—and with great pleasure, since it will be for my master.

KING: Then you have a secret?

MOLIÈRE: Yes.

KING: Tell me.

MOLIÈRE: A while ago, while helping my father with his accounts—in an effort to pacify the dear man—I received a scrap of paper from Cardinal Mazarin. The Cardinal signed for some work done by my father, but he evidently did not notice that there were some notations on the other side of the paper. I know that the Cardinal is very economical, but in this case he should have used a fresh piece of paper. Would your Majesty perhaps like to glance at the other side of the paper?

KING: (*Reading*) "In Lyon—three million francs. Bordeaux—seven million. Madrid—four million. Rents and income—seven million—and so forth, and so forth—total thirty-nine million francs." Ah, ha, Mazarin could not resist the pleasure of scribbling down his fortune in order to please his eyes. But he was so thrifty—and so distracted—that he used the same paper for your father's voucher. As a thrifty man, I can entrust him with affairs of state, but if he is becoming distracted, it's time for me to take charge. Thank you, Monsieur Molière, I shall not forget your advice. (*Hands back paper as hunting horns sound outside.*) It's time to leave for the hunt. Now, please listen to me, Molière: although a poet likes to float in the clouds, a poet must also eat. Beginning today, you are my honorary valet de chambre at three thousand a year.

MOLIÈRE: Oh, Sire, my deepest thanks.

KING: As for the theatre—ask me about it whenever you like.

MOLIÈRE: Sire, to kiss the royal hand is the only wish I have.

(*Fanfares. The* KING *extends hand.* MOLIÈRE *respectfully kisses it, then exits. As the door opens we see a group of men and women in hunting costumes. They pour into the room.*)

KING: Ladies and gentlemen—to the hunt! I hope the day finishes as well as it started.

Curtain

Act II

The forest of Vincennes. At left is the St. Louis oak tree. At right, a grotto covered with greenery. Trees and foliage in background. People are gathered in groups. Under the oak tree are ANNE OF AUSTRIA, HENRIETTA, *who are seated on a bench,* MLLE. DE LA MOTTE, BERINGHEN, *and* LE TELLIER, *standing or sitting on ground. The group, in and around the grotto, consists of the* KING, MARIE DE MANCINI, D'ANJOU, DE GUICHE, VILLEROI *and* DANGEAU. *A third group is upstage:* MAZARIN, FOUQUET, GRAMMONT *and* GUITAUT. *Other hunters may be used at will.*

MONTGLAT *is busily urging two servants to take the remains of the lunch away.*

In the background we can hear the sounds of hunting dogs.

MONTGLAT: Quickly! Quickly! Clear everything away. The hunt must go on. (*Excitedly, to* KING) I hope your Majesty will be indulgent. It isn't easy to serve a meal in the middle of a forest.

KING: It was an excellent lunch, Montglat, but I am sure you will think of improvements during the next two weeks. There will be many more hunts.

MONTGLAT: (*Horrified*) Oh!

(*Goes busily about his work.*)

MARIE: (*She is watching* DANGEAU *make notes on a pad.*) Sire, ask Dangeau what he is writing. I'm willing to wager it's a madrigal in honor of your passion for Mademoiselle de la Motte.

KING: La Motte?

MARIE: Yes, she is watching you with an eagle's eye, and she is mak-

195

ing sure the Queen doesn't hear what we say, even though the Queen is watching every movement.

KING: Marie, you know very well that Mademoiselle de la Motte is no longer my passion. If I have no power as a King, I at least have power over my heart.

MARIE: But you did love La Motte.

KING: Who knows? But she was in love with Chamarante, and therefore she could be nothing to me. I learned of her lover from my secret agent. But I can tell you, even without my secret agent, that Dangeau is not writing verses.

MARIE: Then I told two lies.

KING: Lies never came from such beautiful lips as yours, Mademoiselle de Mancini.

MARIE: I have never been given such a gallant scolding.

KING: My dear, I could never scold you. When I look in your eyes, I'm speechless.

ANJOU: De Guiche, does it amuse you to hear love talk so constantly?

DE GUICHE: To hear it—no! To speak it—yes.

MARIE: I've been thinking—how do I really know that La Motte is no longer your love? And how do you know that Dangeau is not writing poetry?

KING: The answer to the first question is that a woman never mistakes the feeling she inspires.

MARIE: You mean—?

KING: I mean that you can see the love I have for you as easily as a diver can see a pearl at the bottom of the sea.

MARIE: Oh, it's you who are the poet! If you tried, you could write beautiful verses.

ANJOU: What is your opinion, De Guiche?

DE GUICHE: The King is the King—he can do as he likes. But poetry is a woman, and like all women it can be unfaithful.

KING: De Guiche, I warn you, if you continue to speak ill of women, I shall exile you. (*He laughs.*)

DE GUICHE: (*Sullen, takes a step away, muttering.*) Like Chamarante?

KING: What did you say?

DE GUICHE: I said it wouldn't surprise me if you exile me.

ANJOU: I know very little about verses. I like them better than sweets, but less than lace and diamonds and perfume. I would give my birthright for jewels even if I were Esau instead of Jacob.

MARIE: (*To* ANJOU) Doesn't your governess ever punish you by making you memorize verses?

ANJOU: (*Behind* MARIE) Mademoiselle, I have not had a governess for two years. I govern myself now. The only punishment I receive is when your dear uncle Mazarin refuses me money. But, Mademoiselle, I must say—considering that you are the Cardinal's niece—that is a very fetching English tweed you are wearing.

MARIE: Her Majesty Queen Henrietta gave it to me.

ANJOU: Does my poor aunt still have something to give away? I thought the two Cromwells had taken everything.

VILLEROI: Come now, let's not get into politics.

MARIE: Sire, you haven't yet told me if Dangeau is writing verse or prose.

KING: We'll find out. Come here, Dangeau. (DANGEAU *approaches.*) Mademoiselle de Mancini claims you are writing poetry, and I claim you are writing prose.

ANJOU: Perhaps it's neither one nor the other.

KING: Which of us is right?

DANGEAU: You as always, Sire.

KING: Take care—there are certain persons who must always be right against me, even when they are wrong.

DANGEAU: Sire, my position as Royal Historian does not allow me to lie.

ANJOU: Or to flatter.

DANGEAU: I am writing history, and history is not written in verse.

KING: Read what you have written. We'll decide for ourselves.

DANGEAU: Permit me to finish a phrase.

LA MOTTE: (*To* ANNE) You see—he can scarcely keep his eyes off her.

ANNE: Yes—I see. But then, only two or three weeks ago they were saying the same about you.

KING: Are you finished, Dangeau?

DANGEAU: Yes, Sire.

KING: We're listening.

DANGEAU: (*Reading*) The 25th of September, 1658, his Majesty, Louis XIV, before going on a hunt, had lunch in the forest of Vincennes, under the oak tree known as the Oak of Saint-Louis. The hunters ate on the ground, and were divided in several groups. The King's group consisted of—

KING: (*Laughing, interrupts him.*) Enough! Enough! We're convinced that you were not writing poetry.

(*They all laugh.*)

ANJOU: Dangeau, your history of my brother's reign is going to be sensational if it contains many paragraphs like the one you just read.

(*The* KING *suddenly takes* MARIE'*s hand and kisses it.*)

DE GUICHE: Oh!

(*Clenches his fist and walks away.*)

ANJOU: What's wrong with De Guiche? A while ago he was grumbling, now he's angry.

MARIE: How would I know?

KING: If you don't want to tell us, I'll ask my secret agent.

MARIE: Pardon, Sire, but that's the second time you have spoken of your secret agent. May I ask how you employ this mysterious confidant?

KING: He tells me all that is said, done, and thought at court. For instance, he will tell me what my cousin Henrietta—who hasn't said a word—is thinking. And he will tell me what Mazarin is whispering to my Captain of Musketeers at this very moment.

MARIE: You're joking with me.

ANJOU: Monsieur Dangeau, here's an entry for your journal: my brother Louis has a friendly ghost that haunts him by day and visits him at night.

ANNE: Philippe! (ANJOU *goes to his mother's side.*) What were you just saying?

ANJOU: My dear brother says he has a secret agent that tells him everything. In the future, no one will be able to hide a thing.

HENRIETTA: Good heavens!

ANJOU: Why are you so frightened, Henrietta? Do you have something to hide? (*He goes to* LA MOTTE, *kneels and speaks low to her.* HENRIETTA *speaks in undertone to* ANNE.)

HENRIETTA: Did you hear what they are saying? The King has a secret agent. If that's true, the King must know that Charles is in Vincennes. Perhaps I ought to warn him.

ANNE: Don't be afraid, my dear. First of all, that friendly ghost probably doesn't exist. In the second place, if Louis learns that the King of England has broken the ban which exiled him from France, he will not be angry. Louis has the most tender regard for your brother.

HENRIETTA: I'm not afraid of Louis, but of Mazarin.

ANNE: I shall admit that Mazarin is a friend of Cromwell, and therefore an enemy of the rightful King of England.

HENRIETTA: That has been proved. My mother thought that when Oliver Cromwell died, Mazarin would support Charles. But what happens? He recognizes Richard Cromwell, and my brother is kept from his legitimate throne.

ANNE: Don't give up hope. Remember when the King and I, and your mother and you were almost dead from hunger during the war? But quiet—people are trying to hear what we are saying.

LA MOTTE: (*Taking* ANJOU's *arm*) Tell me honestly, Philippe, please—what has the King been saying to Marie?

ANJOU: First he told her how perfectly lovely she looked—and I agree. I have never seen an outfit cut so beautifully as hers. It does wonders for her. Don't you think so? I'm sure you do.

LA MOTTE: I hadn't noticed. But I thought I heard him speak of her eyes. Did he by chance tell her that she had the most magnificent eyes in the world?

ANJOU: Naturally! Don't you think Marie's eyes are magnificent? I'm sure you do. (*Looking at her diamond clip*) Oh, what a charming diamond clasp.

LA MOTTE: Don't you recognize it?

ANJOU: Yes. I think I once saw it on Louis' hat.

LA MOTTE: Not so loud—Marie will be jealous. What did he really say about her eyes?

ANJOU: That they were as blue as the sea.

LA MOTTE: And what did she say?

ANJOU: "Bad comparison," she said. "The sea is treacherous, but my eyes never promise something that is not fulfilled." "Well then," said Louis, "they are as blue as the sky which is over our heads." "That I accept," replied Marie, "even though the sky is spotted with clouds at this moment."

LA MOTTE: You're making that up.

ANJOU: Of course I am! You know very well that Marie's eyes are as brown as chestnuts. But you ask a lot of questions. Could it be you are no longer in love with Chamarante?

LA MOTTE: Perhaps no more than Marie de Mancinci is in love with De Guiche.

ANJOU: Oh, ho! De Guiche and Marie de Mancini? What are you saying, beautiful serpent?

LA MOTTE: I'm simply saying that you need only watch the way De Guiche keeps looking at Marie, and the way Marie avoids looking at De Guiche.

ANJOU: What you are really trying to say is that someday things will be finished between the King and Marie, just as they are finished between the King and you.

(*He turns away as* GEORGETTE *enters, carrying an armload of flowers.*)

GEORGETTE: Help! Help! My bouquets are falling.

THE LADIES: Oh, what charming flowers.

THE MEN: What a pretty girl.

KING: Georgette, is that you behind all those flowers?

(*He rises.* ANJOU *comes to* MARIE, *whispers.*)

ANJOU: Take care of your wool, my lamb—there are some wolves here.

GEORGETTE: It's me, Sire. My father said, "Georgette, we're not going to be like those people who save their best wine for themselves. I'm going to cut all my best flowers, and you can make bouquets and carry them to the ladies. That will please the King." No sooner said than done. Here I am with the bouquets. But they are going to fall if someone doesn't help me.

KING: Ladies, you can see Georgette's predicament. Be good enough to accept the flowers she has brought. The gardener who gives his flowers, and the King who gives his crown are equal before the Lord.

(*The women gather around and take a bouquet, but* GEORGETTE *clings tenaciously to one.*)

GEORGETTE: No, not this one, ladies. It's for the King. (*Low to the* KING) Or rather, it's for Mademoiselle de Mancini.

KING: Why for her?

GEORGETTE: Because she's the prettiest.

KING: But why should her bouquet be prettier than the others?

GEORGETTE: Because, when I was under the table, I heard the Queen's servant tell her that Marie was at her window all morning. If she was waiting for you, she must love you, and if she loves you, I love *her*.

KING: You're a dear girl. Go take the bouquet to Mademoiselle de Mancini.

GEORGETTE: (*Changing her tone*) I will—but the flowers are only a pretext. I want to tell you that Princess Marguerite just arrived with her mama and a maid of honor named Charlotte.

KING: Good work! Now take the flowers to her.

GEORGETTE: (*To Marie*) Here, Mademoiselle—I give you these on behalf of the King.

DE GUICHE: (*Low to* MARIE) Marie, I must speak to you.

(ANNE *whispers to* BERINGHEN, *who goes to the* KING *and makes sign that* ANNE *wishes to talk to him. There is a sound of hunting horns offstage.*)

KING: Ladies and gentlemen, the hunt is about to start. (*People start moving off as* KING *goes to* MARIE.) My dear, I must remain for a few moments to speak to my mother.

MARIE: Has the King been disobedient?

KING: It appears so.

MARIE: And will they punish him?

KING: They will try. (MARIE *moves away, backstage.* KING *and* ANNE *walk forward, talking in undertone.*)

ANNE: What is this foolish talk about a secret agent? How long have you had this good genie in your service?

KING: Truthfully, only since eleven o'clock this morning.

ANNE: And has this ubiquitous friend revealed many secrets to you since this morning?

KING: Only one, but important enough to merit all my attention.

ANNE: Really?

KING: Yes. And the secret has doubled my respect and admiration for you, mother, because it proves to me that you are always busily working for my happiness.

ANNE: You're thanking me for something, but I can't imagine what.

KING: Admit frankly, mother—there is one particular thing that obsesses you of late.

ANNE: What are you talking about?

KING: I refer to a certain feeling of mine that you fear might become too tender.

ANNE: You are right—but I'm not afraid it will become too tender, but too serious.

KING: So, with your profound regard for me, and thinking only of my welfare, you had the idea of inviting your sister-in-law to Vincennes, under pretext of a casual visit. And of course she will bring her charming daughter, Marguerite, whose blue eyes you hope might combat the influence of Marie de Mancini's dark eyes.

ANNE: How did you know all that?

KING: My secret agent! Did you think he was a myth! I also know that Princess Marguerite is pious and gentle, has sad eyes, a straight nose, white teeth, skin slightly olive—and other features which I shall examine after the hunt.

ANNE: After the hunt?

KING: Yes! Thanks to my secret agent, I can be the first to give you news that you have been impatiently waiting. Marguerite and her mother arrived at Vincennes a few minutes ago.

ANNE: Without my knowing it? Impossible!

KING: I assure you they are at the chateau—Marguerite's maid, Charlotte, also. My secret agent never makes a mistake. Pardon me, I must rejoin Marie. (*Turns to* MARIE, *who comes nearer.* KING *speaks pointedly towards his mother.*) I'll take you to your horse, Marie. I must return to speak to your uncle on an important matter. Please take my place at the head of the hunt. You might as well be queen when I am not there—you are my queen when I am near you. But come back in less than ten minutes. I shan't need more time than that.

(*They go out of sight together.* ANNE *is furious, and beckons* MAZARIN *to come to her.*)

ANNE: You told him everything!

MAZARIN: I told him nothing!

ANNE: But he knows every detail—that I am concerned about his new love, that I am trying to bring Princess Marguerite to his attention.

MAZARIN: Peccato! Who could have told him?

ANNE: Pardon this thought if it is false, but who could be more interested than you in preventing a union between Louis and Marguerite?

MAZARIN: I don't understand you.

ANNE: Doesn't the King love your niece?

MAZARIN: He has loved other nieces of mine, but those romances have meant nothing.

ANNE: Yes, I know—but this new love is becoming serious.

MAZARIN: In that case I must marry the girl to some prince or other, as I did her three sisters.

ANNE: Marry her to whomever you like, Cardinal, but I warn you, do not attempt to marry her to the King.

MAZARIN: Buon Dio! Who could think of such a thing? The King, perhaps, but not me, that is certain.

ANNE: I do not believe the King capable of such folly, but if he should make such a decision, all of France will revolt against you—and I will head the revolt myself. Come Beringhen.

(BERINGHEN, *who has been far upstage, joins* ANNE *and they exit. The* KING *has appeared on the last words. He smiles and approaches the* CARDINAL.)

KING: I have something to ask you, my dear Cardinal.

MAZARIN: Speak, my boy. Oh, pardon me, I was speaking to you as I did when your mother was regent, and you were no higher than this. (*He demonstrates.*)

KING: Haven't you still the right to speak to me like that? If I am King of France, it is because of you. After God, I owe my crown to you.

MAZARIN: Are you really convinced of what you say?

KING: But it's history, Monsieur de Mazarin.

MAZARIN: History often lies. But you said you had something to ask me, my dear Louis.

(*The* KING *puts his hand on* MAZARIN's *shoulder in the most friendly fashion.*)

KING: Well, my dear Cardinal, I need money.

MAZARIN: (*Taken off guard*) Money?

KING: Yes, money!

MAZARIN: Pardon me, I thought I misunderstood. And why do you need money?

KING: To amuse myself, that's all.

MAZARIN: Do you think you became a King simply to be amused?

KING: My dear Cardinal, a King must either rule or amuse himself. Since it is you and my mother who rule, I must find amusement. If not, I might start meddling in affairs of state. That wouldn't be amusing but it would be a distraction. I might even start tomorrow. You'll be able to rest. After thirty years of devoted work for France, you deserve a breathing spell, and after six years of doing nothing, I need to do a little work.

MAZARIN: How much do you need? A large sum?

KING: No.

MAZARIN: If it's only a small amount, perhaps it can be arranged.

KING: A small amount for a King, especially when the King is surrounded by rich ministers.

MAZARIN: But what is the sum? It all depends on the sum.

KING: I believe that with a million—

MAZARIN: A million?

KING: Is that too little for a King of France?

MAZARIN: A million! Where do you think I could touch a million, my boy?

KING: That's for you to decide. You could draw on the three million you have in Lyon, or on the seven million you keep in Bordeaux, or even the four million in Madrid. Or, if you don't care to dislodge such well-placed gold, you could borrow the sum on your nine millions of property, and I would pay you interest to the last centime.

MAZARIN: I'm betrayed—ruined!

KING: It seems to me that a minister who has such vast hordes of assets—thirty-nine million, to be exact—would not mind lending a paltry million to his King.

MAZARIN: But who told you? Who could have told you?

KING: My secret agent, of course.

MAZARIN: But the figure is exact.

KING: Of course—my secret agent is scrupulously correct.

MAZARIN: When do you want this million?

KING: This evening, my dear Cardinal.

MAZARIN: What do you intend to do with it?

KING: I'm going to tell you, because I have no secrets from you. I am in love, and I want to please the woman I love.

MAZARIN: A King—a handsome and young King like you—has no need of a million to make a woman mad for him.

KING: Perhaps. But a million spent on parties—of which she will be the queen—will certainly not make her care less for me.

MAZARIN: You intend to make a Queen of the one you love?

KING: Queen of my parties, I said. Perhaps later she will become Queen of my kingdom.

MAZARIN: Since you give me such good reasons, you shall have the million tomorrow.

KING: Tonight, my dear Cardinal. My love is so overwhelming, that it can't wait.

MAZARIN: If your love is overwhelming, that is another thing. Well—

KING: Well?

MAZARIN: I will do my best to get you the million this evening.

KING: You are the most generous man I know, Cardinal. Until this evening, then.

MAZARIN: Are you going to remain here?

KING: I shall join the hunt in a moment. (MAZARIN *goes off. The* KING *looks offstage. He raises his arms even before* MARIE *appears. She comes to his arms, he kisses her.*) Marie, come here. (*He takes her to the bench under the oak tree. They sit.*) At last we are alone. I've been dying to hear your voice without a torrent of other voices around me. I want to see your face in the private mirror of my eyes. You are like a goddess that chases away all the evil demons. Marie, you make me very happy.

MARIE: I'm grateful for the place I occupy near the King.

KING: Marie, do you know of anything in this world but a charming woman that can make a King forget that he is a King?

MARIE: Do you really believe that being a king is so dreadful that you must forget it?

KING: Marie, the only crown that God places on his chosen ones is the crown of love. Any other crown chafes and burns the head that wears it.

MARIE: Perhaps the crown you value so highly could be yours if you would only ask.

KING: If I asked, would it be the King or the lover that received the crown? Perhaps an ambitious love might replace a tender love. Sometimes I regret not being born the lowest of my subjects rather than a king. Then, if beautiful lips like yours said, "Louis, I love you," I would be sure of being loved for myself.

MARIE: Have you ever thought that the woman you will love might also be tormented by doubts? If you were poor and insignificant, the woman who loved you would feel that you were hers until death. But a woman who loves a king never knows if it is for always or if it is a caprice of the moment. Every beautiful woman of the court is her rival for the king's affection. Suddenly she may discover that she is a Queen but not a wife. I tell you this sincerely—a woman who is in love with a king—a young and handsome king—if she had a smattering of wisdom in her head—a shadow of dignity in her soul—she would stuff her love into a remote corner of her heart instead of letting it grow.

KING: Do you mean that?

MARIE: I speak for myself. I am not of royal birth. Your Councillors, your mother, everyone at court, would be my enemy.

KING: Who can say that a king must marry a princess or a sister of a queen? Is it so necessary to the State? Would France be better off if I marry some princess from Savoy or Portugal or Germany? Do you think I could be happy in my kingdom and unhappy in my love? Impossible!

(*There is thunder and a drizzle of rain. The* KING *puts his cloak around* MARIE *and leads her gently to the grotto.*)

MARIE: Even kings can be unhappy.

KING: But I mean to be happy, and I tell you that I mean to be a king! If I say "I wish," it is all I need say. I will marry the woman I love, and yet I want that woman to love me for myself alone. I want her to say "I love you," and I will say to her, "Here is my heart," and to France I will say "Here is your Queen!"

MARIE: If a woman believed such a promise she would be foolish.

KING: Why?

MARIE: Madame de Fontenac loved you.

KING: She had a husband.

MARIE: My sister Olympe loved you.

KING: I was a child.

MARIE: Mademoiselle de la Motte loved you.

KING: I did not love *her!*

MARIE: But me—what about me?

KING: That's different! I love you! I love you with all my heart. I love you more than I am able to say.

(He kisses her passionately. There is a clap of thunder. Several of the hunters appear in the background, seeking shelter. They come no further when they see MARIE *and the* KING.)

MARIE: I love you, Louis, I swear it!

(He takes his cloak and spreads it in a corner of the grotto. Gently he puts his arms around MARIE *and they lie on the ground together. More hunters have assembled, among them* ANJOU. *He is the only one who approaches the grotto. His eyes widen and he tiptoes away, going towards the hunters.)*

ANJOU: I believe the storm has passed. We can return to our horses.

Curtain

Act II

SCENE 2

The Council Room, same as first scene. MAZARIN *is at the table writing, and muttering.*

MAZARIN: A million! *Questo è il colmo!*

(BERNOUIN, *agitated, comes in center door.*)

BERNOUIN: Your Eminence, I have some important news.

MAZARIN: So it appears. Calm down, Bernouin. What's wrong?

BERNOUIN: Two vital matters, sir. First, the Prince de Condé has sent his submission to the King. Of course I knew that you would wish to see it first.

(*Hands him a paper, which he looks at.*)

MAZARIN: Naturally. We must not trouble the King with trifles. So Condé wants to come back? He is tired of fighting against us, and now he wants to fight for us.

BERNOUIN: But the messenger said that Condé is sick in Brussels— very sick.

MAZARIN: Then it is a matter for my good doctor Guénaud. Condé must be healed—and very slowly. Bernouin, if you ever become a statesman, remember that the first great secret of diplomacy is contained in these words: "Know how to wait!" Send for Captain Guitaut.

BERNOUIN: Yes, Your Eminence.

(*He opens center door and speaks to guard.*)

MAZARIN: What was the other important matter?

BERNOUIN: King Charles II—or should I say, former King Charles II—is in Vincennes.

MAZARIN: Charles in Vincennes? Are you sure? Who saw him?

BERNOUIN: I did—at the Hotel of the Crowned Peacock.

MAZARIN: That is not good news, Bernouin. Charles should not be in France. Richard Cromwell rules England now, and we have a treaty with him. Where is Guitaut?

BERNOUIN: He's coming. Are you going to arrest King Charles?

MAZARIN: Of course not—I am simply going to invite him to leave France.

BERNOUIN: And if he doesn't want to leave?

MAZARIN: Then I will act. If you ever become a statesman, Bernouin, remember that the secret of getting out of any difficulty is contained in these words: "Know when to act."

BERNOUIN: How does Your Eminence reconcile his second maxim with his first one?

MAZARIN: I don't reconcile them—put them face to face. I wait, or I act, as the need arises. (GUITAUT *enters and* BERNOUIN *retires.*) Good evening, my dear Guitaut.

GUITAUT: Good evening, Your Eminence. You sent for me?

MAZARIN: Yes, I have several things to tell you. But first, let me say that I scarcely ever hear you speak of Lieutenant Comminges.

GUITAUT: He is well, and always at your service. Is there someone you want arrested?

MAZARIN: I was thinking that there was talk of a marriage between Lieutenant Comminges and your daughter. You know, that if this marriage takes place, I intend to give the bride a wedding gift of ten thousand francs.

GUITAUT: That would be very interesting, Your Eminence, because, until now, we have received only bullets and sword thrusts in the service of royalty. Do you want someone arrested?

MAZARIN: Do you always think there is someone to be arrested?

GUITAUT: Well, when one calls the Captain of the Guards, and when one promises him ten thousand francs for his daughter's dowry, it appears that one has need of the Captain of the Guards.

MAZARIN: Yes, I need you, Guitaut, but not to arrest anyone.

GUITAUT: Oh? To do what, then?

MAZARIN: First I want you to see that Doctor Guénaud is made ready to leave at once for Brussels.

GUITAUT: Brussels?

MAZARIN: Yes. The Prince de Condé is very sick there. I want Guénaud to cure him—but not too quickly. Fast cures are not safe. It must take a month or two months. Do you understand?

GUITAUT: Perfectly. But what about your health during that time?

MAZARIN: Don't worry about my health. I was never better. Besides, it is my duty to sacrifice myself in this case. Now, for the second matter I wish you to handle.

GUITAUT: Yes, Your Eminence.

MAZARIN: I want you to warn a foreigner who is at the Hotel of the Crowned Peacock, the I know he is here.

GUITAUT: Very well—you know he is here—and you want—?

MAZARIN: I want him to leave the hotel.

GUITAUT: Shall he find lodging elsewhere in Vincennes?

MAZARIN: I want him to leave Vincennes, if that is not too much trouble to him.

GUITAUT: Very well. Then he should return to Paris?

MAZARIN: Paris is too close to Vincennes. I should like him to leave Paris also, if that does not inconvenience him too much.

GUITAUT: And in what part of France shall he be permitted to stay?

MAZARIN: I should like to see him leave France, if that is not too disagreeable to him.

GUITAUT: You mean that you want to exile him?

MAZARIN: Oh, buon Dio, no! I simply send him back where he comes from, that is all.

GUITAUT: And if he should refuse to go?

MAZARIN: In that case you must use force—but with the utmost delicacy and regard.

GUITAUT: Then this is a great lord you speak of?

MAZARIN: Very great.

GUITAUT: Greater than Condé?

MAZARIN: Much greater.

GUITAUT: Is he perhaps a king?

MAZARIN: He is a king, and he is not a king. Do you understand, Guitaut?

GUITAUT: I'm afraid I don't.

MAZARIN: In your opinion, Guitaut, is it the fact or the right that makes a king?

GUITAUT: The right, Your Eminence.

MAZARIN: Well, I am not entirely of your opinion. To my eyes, Richard Cromwell is the real ruler of England—at least until General Monk decides otherwise.

GUITAUT: Then you are speaking of Charles II of England?

MAZARIN: Quite right! You see now why I insist on such politeness and finesse. Charles is the cousin of Louis XIV. You will conduct him in a fine carriage with excellent horses. You will enter the carriage after him, and you will sit at his left—remember, Guitaut, the left. You must not be lacking in etiquette with a king. You will place two guards on the opposite seat—the most amiable men you have available, if you please. And you will conduct the king to the frontier of Holland.

GUITAUT: But what will King Louis say—and the Queen-mother?

MAZARIN: It's needless to tell them about it, Guitaut. It would upset them, and we wouldn't want that, would we? Here is your written order. Remember—great delicacy and regard.

GUITAUT: Yes, Your Eminence.

MAZARIN: And always on the left—always the left—and address him as "Your Majesty".

GUITAUT: Rest easy, Your Eminence. Your orders will be carried out to the letter.

(GUITAUT *goes out center.* MAZARIN *starts to go in door to his quarters and we see* BERNOUIN *inside.* GEORGETTE *is seen peeking from under the table, and starts to sneak out to door, but door at right opens and she barely has time to crawl under table again.* MARIE *enters at right and interrupts her uncle's exit.*)

MARIE: May I come in, Uncle?

MAZARIN: (*Turning from door, which* BERNOUIN *closes.*) Of course, my little one.

MARIE: You're in a very good mood this evening, Uncle.

MAZARIN: Do you know' something, Marie? Of all my nieces—and thanks to the Lord, I have many of them—you are the one I love the most.

MARIE: Really, Uncle? But why have you kept this secret hidden for fifteen years?

MAZARIN: I didn't want to cause any jealousy.

MARIE: Well, I guessed your affection, and I've been as fond of you as if I had known your preference.

MAZARIN: I didn't want to make you too proud. Pride is a mortal sin. But all the time that I have watched you and your sisters grow up, I said, "Marie will be the glory of the family."

MARIE: Do you think the hour of fulfillment has arrived, Uncle?

MAZARIN: I believe it is drawing near. This morning I was saying to Bernouin: "The others have married counts and dukes and princes, but I will not be satisfied unless my little Marie marries a king."

MARIE: A king?

MAZARIN: Yes. I do not know which one—yet. But I repeat, you will marry a king.

MARIE: Your desires on my behalf make you appear very ambitious, Uncle.

MAZARIN: Perché? Aren't you as pretty as a royal princess? If you had a diamond necklace around your lovely neck, diamond earrings on those precious ears, and a diamond tiara on your head, wouldn't you look as much like a queen as that Princess of Savoy that Anne of Austria wishes to become the Queen of France?

MARIE: Yes, Uncle—if, if, if. But these ears and this neck must be content with the simple charm that nature has given them. And I think that has always satisfied my dear Uncle, or he would not have preferred me to the others, as he says.

MAZARIN: I am going to prove that you are ungrateful. Bernouin! Bernouin! (BERNOUIN *appears.*) Bring me the little chest that I had brought from Paris especially for—tell us, Bernouin— especially for whom?

BERNOUIN: For Mademoiselle de Mancini.

MAZARIN: You see? I didn't force him to say it. Bring it in! (BERNOUIN *leaves and returns with chest.*) You will see if your uncle prefers you or not—you will see.

BERNOUIN: Here it is, Your Eminence.

(MAZARIN *takes chest, puts it on table.*)

MAZARIN: You know, Marie, I have always loved jewels—but especially diamonds. It is the only gem that carries its own ray of sunshine. (*Takes some diamonds from chest, holds them to his breast.*) These diamonds are my sun. Sometimes, in the evening, when the day has been rude, or in the morning, when the night has been bad, I take them to bed with me. I lie there and I caress them, and admire them, and hold them to my heart. But I always say to myself: "Someday these diamonds will be Marie's."

MARIE: Really—you say that?

MAZARIN: I do, I do! You would have them already if it did not hurt so much to part with them.

MARIE: I'm afraid you love your diamonds more than me.

MAZARIN: Oh!

MARIE: Admit it!

MAZARIN: No! Here they are! Tonight I want you to be lovelier than that little Princess Marguerite who arrived from somewhere or other. Tonight, I—I—

MARIE: Yes?

MAZARIN: You will promise me to be lovelier, won't you?

MARIE: I swear, I'll do my best. If I don't succeed, it won't be my fault.

MAZARIN: Well, my dear niece—here are the diamonds. They are worth more than a million. They will make you more dazzling than Princess Marguerite tonight. Take good care of them—I—I—(*He starts toward the door at left.*) I am lending them to you.

(*He goes out.*)

MARIE: (*Laughing*) He is lending them to me! Did you hear that, Bernouin? That astonishes me as much as if he had given them to me.

BERNOUIN: Take them, and don't question the gift.

MARIE: But you heard—he said, "I am lending them to you."

BERNOUIN: Mademoiselle, I have been very close to the Cardinal for thirty years, and in thirty years I have heard him use the word, "lend," only three times. I have heard him use the word, "give," only once, and that was when he was giving sympathy to a friend. Do as the Cardinal said—make yourself beautiful.

(*He goes into the room at left, leaving* MARIE *to examine diamonds. The*

DUKE D'ANJOU *comes in the door right without* MARIE *hearing him. He stands behind her.*)

ANJOU: Oh, what lovely diamonds!

MARIE: (*Startled*) What?

ANJOU: Don't be afraid—it's nobody.

MARIE: Look at these—look at these.

ANJOU: I see them. Did they fall from heaven?

MARIE: My uncle gave them to me.

ANJOU: What uncle? Do you have two uncles?

MARIE: My uncle Mazarin.

ANJOU: Impossible! You know that as well as I.

MARIE: But it's true just the same.

ANJOU: I believe I know the reason.

MARIE: What?

ANJOU: My brother's secret agent must have told him that Mazarin has millions in his cellars. Our dear Cardinal is afraid they will take some of it from him, so he's beginning to cut his losses. That secret agent is changing things in this old castle. Take good care of these diamonds, Marie—you will need them.

MARIE: For what?

ANJOU: To corrupt my brother's secret agent, if you ever discover who he is.

MARIE: Corrupt him? Why?

ANJOU: So he won't tell the King—

MARIE: Tell the King, what?

ANJOU: Whatever you don't want him to know.

MARIE: (*Troubled*) What do you mean?

ANJOU: Don't worry, my dear—I may be as mean as my brother's agent, but I'm much more discreet. (*Picks up some jewels.*) Oh, this strand of diamonds would make a lovely hat-band.

MARIE: And look at this wonderful necklace.

ANJOU: And this perfectly gorgeous clasp—I love it.

MARIE: And these earrings.

ANJOU: I would adore them for cuff-links.

MARIE: But this tiara is the most splendid of all.

ANJOU: It's delightful! You must let me wear it sometime.

MARIE: And look at this!

(*Each one is digging in the chest with cries of joy as the* KING *appears at door center.*)

KING: Has someone been pilfering the royal jewels?

MARIE: Oh! The King!

(*Distracted, she picks up chest, runs out right.*)

KING: Marie! Why did she run away, Philippe?

ANJOU: Because you came in unexpectedly—before the sun had time to shine in its full brightness. So the sun has hidden behind a cloud, but it will be back again, brighter than ever.

KING: What were you two doing?

ANJOU: We were drooling over Mazarin's diamonds.

KING: I don't understand.

ANJOU: Neither did I. But listen to this absolutely unbelievable news: Mazarin just gave Marie a heap of diamonds worth at least a million.

KING: They must be imitations.

ANJOU: I thought so at first—I said they couldn't be real. But now I know a secret, brother. We've both been mistaken. The Cardinal is a prodigal, and I have a suspicion that he might be in the mood to make me a handsome gift. In fact, here is Bernouin with a pouch.

(BERNOUIN *enters.*)

BERNOUIN: Oh, the King!

KING: Come in, Bernouin.

BERNOUIN: (*To* ANJOU) Your Highness, the Cardinal left instructions to give you this ten thousand pocket money, and he invites you to come to the games he has arranged for this evening.

ANJOU: You see, brother, I was right. Hand it over, Bernouin. (*He empties the pouch in his hat.*) All this is for me?

BERNOUIN: Yes, your Highness.

ANJOU: Have some for yourself.

(*Gives him some coins*)

BERNOUIN: Thank you, your Highness.

ANJOU: Do you want some, Louis. Take it, take it! When I'm rich, I'm extravagant!

BERNOUIN: His Highness need not deprive himself in favor of the King. The Cardinal ordered me to give the King this portfolio containing a million.

KING: (*Taking portfolio*) Thank you, Bernouin

(BERNOUIN *bows and exits left.*)

ANJOU: Diamonds for Marie, a million for you, and ten thousand for me—and all from the Cardinal. (*Calling*) Guénaud! Guénaud!

KING: What are you doing?

ANJOU: I'm calling the doctor. I'm sure the Cardinal has gone mad. Guénaud!

(*He runs out right.*)

GEORGETTE: (*Crawling out from under table*) Were you calling the doctor?

KING: Georgette! What an unexpected—or should I say expected—pleasure. No I wasn't calling the doctor. It was the Duke d'Anjou.

GEORGETTE: It's useless to call Doctor Guénaud, because he won't come.

KING: Why not?

GEORGETTE: Because he left on a long trip.

KING: To where?

GEORGETTE: To Brussels—in order to take care of the Prince de Condé who is very sick.

KING: Condé is sick? Who told you?

GEORGETTE: Nobody told me, but I heard it. Guitaut is taking care of everything. Condé wants to come back to France, but the Cardinal wants his doctor to take care of him for a month or two because he's so sick. And Guitaut is going to get one of his best carriages to escort a king to the frontier of Holland.

KING: A king?

GEORGETTE: His name is Charles, and I think he's the king of England. He's in Vincennes, but Mazarin wants him to go home.

KING: Charles II is here? Then he is trying to see his sister.

GEORGETTE: Did I bring you good information? I hope so, because I'm stiff from hiding under that table.

KING: Very good information, Georgette, and I thank you. Cardinal Mazarin didn't mention either of those matters. He treats me like a child, Georgette—just as he did when we played in the garden together.

GEORGETTE: But you're the King!

KING: I'm a royal cipher, Georgette, but someday I'll be a king.

GEORGETTE: I know you will.

KING: Georgette, I must find you a good husband, and give you a dowry.

GEORGETTE: Why?

KING: Do you mean, why a dowry?

GEOGETTE: No—why a husband?

KING: To get married, of course.

GEORGETTE: But I don't want to get married.

KING: Why not?

GEORGETTE: Don't you remember—I want to be an actress.

KING: Can't you be both an actress and a wife?

GEORGETTE: Not at the same time. I want to be an actress first. Husbands are easy enough to find.

KING: For a girl like Georgette, I'm sure it would be very simple. Well, I haven't forgotten about speaking to Molière on your behalf. Be patient. But right now, I have something important to do, and you can help me. As you leave, tell the guard to send the Marquis de Montglat here immediately.

GEORGETTE: The Marquis de Montglat? The King's wish is my command! (*She stands rigidly at attention, then throws a kiss to him, runs out.*) Good-bye, dear Louis.

(*The* KING *smiles, picks up portfolio and feels its weight.*)

KING: I wonder if the Cardinal imagines I will be satisfied with only one of his millions, and one of his nieces.

(MONTGLAT *enters, flustered as usual.*)

MONTGLAT: Your Majesty wishes to see me?

KING: Indeed, my Grand Master of Ceremonies. Is everything in readiness for the Cardinal's games this evening?

MONTGLAT: Yes, Sire.

KING: Good. But that is not what I wanted to see you about. I want a passkey that will open all the exterior doors of the chateau.

MONTGLAT: Which doors?

KING: All of them, without any distinction.

MONTGLAT: You shall have the key in an hour. Are there any further orders?

KING: No. You are free to go.

MONTGLAT: Your Majesty, I've been wondering if you will be requiring a room or an entire apartment.

KING: For whom?

MONTGLAT: For the new dignitary.

KING: What dignitary, Montglat?

MONTGLAT: His Majesty's secret agent.

(*The* KING *cannot suppress a smile.*)

KING: Oh, I see. But I didn't ask for a room or an apartment.

MONTGLAT: Sire, it is my duty, not only to carry out your wishes, but to anticipate them.

KING: Thank you for your interest, my dear Montglat, but the person of whom you speak will not be lodging in the chateau.

MONTGLAT: I see. And if this agent—if he—if she—if it should come to see the King, what title should be used to announce it?

KING: *It* has no title, Marquis.

MONTGLAT: Shall it be admitted through the main entrance?

KING: It shall be admitted wherever it wishes to enter. It has the keys to my apartment.

MONTGLAT: Keys to your Majesty's apartment?

KING: Why, yes. You understand, my dear Montglat, that if this agent were lodged at the chateau, and if he had a title, and if he had to wait for you to announce him—well—he wouldn't be a secret agent any longer—would he?

MONTGLAT: I suppose that is correct. But I must say that what the King is doing is contrary to accepted custom. I know of no such example in Court protocol.

KING: Excellent, my dear Marquis—I'll be establishing protocol instead of following it.

(ANNE OF AUSTRIA *enters right.* MONTGLAT *bows.*)

MONTGLAT: Her Majesty the Queen!

(*He goes out center.*)

KING: Mother, I was coming to talk to you.

ANNE: Instead I came to you. Am I not your most loyal subject, Louis?

KING: (*He kisses* ANNE, *offers her a chair.*) Excuse me if I seem irritated, mother, but I am quite disturbed.

ANNE: Because of me?

KING: No, but because of another person whose conduct you approve.

ANNE: The Cardinal?

KING: Naturally. He has intercepted the submission of Condé, who wants only to return peacefully to the court. He has also discovered that Charles of England is in Vincennes, and he has ordered Guitaut to conduct him to the frontier. And all this without a word to me. Are you aware of the facts?

ANNE: No. Do you disapprove of them?

KING: Yes. A minister does not take such actions without the consent of his King.

ANNE: Then you must talk to the Cardinal, and not to me, my son.

KING: I wanted to know first if Mazarin consulted you. I have no desire to blame him for acts which you initiated.

ANNE: But I assure you I know nothing about these matters. Why don't you speak to the Cardinal?

KING: Because I'm afraid that I may be carried too far by anger. I do not wish to forget that the Cardinal—

ANNE: Is the uncle of Marie de Mancini?

KING: And the protégé of my mother.

ANNE: If I protect the Cardinal it is because of the great service he has done for France. And I'm convinced that even now he has the interest of France at heart. The presence of Charles II in France would cause grave complications since you have a treaty with Richard Cromwell.

KING: I was a child when that treaty was made. Now I am a man.

ANNE: Do you count on making war with England?

KING: I count on doing whatever is necessary to be respected in this world. As for the Prince de Condé—

ANNE: He fought against you with the Spaniards.

KING: And he was beaten. But every time he fought for me, he was victorious. I played in the gardens of Saint-Germain with little Georgette while he was winning one battle after another. If now he wants to come to me in peace, I am the one, and the only one, to judge him.

ANNE: Do you believe in his sincerity?

KING: When a man like Condé offers his submission, it is good politics to believe in his sincerity.

ANNE: Your father never pardoned anyone, and yet he was called "the Just."

KING: Those were different times. Those were days when an axe, not a scepter, was the symbol of a king's authority. Thank God, the days of Richelieu are gone. I am King of a new era. I must build a new society from the debris of the past. When the father destroys, the son must rebuild. A man is fortunate to be called by Providence to regenerate a people. Augustus did it in ancient times. Charlemagne did it in modern times. There were eight hundred years between Augustus and Charlemagne, and there are eight hundred years between Charlemagne and Louis XIV. If I commence as they did, by clemency, then with God's help, I might finish as they did. And my first act of clemency is a pardon for the great Condé.

ANNE: My son, your declaration astonishes me, but it augurs well. It assures me that you will never do anything to compromise your royal dignity, and that you will hold your crown so high that no one of lower rank can aspire to sit by your side.

KING: Exactly what are you trying to tell me, mother?

ANNE: Simply that I am sure the queen you choose will be worthy of your person and your blood. And even the wiles of Cardinal Mazarin will not weaken your resistance.

KING: That signifies what?

ANNE: That what worried me yesterday does not worry me today. I know now that you would never consider making Marie de Mancini Queen of France.

KING: If Marie de Mancini is worthy and capable of being Queen of France, she will be. The decision is mine alone.

ANNE: And this Cardinal Mazarin who dominates your life will become one of your family?

KING: Are you certain he hasn't been one of the family for a long time, mother?

ANNE: My son!

(MARIE *enters, dressed magnificently, adorned with diamonds.*)

KING: Pardon me, mother, but here is Mademoiselle de Mancini. I have been waiting for her here. She counts on my being her cavalier for the evening's games. (*The* KING *takes* MARIE *by the hand.*) Come my dear. You look wonderful, and I love you.

(*He kisses* MARIE *and goes out with her, leaving* ANNE *smouldering in her chair.* CHARLOTTE *enters at right.*)

CHARLOTTE: Your Majesty, the Duchess of Savoy requests that you visit her in her apartment.

ANNE: Yes? And who are you?

CHARLOTTE: Charlotte, maid of honor to Princess Marguerite.

ANNE: Oh yes, of course. Tell the Duchess—never mind—I'll see her myself this very moment.

(ANNE *goes out right.* CHARLOTTE *goes to center door, calls in low voice.*)

CHARLOTTE: Bouchevannes!

BOUCHEVANNES: (*Entering center door*) Charlotte, I'm so happy to be alone with you for a moment.

CHARLOTTE: My dear, I can't stay. The Princess is not going to the Cardinal's games. I'm afraid we'll be leaving tomorrow, and I don't know how or when I can see you before I leave.

BOUCHEVANNES: Then listen to me. I'll be on guard in the courtyard from eleven until midnight. There is a door in the Princess' apartment that leads to the courtyard. Throw a cloak on your shoulders and meet me there tonight.

CHARLOTTE: Good! I'll do my best to come.

(DE GUICHE *enters, very agitated.*)

DE GUICHE: Pardon me, Bouchevannes, it's very urgent that I meet a certain person tonight. Will you let me take your place on guard duty tonight?

BOUCHEVANNES: Impossible, Count. I have a rendezvous myself, and it's too important to miss. (*To* CHARLOTTE) This evening, Charlotte.

CHARLOTTE: Till then.

(*She kisses him and goes out right.*)

DE GUICHE: Who is on guard after you?

BOUCHEVANNES: Tréville.

DE GUICHE: At what time?

BOUCHEVANNES: Midnight.

DE GUICHE: Where can I find him?

BOUCHEVANNES: In the Guard Room.

DE GUICHE: Thanks.

(*He rushes out door center, followed by* BOUCHEVANNES. MONTGLAT *enters at the same time, talking to himself and not even noticing them.*)

MONTGLAT: Let me see—after thirty years at court, that will be at least ten thousand days. That means ten thousand breakfasts, ten thousand dinners, and ten thousand suppers. During those ten thousand days, and those ten thousand breakfasts, and ten thousand dinners, and ten thousand suppers, I will see the same faces and hear the same conversation, except that the faces will get older, and the conversation will get more boring.

(GUITAUT *and* BERNOUIN *enter center.*)

BERNOUIN: Excuse me, Monsieur de Montglat, but we have very private business to discuss with the Cardinal. Won't you please come back in five minutes?

MONTGLAT: But I am waiting for the King, and I have equally private business with him.

BERNOUIN: But I assure you, we'll be only five minutes. You won't miss the King. (MONTGLAT *goes out in a huff. To* GUITAUT) I'll tell the Cardinal you are here.

(*Goes in door at left.*)

HENRIETTA: (*Entering right*) Oh, Monsieur Guitaut, at last I've found you.

GUITAUT: Your Royal Highness.

HENRIETTA: Be kind enough to tell me the names of the Musketeers who will be on duty in the courtyard after the Cardinal's games.

GUITAUT: From ten to eleven, Brégy—from eleven to midnight, Bouchevannes—from midnight until one in the morning, Tréville.

HENRIETTA: Thank you, dear Guitaut. Oh, the Cardinal!

(*She rushes out right as* MAZARIN *enters with* BERNOUIN, *left.*)

MAZARIN: Bernouin, what news is there from the Spanish Ambassador?

BERNOUIN: He wants to see you tonight. He has something important to tell you.

MAZARIN: Tonight, eh? We shall meet him, but he must get no further than the watch tower. I will give you a message for the Ambassador. (*As he writes*) Well, Guitaut, what news of King Charles?

GUITAUT: He listened to reason, and agreed to leave Vincennes tomorrow.

MAZARIN: And Princess Henrietta?

GUITAUT: What about her?

MAZARIN: Have you said anything to her?

GUITAUT: Your Eminence knows me better than that.

MAZARIN: Good! You are a faithful subject, and I won't forget that five thousand francs for your daughter.

GUITAUT: I believe Your Eminence said ten thousand.

MAZARIN: (*Pretending to be absorbed in his writing*) This is correct—five thousand. Guitaut, give this order to your guards. (*Reads*) "Allow entrance by the little door of the watch tower to the person who knocks three times and says "Spain and France." (*Hands paper to* GUITAUT, *says to* BERNOUIN) Here is the message for the Ambassador (*Hands* BERNOUIN *a paper.*) Now I must get ready for the games. (*He goes to his quarters.*)

MONTGLAT: (*Coming in without paying attention to anyone.*) Thirty years—ten thousand days—what a waste.

GUITAUT: What are you muttering, Montglat?

MONTGLAT: I was just saying that when I've been Grand Master of Ceremonies for thirty years, that will be ten thousand breakfasts, dinners and suppers. And think how humiliating it is to know that there is someone entering and leaving without my knowing who it is or when he comes and goes. The next time I see the King, I'm going to tell him what I think—with all due respect, of course.

BERNOUIN: What will you say to him?

MONTGLAT: I'll say: "Your Majesty has taken measures which sadden the hearts of your loyal subjects. Your Majesty carefully guards the identity of your secret agent—(*The* KING *enters but* MONTGLAT *does not see him.*)—but in spite of Your Majesty's silence, this agent is known. His name is—

KING: Montglat!

(MONTGLAT *almost falls in a heap.*)

MONTGLAT: Your Majesty, I was—

KING: Never mind! (*Draws him aside and whispers.*) Have you the key I asked for?

MONTGLAT: Here it is, Sire. And I have a message from Mademoiselle Georgette. It's cryptic She said: "News—tonight—stairway to heaven."

KING: (*Smiling*) Thank you. I understand very well.

(*He goes out.*)

BERNOUIN: What was the King whispering to you?

GUITAUT: What did he say?

MONTGLAT: The King did me the honor of confiding the name of his secret agent.

GUITAUT: What is his name?

MONTGLAT: (*Haughtily*) The King swore me to secrecy. Why don't you find out for yourself? You're a policeman!

Curtain

Act III

Courtyard of the chateau, late at night of the same day. At left, a residential section of the chateau, with arched entrance downstage. Upstage, there must be one operative window with balcony. A bench is under the balcony. Upstage, this section terminates in a turret in which there is a window and a door. At rear is a wall topped by battlement. There is a small door midway in the wall. At right is a continuation of the wall which terminates downstage in a massive watch tower. This must have a window, high off the ground, but from which a man can jump. Entrance to the watch tower is unseen, but there is a covered passageway which leads to it at extreme downstage point.

BOUCHEVANNES *is on guard: He walks back and forth.* GUITAUT *marches in briskly, flanked by two* MUSKETEERS, *one with a lantern. When they come to* BOUCHEVANNES, *they stop.*

GUITAUT: The password?

BOUCHEVANNES: Fortune and Fontainebleau.

GUITAUT: Order of the day?

BOUCHEVANNES: Admit into the watch tower the person who knocks three times and says "Spain and France."

GUITAUT: Thanks! Carry on! Enjoy yourself, Bouchevannes.

BOUCHEVANNES: I shall. Sometimes these night guard duties are most enjoyable.

(GUITAUT *and* MUSKETEERS *continue around the courtyard on inspection, then return to passageway down right and go out.* BOUCHEVANNES *walks to the turret up left, looks up for signs of* CHARLOTTE, *then walks back near balcony, meeting* HENRIETTA *coming in from left.*) Who goes there?

HENRIETTA: Look carefully and you will see.

BOUCHEVANNES: Princess Henrietta!

HENRIETTA: Monsieur Bouchevannes, I've come to ask a great favor.

BOUCHEVANNES: All your Highness must do is give me an order.

HENRIETTA: That is very kind of you, but you know that we give no orders here any longer. On the contrary, we are subject to some rather harsh orders ourselves.

BOUCHEVANNES: What brings you here at this time of night?

HENRIETTA: I was looking for you.

BOUCHEVANNES: For me?

HENRIETTA: You are a friend of my family. It was my mother, you remember, who once aided you in obtaining a position with the Duchess of Savoy.

BOUCHEVANNES: I shall always be grateful, and I ask nothing more than the opportunity to be of service to you.

HENRIETTA: If you were proscribed and a fugitive, and separated from your sister, you would want her to confide in a friend if that friend could help her to see you.

BOUCHEVANNES: Yes, of course.

HENRIETTA: My brother is an exile and a fugitive, and I have not seen him for three years.

BOUCHEVANNES: King Charles II?

HENRIETTA: Yes, Monsieur, poor Charles, a wandering king. He is on the other side of that wall. Mazarin has ordered him to leave France tomorrow. Monsieur Bouchevannes, I must see my brother again if only to tell him good-bye.

BOUCHEVANNES: And that is all you ask of me?

HENRIETTA: Yes, that is all.

BOUCHEVANNES: I am ashamed that you ask so little when I would willingly risk imprisonment—even my life—for you. Come with me. (*They go to the little door in rear wall, which* BOUCHEVANNES *unlocks.*) Enter, your Majesty.

(CHARLES *enters, grasps* BOUCHEVANNES' *hand.*)

CHARLES: Henrietta!

HENRIETTA: My dear brother!

(*They embrace.*)

BOUCHEVANNES: I shall watch out for you both.

(*He walks to the archway and stands at attention.*)

CHARLES: My dear Henrietta, how can I thank you for doing this? Where is mother, and how is she?

HENRIETTA: She is well, and she is waiting to see you. Come with me. (*They pass to archway where* BOUCHEVANNES *is.*) Oh, Monsieur Bouchevannes, how can I thank you?

BOUCHEVANNES: There is no need. Go quickly, and do not forget that I will be replaced by another guard at midnight.

HENRIETTA: We'll return long before that. Follow me, Charles.

(*They exit and* BOUCHEVANNES *goes upstage by the turret.*)

GEORGETTE: (*Appearing on wall at right, immediately after the watch tower. She tries to lean close to window of tower.*) Your Majesty! Oh, I can't see him, and I can't hear him!

(*She picks up a branch and strikes the window.*)

KING: (*At window*) Is that you, Georgette?

GEORGETTE: Yes!

KING: What did you want to tell me?

GEORGETTE: Shh—quiet! There's a guard over there.

KING: I know.

GEORGETTE: Cardinal Mazarin told my father to make the watch tower ready for him tonight.

KING: Why?

GEORGETTE: He's meeting someone.

KING: In this tower?

GEORGETTE: Yes, so you'd better come out.

KING: Through the window?

GEORGETTE: You used to crawl through windows at Saint-Germain.

KING: When will he be here?

GEORGETTE: Any minute! Shh—! I hear someone.

(KING *goes away from window.* MAZARIN *enters left, enveloped in long cape.* BERNOUIN, *beside him with a lantern.*)

BOUCHEVANNES: (*Seeing figures, comes forward, confronts them.*) Who goes there?

MAZARIN: Fortune and Fontainebleau.

BOUCHEVANNES: Pass.

MAZARIN: Do you know your orders, Bouchevannes?

BOUCHEVANNES: Admit the person who knocks three times, and—

MAZARIN: Good! Good! You are a fine guard, Bouchevannes. When the person arrives, bring him immediately to the watch tower.

(MAZARIN *and* BERNOUIN *go into passageway at right. We hear a heavy door open and shut.*)

GEORGETTE: (*Knocks with branch on window,* KING *comes quickly and crawls through, jumping to ground.*) The King is saved!

(*The* KING *hides in shadows of tower as light appears in window; then we see* BERNOUIN *close shutters.*)

GEORGETTE: (*Seeing* BOUCHEVANNES *coming*) The guard! The guard!

BOUCHEVANNES: (*Confronting the* KING) Who goes there?

KING: The King, Bouchevannes. May I have your hat, your cloak, and your weapon. I shall finish your guard duty for you.

BOUCHEVANNES: But, Sire—I don't understand.

KING: Don't try! What is the password?

(*The* KING *is putting on the articles that* BOUCHEVANNES *hands him.*)

BOUCHEVANNES: Fortune and Fontainebleau.

KING: Any special orders?

BOUCHEVANNES: Admit the one who knocks three times at the postern, and says "France and Spain."

KING: Who relieves you?

BOUCHEVANNES: Monsieur de Tréville.

KING: Very well. Not a word! Retire to your room, and come to see me tomorrow for your commission as captain.

BOUCHEVANNES: Your Majesty!

KING: Go quickly now.

(BOUCHEVANNES *exits through archway.*)

VOICE: (*from behind wall*) Georgette!

GEORGETTE: My father is calling me.

KING: You had better go.

GEORGETTE: Louis, you make a very handsome Musketeer. Goodbye!

(*She disappears on other side of wall.*)

CHARLOTTE: (*At turret window*) Bouchevannes!

KING: (*Turning sharply*) Huh?

CHARLOTTE: Are you there?

KING: Yes, but—

CHARLOTTE: It's me—Charlotte. The Princess is asleep and I can slip out now. Shall I come down?

KING: Of course.

CHARLOTTE: Are you alone?

KING: Yes. (*He pulls hat down as far as possible, and holds cape to face, as* CHARLOTTE *appears.*) Come over by the wall where no one can see us. Not too close to me. We may be surprised by Guitaut, the captain.

CHARLOTTE: I'm so happy to see you again.

KING: I too.

CHARLOTTE: I thought I might have to leave without even telling you good-bye.

KING: Why?

CHARLOTTE: You know we aren't going to stay at Vincennes.

KING: I don't understand.

CHARLOTTE: Why don't you understand? Can't you see we've made a useless trip? The King is mad about Marie de Mancini—he has no desire to pay attention to Marguerite.

KING: Really?

CHARLOTTE: The Queen-mother is furious. She thinks the King wants to marry Marie. I imagine that crafty Cardinal is behind it all. The Duchess was in tears all evening. It was only natural. She thought her daughter was already the Queen of France.

KING: How did Marguerite accept it?

CHARLOTTE: Oh, she pretended to be very sad.

KING: Pretended?

CHARLOTTE: Yes, but I'm sure she's very pleased the way things turned out.

KING: You mean she dislikes the King?

CHARLOTTE: No, she's in love with someone else.

KING: Who?

CHARLOTTE: Must we talk about her, dear Bouchevannes?

KING: I'm curious. With whom is she in love?

CHARLOTTE: The Duke of Parma. And I'll tell you a deep secret—the Duke has promised me a present of ten thousand francs when he marries the Princess.

KING: But would she rather marry the Duke of Parma than the King of France?

CHARLOTTE: Naturally—she loves him! Don't you think I would rather marry you than the infant King of France?

(*She kisses him on the cheek.*)

KING: Charlotte, I tell you with all my heart that I am very happy to be Bouchevannes at this moment, and not the King of France.

CHARLOTTE: I don't want you to be a king—just a captain.

KING: What?

CHARLOTTE: You said we'd be married when you become a captain. Yes, you told me that.

KING: I did?

CHARLOTTE: Don't tell me you've forgotten!

KING: Of course not. Tomorrow I'll be a captain.

CHARLOTTE: Tomorrow?

KING: The King promised me. The commission is as good as mine.

CHARLOTTE: But has he asked Mazarin's permission?

KING: I'll be a captain, I tell you. The King always keeps his word.

CHARLOTTE: Oh, I'm so happy. And then you will marry me?

KING: Of course.

CHARLOTTE: Then kiss me in proper fashion.

KING: Charlotte! (*He opens his arms, then stops abruptly.*) Someone is coming! You must run! Please, hurry! Until tomorrow! (CHARLOTTE *dashes to turret door and exits.*) Ah, my dear Bouchevannes, you have fallen into holy matrimony. May you be blessed with many offspring.

(HENRIETTA *and* CHARLES *come in from left,* KING *confronts them.*)

KING: Who goes there?

HENRIETTA: Don't you recognize me, Bouchevannes? It's Henrietta.

CHARLES: My deepest thanks, Monsieur. I owe you the sweetest moments I have spent for a long time. I had promised Cardinal Mazarin not to see the King or the Queen-mother, but I did not promise not to see my own mother and sister.

HENRIETTA: I swear to you, Bouchevannes, if anyone learns what you have done for us—I mean, if they try to punish you for helping two poor exiles—I will throw myself at the feet of King Louis. He is good and kind, and he will protect you.

KING: Thank you.

CHARLES: Good-bye, sir, and may God be with you. Come, sister, we can talk a few minutes longer. I don't want to leave a moment before my time is up. (*They walk away but we can see that the* KING *is listening.*) Henrietta, I regret not being able to see Louis.

HENRIETTA: If there is anything you would like to ask him, tell me and I shall carry the message to him.

CHARLES: Listen carefully, then. Now that Oliver Cromwell is dead, England has become a gambling house where the players throw dice for my crown. One of these players is General Monk. With a word, he could overthrow Richard Cromwell, and put me back on the throne. It would require only a million to make an ally of him.

HENRIETTA: A million! Only Mazarin has millions.

CHARLES: Perhaps cousin Louis would lend us the money. Then I could become a real king, and you a royal princess.

HENRIETTA: Then perhaps dear Louis would pay a little attention to poor Henrietta. Now, he scarcely knows I'm alive.

CHARLES: Wait and hope—that is all we can do. I must say good-bye, Henrietta. Tomorrow morning I must leave France. I gave my word.

HENRIETTA: Good-bye, Charles.

CHARLES: Tell mother that when I become king, I'll make up for all she has suffered. (*They embrace.*) Monsieur Bouchevannes, will you unlock the door, please? (*The* KING *unlocks the door.*) I shall never forget what you have done for us.

(*He goes out,* KING *locks door.*)

HENRIETTA: Nor I, Monsieur Bouchevannes. Good night.

(*She goes out the archway.*)

KING: Good night, Princess. (*Midnight sounds.*) Midnight already— and I haven't had time to let Marie know I am here. (DE GUICHE *enters with two* MUSKETEERS.) Who goes there?

DE GUICHE: Fortune and Fontainebleau. I've come to relieve you.

KING: When did you become a Musketeer, Monsieur de Guiche?

DE GUICHE: I asked Tréville to allow me to take his turn on guard duty. It doesn't concern you, Bouchevannes.

KING: (*Taking off his hat*) It concerns the King!

DE GUICHE: The King!

KING: De Guiche, go to your quarters, and consider yourself under arrest. I will do Tréville's turn at guard, just as I have done Bouchevannes'.

DE GUICHE: But, Sire—

KING: To your quarters! And not a word of this to anyone—do you understand? (*To the two* MUSKETEERS) That goes for all of you.

ALL: (*Bowing*) Sire!

(DE GUICHE *and the* MUSKETEERS *exit. The* KING *goes to window with balcony, stands on bench and taps on window with his weapon. The window opens and* MARIE *appears at window.*)

MARIE: Is that you, De Guiche?

KING: (*In his throat*) De Guiche?

MARIE: (*Coming on balcony*) Oh, there you are, Armand.

KING: Were you waiting for me?

MARIE: Of course.

KING: Have you decided to grant me the favor I have been hoping for?

MARIE: You mean—? Of course, I know what you mean. An explanation? Yes, Armand, the time has come for an understanding. I can no longer deceive you with the King, and deceive the King with you. Since the King has been paying attention to me, you have made me shudder a hundred times because of your jealousy.

KING: I have reason for jealousy.

MARIE: Not if you really love me. You should want me to do what is best for me. I met you tonight because I can't allow this double intrigue to go any further. I've told you I love you, but you must sacrifice that love to my future. If I thought I would become simply the mistress of the King, I would not ask this sacrifice. But the King loves me seriously.

KING: Are you certain?

MARIE: He has not given his word, but I am certain he is ready to give it.

KING: But do you love the King?

MARIE: I don't love him as a king—I love him as a handsome, gracious young man. I would love him even if he were not a king. But he is the King, and he is ready to marry me. Would you want to snatch a crown from my head? Oh, Armand, our love was sweet, but don't make me regret it. Return my letters, and I shall return yours. Leave the court under some pretext—at least for a while. Don't allow the King to become suspicious. You know what happened when he discovered that Mademoiselle de la Motte was in love with Chamarante. Let me follow my star, and I will bless you for it.

KING: (*Seriously, and full of emotion*) Marie, let me speak frankly. I came here full of joy and hope, but you have destroyed the happiness I thought was mine. You have snuffed out the very flame of youthful love that you caused to burn in my heart. Don't be angry if I agree to your wishes too easily, but I am like the King—I do not wish a love that is shared. The body, the heart and the soul of the woman I love must belong to me. You are free to do as you wish.

MARIE: Armand! Thank you! Here are your letters.

(She lets a packet of letters drop. KING *picks them up.)*

KING: Good-bye, Marie. Tomorrow you shall have all your letters, and this jealous man who might jeopardize the love of a King will leave the court, and you shall never see him again. *(There are three knocks on door of rear wall.)*

MARIE: Armand.

(She tries to reach his hand.)

KING: Marie, your uncle is in the watch tower, waiting for the man who just knocked at the gate. My orders are to open to him. Close your window. No one must see that we met here.

MARIE: And tomorrow—my letters?

KING: Word of a man who loved you. (MARIE *goes in and closes window.* KING *goes toward rear.)* Well, it seems that De Guiche just exiled himself. *(More knocking at gate)* Coming, coming. *(He unlocks rear door.)* Are you the person to see Cardinal Mazarin?

PIMENTEL: *(Entering)* Yes.

KING: The password?

PIMENTEL: Spain and France.

KING: Do you bring news from Madrid?

PIMENTEL: The most important.

KING: Has the Queen of Spain had a child?

PIMENTEL: Yes.

KING: A boy or a girl?

PIMENTEL: A—but why are you bombarding me with questions? This information is to be confided only to the Cardinal.

KING: I was hoping that you would be good enough to tell me before you tell him.

PIMENTEL: Who are you to speak to the Spanish Ambassador in this way?

KING: King Louis XIV of France.

PIMENTEL: King Louis—(*The* KING *removes his hat.*) Oh! My excuses, Sire. How was I to recognize you in that disguise?

KING: Ambassador, will you kindly wait for me under the archway before I conduct you to the chateau? I have some orders to give the Captain of the Guards who is making his nightly round.

(PIMENTEL *goes to archway, down left, as* GUITAUT *and* TWO MUSKETEERS *come in the passageway. One has a lantern.*)

KING: Come here, Monsieur Guitaut. Do you recognize me?

(*He takes off hat. The man with lantern raises it.*)

GUITAUT: The King! Does your Majesty want someone arrested?

KING: Yes! Arrest the Count de Guiche immediately. And give these garments and this weapon to Bouchevannes. You might also give this packet of letters to De Guiche. (*He hands the things to* GUITAUT.) He wrote them all. Tell him to give you the letters he had in answer. Bring them to me.

GUITAUT: Yes, Sire.

KING: Tell Tréville to finish his regular turn on guard.

GUITAUT: Yes, Sire.

KING: (*Turning to* PIMENTEL) My dear Ambassador, please come with me.

PIMENTEL: But what about Cardinal Mazarin?

KING: A very good question. What about him? This way, Your Excellency.

(*They go out through archway.*)

GUITAUT: Well, I think our King Louis is becoming—

MUSKETEER: What?

GUITAUT: Becoming a King!

Curtain

Act III

The King's reception room, sparsely furnished as the others. At left, under canopy, three armchairs. At rear, door to King's quarters. Door, right, from which people of court enter. Small table and two chairs, center. KING *is standing, speaking to* MOLIÈRE.

KING: Monsieur Molière, here is the list of persons I wish to receive before breakfast.

MOLIÈRE: Yes, your Majesty.

(Takes the list)

KING: In the last twenty-four hours—thanks to the advice you gave me—events have toppled upon each other with such rapidity that the comedy you created for me has almost reached the final curtain. You saw the beginning, now you shall witness the closing scene.

MOLIÈRE: When the comedy is finished, your Majesty, may I request permission to take up my life in the theatre? I am not a man of the court, I am a poor Bohemian. In the wings of a theatre I am honored like an emperor, but in the halls of your palace, I am shunned like an outcast. For example, if the King did not sleep well last night, it was not because of insomnia, but because of the way his bed was made up.

KING: Yes, I know that my valet refused to allow you to help him make my bed. No doubt you thought he considered a poet beneath his dignity. Actually, he probably considered himself unequal to a poet. What you took for pride was simply humility. I

243

shall speak to my valet about it. Meanwhile study the list, and admit no others.

(MOLIÈRE *exits right.* KING *arranges clothes, sits in center armchair under canopy.* MOLIÈRE *enters with* GUITAUT.)

MOLIÈRE: Captain Guitaut!

(*He goes out.*)

KING: Guitaut, what did De Guiche say when you arrested him?

GUITAUT: What they all say: "What is the reason for this?" But when I asked him for the letters from the person who had returned his, he appeared to understand clearly, and he gave me the letters without a word.

(*Hands him a packet of letters.*)

KING: Well done, Guitaut. Tell De Guiche that he is free, on condition that he reports back to the army immediately. Advise him not to return to Paris without my express permission.

GUITAUT: Yes, Sire. Your orders will be carried out.

(*He exits,* MOLIÈRE *enters.*)

MOLIÈRE: Her Royal Highness, Princess Henrietta.

KING: Admit her.

(MOLIÈRE *exits,* HENRIETTA *comes in.*)

HENRIETTA: Sire!

KING: Come here, my dear Henrietta, and let me look at you.

HENRIETTA: Good heavens! If you did not look so kind, and sound so affectionate, I should be very frightened.

KING: Why?

HENRIETTA: You asked to speak to me alone. You have never done that before.

KING: I have something to tell you.

HENRIETTA: What?

KING: I want to tell you that you not only have beautiful eyes, a charming mouth, and lovely hair, but a noble heart as well.

HENRIETTA: Oh, my dear cousin.

KING: I want to say also that I have great admiration for a sister who would comfort an exiled and fugitive brother who has been forced by an unjust order to leave France, and especially since the comfort of your presence was all you were able to give him before he departed.

HENRIETTA: Oh, good God! Your secret agent has—! Pardon, Sire, pardon!

KING: Not only do I pardon you, but I congratulate you with all my heart.

HENRIETTA: I must be dreaming.

KING: I'm going to prove that you are awake. Last night, as your brother was leaving, he told you that he needed a million to obtain an alliance with General Monk.

HENRIETTA: But you know every word that Charles said.

KING: Every word. (*Holds out portfolio*) In this case is the million your brother needs. Send it to him, and tell him that I regret not being able to do more.

HENRIETTA: A million? I can't believe it! (*She kneels, takes his hand, kisses it.*) Oh, thank you. Please allow me to take it to him myself.

KING: I wish it! Take it to him at once.

(*He rises and escorts her to the door.*)

HENRIETTA: You are so good!

KING: You are so lovely!

(*She goes out as* MOLIÈRE *enters.*)

MOLIÈRE: Your Majesty—the Duke d'Anjou is not on the list, but he insists on seeing you.

KING: It would be difficult to keep him out. Let him come in. (MOLIÈRE *exits, in a moment* ANJOU *enters.*) You look sad, Philippe. Almost as sad as I am.

ANJOU: I am sad! And it's not for nothing.

KING: Sad? With ten thousand in your pocket, diamonds in your cuffs, and diamonds on your hat?

ANJOU: I'll tell you why I'm sad. Do you know what happened to the ten thousand that Marzarin gave me?

KING: No—what?

ANJOU: Well, they returned to the old miser's coffers.

KING: You mean he took them back?

ANJOU: No! He won them gambling with me last night. And when I was down to my last sou, do you know what the miserable bastard said? He said: "It's very ugly to be a gambler at your age."

KING: So you have no money?

ANJOU: None! Yesterday I offered you some of mine. Could I be so piggish as to ask you for some of your million today?

KING: Poor Philippe—you came at the wrong time.

ANJOU: Did the Cardinal win your money too?

KING: No, I didn't gamble last night, but I gambled the entire million for very big stakes this morning.

ANJOU: When will you get some more?

KING: When I really become a king.

ANJOU: When will that be?

KING: Who knows? Today, perhaps.

ANJOU: Let me be the first to wish you success in your royal future. You won't forget me when you get your hands on some gold, will you?

KING: Of course not, little brother. In the meantime, take this.

(*He takes off a ring and hands it to* ANJOU.)

ANJOU: For me?

KING: Yes. For being the first to wish me well.

ANJOU: Oh, what a lovely ring, Thank you, Louis. (*He opens door,* MOLIÈRE *steps in.*) Look at this beautiful ring, Molière! It's mine! (*He dashes out.*)

MOLIÈRE: Mademoiselle Charlotte is here, your Majesty.

KING: Show her in.

(*He returns to his formal chair.* MOLIÈRE *goes out and returns with* CHARLOTTE, *then exits.*)

CHARLOTTE: There must be some mistake, your Majesty. They told me your Majesty was doing me the honor of giving me an audience.

KING: Why do you think there is a mistake?

CHARLOTTE: I mean—I mean—I have nothing to say to your Majesty.

KING: Perhaps I have something to say to you.

CHARLOTTE: To me? What can the King have to say to me?

KING: I can ask you news of Princess Marguerite and her mother.

CHARLOTTE: They are very well, your Majesty.

KING: They are leaving today, are they not?

CHARLOTTE: Yes—at noon.

KING: How do you feel about leaving?

CHARLOTTE: They are very sad, of course.

KING: You mean the Duchess is sad. But Princess Marguerite is very happy.

CHARLOTTE: Happy? Why should she by happy?

KING: Because she will soon be near the man she loves.

CHARLOTTE: Oh!

KING: I mean the Duke of Parma.

CHARLOTTE: Oh!

KING: Who has promised a certain maid of honor a handsome gift when he marries.

CHARLOTTE: Oh!

KING: A gift of money. Ten thousand francs, to be exact.

CHARLOTTE: Oh!

KING: And then the maid of honor will be able to marry her dear Bouchevannes—when, and if he becomes a Captain of Musketeers.

CHARLOTTE: I'm going to faint!

KING: Please don't faint before you take this paper.

(*He hands her a document.*)

CHARLOTTE: Of course—but my legs are very weak. (*She looks at the paper, filled with fear.*) I can't read it! I can't!

KING: My dear child, that document is not your death warrant—it's a Captain's commission for Bouchevannes.

CHARLOTTE: His Captain's commission? Oh, thank you, your Majesty.

KING: There is a condition attached. He must be married to you within six weeks. Will you kindly convey that bit of information along with the commission? You may go now.

CHARLOTTE: (*Backing out, still in a daze*) Yes, of course, thank you, thank you—

KING: Wait a moment—I forgot one small thing.

(*He rises, goes to* CHARLOTTE, *kisses her on cheek.*) That was the kiss you gave me last night. I don't want anything that rightfully belongs to your future husband.

CHARLOTTE: (*Almost screaming*) Oh! (*She runs out.* MOLIÈRE *comes in.*)

MOLIÈRE: His Eminence, Cardinal Mazarin.

(MOLIÈRE *goes out as* MAZARIN *enters.*)

MAZARIN: You wished to speak to me?

KING: (*Returning to his chair*) About two things: your refusal to allow Condé to enter France, and your order to force Charles II to leave.

MAZARIN: You know?

KING: I know that you sent Guénaud to Brussels to take care of Condé, and I know that you ordered Guitaut to escort Charles out of France.

MAZARIN: How did you know?

KING: Is that more difficult to know than the exact amount of your thirty-nine millions?

MAZARIN: I am going to try to justify myself in two words.

KING: Shouldn't you say "explain" rather than "justify"?

MAZARIN: I did not refuse Condé entry into France. I merely postponed it.

KING: Postponed it for what reason?

MAZARIN: I know Condé is a great general. He is also a capable politician. Condé at court means intrigue. Condé has a strong influence on your Majesty. And until your Majesty has made his choice of a wife, he should not be subjected to undue influence. I want nothing more than to keep Condé away until you have made your decision.

KING: I promise you I shall have made an irrevocable decision on my marriage before Condé comes back to court. Now let me speak of Charles of England. Explain why you order a king, who is also my cousin and ally, to leave my domain.

MAZARIN: Charles II is your cousin, true, and I understand your feelings. But Charles is not a king—he is deposed and a fugitive. And he is not your ally. You have made an alliance with Richard Cromwell, the protector of Great Britain. I know it is hateful to you to have a treaty with the man who dethroned your cousin, but this treaty has saved France from a war. You must remember that everything I do is for France, which means that it is also for you.

KING: I do not question what you have done, but simply your secret manner of doing it. You see, I have means of knowing everything you do, just as I knew about your thirty-nine million.

MAZARIN: I beg your pardon—only thirty-eight million now. And they will not belong to me forever. One day they will belong to you, my sole heir.

KING: You are leaving your fortune to me?

MAZARIN: Did I not gain it in your service? I came to France poor, and all I ask of France is a tomb when I die.

KING: But your family?

MAZARIN: I have only nieces and nephews. I know your good heart— you will look after the relatives of a faithful servant.

KING: Cardinal, as my minister and my friend, I must consult you on the most important action of my life.

MAZARIN: I am listening.

KING: I love your niece, Marie de Mancini.

MAZARIN: Oh, my dear King.

KING: I love her enough to make her my wife.

MAZARIN: That is too much honor for the son of an Italian fisher-man. But if the King desires it, I can do nothing but obey.

KING: But I must make a choice.

MAZARIN: A choice?

KING: I must choose between the woman I love and a princess I have never seen. Should I marry the woman I love—that is to say, your niece—or the princess I have never seen—that is to say, Maria Theresa of Spain.

MAZARIN: But you cannot marry Maria Theresa—she is heiress to the Spanish throne.

KING: No longer. She now has a brother who will become King of Spain.

MAZARIN: How can you know that when even I do not know?

KING: You would have known it last night if the Spanish Ambassador had met you where you were waiting for him, instead of being led to my apartment.

MAZARIN: Led? By whom?

KING: By me. Really now, don't you think I deserved to be the first to know the news? The Ambassador confirmed the birth of a son baptised under the name of Charles.

MAZARIN: That does not mean that the King of Spain would agree to your marriage to his daughter.

KING: That, too, has been arranged. I received a letter from Philip IV offering me the hand of the Infanta in marriage. Now—shall I marry Maria Theresa or Marie de Mancini?

MAZARIN: For the glory of my King, and the grandeur of France, I say to you: marry the Infanta of Spain.

KING: Do you sincerely mean that?

MAZARIN: As your minister, yes. If I had said otherwise, you should say to me: "You are ambitious, you are a bad minister." As a man who is your friend, I must say, "Do what your heart desires, do what will bring you happiness." Whatever you do—be great, greater than any of your ancestors, so that posterity might say, "He owes a little of his greatness to the fisherman from Piscina."

(*He inclines on his knees and grasps the* KING's *hand.* ANNE OF AUSTRIA *enters quietly and listens.*)

KING: Not on your knees, sir—come close to my heart.

(*He helps* MAZARIN *to rise, and embraces him.*)

MAZARIN: It is a great honor you do me. (*He turns and sees* ANNE.) The Queen!

(*The* KING *escorts* MAZARIN *to door where he exits.*)

KING: Mother!

(*He kisses her hand.*)

ANNE: It appears that you have announced some joyous news to the Cardinal.

KING: Yes, mother—news that gave him great satisfaction.

ANNE: Relative to your marriage no doubt?

KING: Your usual keen intuition is at work, mother.

ANNE: Then you have made your choice of a Queen?

KING: Yes, I have.

ANNE: And you made this choice without consulting me?

KING: I can only hope that when my choice is known, you will approve.

ANNE: And what if I declare your choice to be unwise, unloyal and impossible?

KING: That would be a misfortune, but it would not change my decision.

ANNE: Then you declare war on me?

KING: War? No! I desire nothing but your blessing.

ANNE: My blessing? When you defy my heart and my pride as well? Let me tell you that you will find me a terrible adversary. My precautions are taken.

KING: (*Becoming angry*) Your precautions? Listen to me, mother. When I am dead, when I am sleeping in a tomb next to my ancestors, when I am no longer here to say "This is my wish," then you may destroy me, or destroy what I have done. But as long as I am living, and as long as I am the King, everyone is subject to my will.

ANNE: Even—?

KING: Even my mother—even my ministers—even destiny.

ANNE: Oh, Louis, what made you like this?

KING: The truth, mother—the truth that is so carefully hidden from kings—the truth I have called to my aid.

ANNE: Louis!

KING: Go into my room and wait. Soon the court will hear news of my marriage, and the name of the woman who will be my Queen. You will take your place at my right—Monsieur de Mazarin will be at my left. I shall expect your blessing. Please go, mother. I am expecting Marie de Mancini, and you would not like to be here when she arrives.

ANNE: Marie de Mancini?

KING: Yes.

ANNE: Continue this game if you like—but I warn you—

KING: No warnings, mother—your hand.

(*He takes her hand, leads her to door, center. She goes in.*)

MOLIÈRE: Mademoiselle de Mancini! (*The* KING *goes to his armchair, motions to* MOLIÈRE.) Enter, Mademoiselle—the King awaits you.

(*He goes out.*)

MARIE: (*Running to the* KING) Louis, I am so happy to be here. All night long I have been dreaming about you, just as I was dreaming yesterday, in the forest. It was so sweet—with the rain falling, and your arms around me.

KING: Yes, that was true happiness, Marie. But a stone has been thrown into the serene pool of our love. Oh, Marie, to have a love for myself alone, I would have fought God. I would have sacrificed anything to keep the flame alive in me.

MARIE: What do you mean? The flame is gone?

KING: You snuffed it out, Marie—you did.

MARIE: I don't understand.

KING: Then remember the night that just passed. Where were you after midnight? For whom did you open your balcony window? Who was waiting for you beneath that window? Who talked to you for a quarter of an hour? Who took his letters and promised to return yours?

MARIE: Good God!

KING: Who was it?

MARIE: There is no use to lie. You know everything. It was De Guiche.

KING: You are wrong! It was not De Guiche! It was I! It was I! Perhaps you are suffering now, but you will never suffer as I did then.

MARIE: It was you! You were spying on me!

KING: No! You have my word as a King that I did not come to spy on you. I came as myself, as Louis, to speak to the woman I loved. It was a mocking trick of fate that made you think I was De Guiche.

MARIE: If that is true, you know I am not guilty. You heard what I said, and how I spoke of you. You know that I never had real affection for De Guiche. The only man I have ever really loved is you, and I will always love you. How can you allow such a black cloud to come between us?

KING: Marie, that black cloud has been noticed by others. That cloud would be a spot on my royal sun that must always shine without a blemish. Caesar's wife must be above suspicion.

(*He is almost in tears, and rises, trying to move away from* MARIE. *Puts hand to his face.*)

MARIE: Caesar did not cry when he left his wife—but you are crying.

(*She takes his hand gently away from his face.*)

KING: Marie! (*He embraces her, but then moves her gently away.*) It's over, Marie! I don't want it to be over, but it is. You must leave. Please leave. De Guiche has the letters you gave me last night. Here are the letters which he is returning to you.

(*He hands her a packet of letters.* MOLIÈRE *opens door slightly, stands listening.*)

MARIE: Before I go, let me tell you one thing. You are not sacrificing me because of jealousy—you are sacrificing me to that cruel divinity of kings. You're driving me out of your heart, not because I had a passing fancy for another man, but because I am neither the sister nor the daughter of a king.

KING: Marie!

MARIE: Let me speak! You will marry a woman you have never seen.

You will ask her for love but you will receive only submission. Then you will long for poor Marie who would have been so happy to love you. You will look around you but she will not be there. You will look for her in every face you see. You will squander your love on twenty mistresses, and as you throw one after the other to the winds, you will still look for Marie—always Marie, your first real love. But Marie will be dead to you. Adieu, Sire. Be happy, if God will permit it.

(She starts out but turns for a last look at the KING. *He has an impulse to go to her, but he controls himself. She turns and goes out, and* MOLIÈRE *stands quietly by the door. The* KING *falls into his chair, his head in his hands, sobbing quietly. Little by little he raises his head.)*

KING: What are you doing there?

MOLIÈRE: I was witnessing the most sublime spectacle permitted to a poet: the struggle of a man against human passions.

KING: *(Almost in tears)* You are mistaken, it was not a man's struggle you witnessed, it was a King's. The man yielded to his passion— the King conquered his. *(Composing himself and assuming his regal air.)* We are at the end of our comedy, Monsieur Molière. All the scenes have been played, and only the denouement remains. How shall it unfold? First, let me say that I have a guest for breakfast. Set two places.

MOLIÈRE: Then I'm still your valet, Sire?

KING: For a few minutes more. I have some documents here. One of them is to be placed on my guest's plate. This is the one. You may prepare the breakfast table.

(Hands MOLIÈRE *a document, rolled.* MOLIÈRE *goes out as* GEORGETTE *comes in with a basket of fruit.)*

GEORGETTE: My father said, "Georgette, pick the finest fruit in the orchard, and take it to the King for his breakfast." I arrived just in time, didn't I?

KING: You always arrive in time, Georgette.

GEORGETTE: Did the King learn all he wished to know last night?

KING: Much, much more than I wished.

(MOLIÈRE *enters with* MONTGLAT *who has a tray with dishes, glasses, silver etc.*)

MOLIÈRE: (*Puts document on table next to plate, which* MONTGLAT *sets.*) Everything is ready, Sire.

KING: Very well—sit down here, Monsieur Molière.

MOLIÈRE: I? At your table?

GEORGETTE: Sit down, Monsieur Molière—the King wishes it.

MOLIÈRE: (*Stunned, to* KING.) At your table?

KING: At my table. You are my guest. (*They both sit.*) Read the paper at your plate. It was for my guest, you know.

MOLIÈRE: (*Reading the document*) It's for my theatre! You have given me my theatre!

KING: Yes—but on one condition.

MOLIÈRE: What is that?

KING: That you engage a young actress of my acquaintance.

MOLIÈRE: Where is she, Sire?

GEORGETTE: Here I am!

KING: This is the girl. You can see she's not timid.

MOLIÈRE: Georgette?

GEORGETTE: Of course, Monsieur Molière. You'll see how hard I will work. I'll show you what great talent I have. I'm so happy!

(*She kisses the* KING, *then* MOLIÈRE.)

KING: Then that matter is settled. Georgette, will you please open that door, and tell the Queen that I should like her to come in now. And Monsieur de Montglat, will you introduce the people who are waiting in the corridor. (GEORGETTE *goes to rear door,* MONTGLAT *to other door. All the people of the play except* DE GUICHE *come in.* MAZARIN *escorts the* QUEEN *to the chair at right of the* KING's *armchair, then sits himself at left.*) I call everyone's attention to the fact that I am having breakfast this morning with Monsieur Molière, whom my valet did not consider worthy of making my bed.

MONTGLAT: Sire, His Majesty Louis XIII issued an edict that actors could not be subjected to censure.

KING: I am confirming that edict, as you can see.

(*He rises, goes solemnly to his armchair.*)

KING: Ladies and gentlemen, the King has gathered you here in order to announce that through the good graces of his mother, Anne of Austria, to whom he will be eternally grateful— (*Looks at* QUEEN, *who is tense.*)—and the fruitful negotiations of Cardinal Mazarin, whose good works he will never be rich or powerful enough to repay, he will marry the Infanta of Spain, Maria Theresa.

(*The people cheer and shout "Long live the King, Long live the Queen!"*)

ANNE: My king!

KING: Say, "my son," mother. (*Unrolls another document.*) And here is the procuration which I give to Cardinal Mazarin to represent me and to represent France at the conferences which will be held to conclude my marriage to the Infanta and a treaty of peace with Spain. Signed, Louis, the King.

(*Gives paper to* MAZARIN, *goes back to breakfast table.*)

GRAMMONT: (*Low to Guitaut*) King! And since when?

GUITAUT: Since midnight, Duke.

DANGEAU: (*Writing in his tablet.*) Then I am correct in this notation for my book: "The King's secret agent was Molière."

MOLIÈRE: (*Laughing, to* KING.) That is the way history is written.

(*Servants bring in food as people of the court move to depart.*)

The End

Three Interludes
for Molière's
The Love Doctor

ABOUT THE PLAY

In 1850 Dumas proposed a project to Arsène Houssaye, manager of the Comédie-Française. Dumas wanted to write a "backstage comedy set in the days of Molière." He visualized young actresses feuding over their roles and their lovers, nobles watching the performance, the candlelighter and the stagehands exchanging jokes, and the divertissements of music and dancing. All this, thought Dumas, would make an interesting combination with one of Molière's shorter plays. Houssaye liked the idea but wanted the play for January 15th, the anniversary of Molière's birth, which was not far off. Dumas bet him he would have it the next day. He won the bet, and the three entr'-actes, or interludes, opened with *The Love Doctor* on Molière's birthday.

Dumas created the entire panorama of a play in Molière's time. He wove his story around two leading actresses of Molière's troupe, Ducroisy and Duparc. Seen as a sort of stage manager is Lagrange, one of Molière's actors. The characters invented by Dumas appear not only between the acts of the Molière piece, but before, after, and during the play. The blending was ingenious, and at the 1850 opening, some of the audience, thinking to castigate Dumas for meddling with their beloved Molière, booed through the entire second act of *The Love Doctor,* believing they were booing Dumas. In reality it was a tribute to the amazing imagination and genius of Alexandre Dumas.

Molière's *The Love Doctor* (*L'Amour médecin*), written in 1665, serves as the play-within-a-play. Written almost as rapidly as were the interludes by Dumas, it was presented before Louis XIV at Versailles, with dancing and singing to the music of Lully.

This blending of Dumas and Molière gives a great opportunity for re-creating a play in Molière's time. Together, the works make up an evening's entertainment. The use of dancing and mime is unlimited.

The text of *The Love Doctor* is newly translated, and many long speeches have been broken up. The interludes by Dumas appear in English for the first time.

The combination of texts is almost exactly fifty percent Molière and fifty percent Dumas.

Characters

DUMAS:

SUBTIL, *the lighting man*
CHANDEL, *a stagehand*
DUCROISY, *an actress*
DUPARC, *an actress*
SAMUEL, *a banker*
THE COUNT, *an impoverished noble*
THE MARQUIS, *a hot-headed noble*
GENTLEMAN, *a morose noble*
PRIEST, *spectator at the play*
TRUFFE, *a country fellow, spectator at the play*
LAGRANGE, *stage manager*
Various members of audience

MOLIÈRE:

COMEDY ⎫
MUSIC ⎬ *Entertainers in Prologue and Epilogue*
DANCE ⎭
SGANARELLE, *a rich man*
GUILLAUME, *a dealer in tapestries*
JOSSE, *a jeweler*
AMINTA, *a neighbor*
LUCRETIA, *Sganarelle's niece*
LUCINDA, *his daughter*
LISETTE, *his servant*
(LISETTE *is played by both* DUPARC *and* DUCROISY.)
TOMES ⎫
FONANDRES ⎬ *Doctors*
MACROTON ⎪
BAHYS ⎭
MEDICINE VENDOR
CLITANDRE, *Lucinda's suitor*
A NOTARY
Dancers and musicians

The scene is a theatre in the time of Molière.

Act I

The scene, which represents a theatre in the time of Molière, is dark as the curtain goes up. On one side of the stage are chairs for the nobility, on the other side, chairs for the musicians. These may be on raised platforms. The stage setting for the Molière play is already in place, and consists of a house at right and a house at left. Each one has a balcony on the second floor. There is a garden between the two houses, and a street in front. A prompter's box is down center. If a working prompter's box is not feasible, the stage manager can do the prompting that is called for in the play.

As the curtain rises, CHANDEL *is leaning against the house at right.* SUBTIL *enters with a lantern in his hand. He stumbles on a chair.*

SUBTIL: Oh! I think I broke my leg.

CHANDEL: Why don't you light up before you come in, idiot? Then you wouldn't tear up Molière's whole set.

SUBTIL: (*Raising light to level of* CHANDEL's *face.*) Oh, it's you, Chandel.

CHANDEL: Of course. Who did you think it was?

SUBTIL: What are you doing here?

CHANDEL: I'm at my post.

SUBTIL: A quarter of an hour before the play?

CHANDEL: Why not? I'm not always late like you.

SUBTIL: Late? Don't talk to me about being late. I've been an actor like the others. I've performed like the others. I've been cheered, and applauded, and—

CHANDEL: And hissed like the others?

SUBTIL: What did you say?

CHANDEL: Nothing. It was an echo. But what are you complaining about? You're the most important person in the troupe. You're the one who makes night and day.

SUBTIL: Yes, it's true I'm the sun and the moon in this establishment, but if the sun doesn't shine at the right time, Apollo is fined—and if the moon's too bright, Diana goes without supper.

(*He lights some candles.*)

CHANDEL: Speaking of supper—how about some food after the show?

DUCROISY: (*She has opened window on balcony of house at left, and leans out.*) Chandel! Psst—!

CHANDEL: Oh, it's you, Mademoiselle Ducroisy.

DUCROISY: Do you have something for me?

CHANDEL: Yes! In a moment.

SUBTIL: What did you say?

CHANDEL: Nothing.

(*He gets a ladder and climbs to balcony.*)

SUBTIL: What are you doing there?

CHANDEL: Just seeing if the stage-left balcony is solid.

(SUBTIL *goes about his business of placing and lighting candles.*)

DUCROISY Have you seen Monsieur Samuel, my banker?

CHANDEL: Oh, yes.

DUCROISY: Did he give you something for me?

CHANDEL: He did. This note.

DUCROISY: That's all?

CHANDEL: (*Reaching into his shirt*) And this little jewel box.

DUCROISY: Well done—well done. Here—this is for you.

(*She hands him a coin.*)

CHANDEL: Thank you, mademoiselle.

(DUCROISY *closes window and disappears.*)

SUBTIL: That's funny—I was thinking Sganarelle's house was on stage-right.

CHANDEL: Yes—when Mademoiselle Duparc plays, but not when it's Ducroisy. You know very well that one will never do what the other does.

SUBTIL: Of course—I know they hate each other.

CHANDEL: Two pretty women—it's only natural.

SUBTIL: It keeps you guessing which one will steal the other's role.

CHANDEL: Or the other's lover.

SUBTIL: Sometimes they do both in one day. But how does it happen that Ducroisy will play the first performance when Duparc is the head actress?

CHANDEL: This is the first performance in the city, you mean. Duparc created the role at court—that's all she cares about.

DUPARC: (*Opening window of balcony on stage right*) Chandel! Psst—!

CHANDEL: Good God! What do I see? Duparc!

DUPARC: Psst—!

(CHANDEL *crosses to right, carrying the ladder.*)

SUBTIL: What are you going to do?

CHANDEL: I want to see if the right balcony is going to cave in.

(*He climbs ladder to right balcony.*)

DUPARC: Could you send this note to the Count?

CHANDEL: Of course. I'll take it myself if you like.

DUPARC: In case he questions you, tell him that I said it's useless to pursue me, and that if he has something to tell me, I invite him to use the kind of ink that Samuel the banker uses.

(*She hands him a letter.*)

CHANDEL: Samuel the banker? Ducroisy's lover?

DUPARC: He could be mine any time I want him.

CHANDEL: Well, I'll tell the Count what you said. (*Holds out his hand.*) Nothing for the messenger?

DUPARC: Ask the Count. It's the man that pays.

CHANDEL: I don't think I can count on that particular Count. He's in debt up to his eyes. But it doesn't matter. He'll get your note all the same. By the way, why are you here? Are you playing Lisette tonight?

DUPARC: Yes.

CHANDEL: But Ducroisy is in the other house.

DUPARC: I know that very well.

CHANDEL: But how—?

DUPARC: Shh—

(*She shuts the window and disappears.*)

CHANDEL: (*Climbing down*) This is going to be curious. (*To* SUBTIL) Have you finished?

SUBTIL: I'd like to see you light forty-eight candles, or I'd like to see you snuff them out. The day I started I only put out fifteen. (*Stops by prompter's box and speaks into it.*) Already in your hole, prompter? You have a very nice job there, being able to examine everyone from head to toe—especially the ladies. You have a great view. (*To* CHANDEL) I'll see you later, Chandel. My job is finished, but yours is just beginning.

CHANDEL: It started thirty minutes ago, and it keeps on.

(SUBTIL *goes out.*)

DUCROISY: (*Appearing at window, left*) Chandel! Psst—!

CHANDEL: Here I am.

DUCROISY: Shh! A note.

CHANDEL: For Samuel the banker?

DUCROISY: No—for the Count.

CHANDEL: That's good! It's Samuel who writes to you, and it's the Count who gets the reply.

DUCOISY: Will you see that this gets into no one's hands but his?

CHANDEL: I'll see to it.

DUCROISY: Do you think it's true that he's courting Duparc?

CHANDEL: I'm sure he hasn't even thought of it.

DUCROISY: Thanks. You're an honest fellow.

(*She closes the window.*)

CHANDEL: Well, if the Count is mistreated at stage-right, he can get consolation at stage-left.

DUPARC: (*At right window*) Chandel! Psst—!

CHANDEL: Here I am.

(*He climbs down the ladder, carrying it with him.*)

DUPARC: I've been thinking it over. Don't take that note to the Count.

CHANDEL: Will it trouble him?

DUPARC: That's right. Return it to me.

CHANDEL: Just a minute. (*Fumbles in pocket for letter.*) Here it is.

DUPARC: And don't speak to him of my displeasure. Poor boy. We can't upset him like that. Here—this is for the bother I've been.

(*She gives him a coin.*)

CHANDEL: Thank you, mademoiselle. It's no bother at all—now.

DUPARC: But listen—

CHANDEL: What now?

DUPARC: Have you heard that the Count is carrying on with Ducroisy?

CHANDEL: Me? Never!

DUPARC: Thank you. You're a good man, Chandel.

(*She closes the window as* SAMUEL *enters with* SUBTIL *as* CHANDEL, *stands near the ladder.*)

SUBTIL: You're looking for Chandel, aren't you, Monsieur Samuel?

SAMUEL: I'm looking for the stagehand who was to deliver a note from me to the girl whose eyes are making me die of love.

SUBTIL: That's a good line for Molière. (*To* CHANDEL) Chandel, my friend, you're doing a good business as a postman.

CHANDEL: What do you mean?

SUBTIL: I mean, now I can understand why you come here so early.

SAMUEL: (*To* CHANDEL) Did you give Mademoiselle Ducroisy my letter?

CHANDEL: I did, sir.

SAMUEL: And my jewel box?

CHANDEL: It's in her hands.

SAMUEL: Did she appear pleased?

CHANDEL: She squealed.

SAMUEL: Squealed.

CHANDEL: With delight.

SAMUEL: And she didn't give you anything?

CHANDEL: As a matter of fact—she did.

SAMUEL: What was it?

CHANDEL: A note.

SAMUEL: Then, let's have it. Give it to me.

CHANDEL: But it's not for you.

SAMUEL: For whom then?

CHANDEL: For the Count.

SAMUEL: For that butterfly? She gave you a letter for him?

CHANDEL: Yes, but it's his final one—it's his dismissal.

SAMUEL: Are you sure about that?

CHANDEL: He'll be here—you'll see how sad he looks.

SAMUEL: If he's sad, will that make you happy?

CHANDEL: If there's not a tip in it, it will make me sad. (*The* COUNT *enters.*) Good evening, Monsieur the Count.

COUNT: Do you have anything for me?

CHANDEL: From whom?

COUNT: From either one of our Lisettes. I'm like our banker— I play two games at once.

CHANDEL: Well, you have scored twice. I have replies from both of them. First, here is Ducroisy's letter.

COUNT: Give it to me, my friend. (*He reads.*) "My dear Count: I ask nothing better than to be near you, even though I stay very close to my banker." (*Looks up.*) That's charming.

SAMUEL: (*Low, to* CHANDEL) He's not at all sad—on the contrary—

CHANDEL: Wait until he reads the postscript.

COUNT: (*Reading*) "P.S. That is what I would have replied to you if you were not paying so much attention to Duparc." (*Looking up*) The postscript seems to destroy the charm of the letter. But what's the difference. We are at a comedy!

SAMUEL: Well, he resisted the postscript. He's not sad.

CHANDEL: He's a man of strong constitution—but you'll see. (*To the* COUNT) Now—from Mademoiselle Duparc—I had a message to go with her letter. She said to tell you that if you write to her, you should use the kind of ink that Samuel the banker uses when he writes to Ducroisy.

COUNT: What kind of ink does he use?

CHANDEL: Black ink like yours, I suppose, but he sprinkles it with powdered gold, and that makes it very distinctive.

COUNT: I'm afraid I understand.

(*He looks dejected.*)

CHANDEL: (*To* SAMUEL) Did you hear?

SAMUEL: I heard. Here!

(*He hands some money to* CHANDEL *who looks at it disgusted.*)

COUNT: Give me her letter.

CHANDEL: I don't have it any longer.

COUNT: But you said you had a letter for me. Where is it?

CHANDEL: She took it back and told me to tell you nothing at all.

COUNT: Do you know why?

CHANDEL: Of course! Because she loves you.

COUNT: What? She loves me? Oh, my good friend, my good friend.

SAMUEL: (*Drawing* CHANDEL *aside*) What are you telling him? He's getting quite happy.

CHANDEL: I hope so. Do you think I can keep him sad for this? (*Holds up money that* SAMUEL *gave him.*) It was your present that was sad.

SAMUEL: Forgive me—I didn't realize what I gave you. I thought it was more. Here! (SAMUEL *hands* CHANDEL *more money.*)

CHANDEL: That's better. You have no idea how sad this will make the Count. Watch! (*To* COUNT) Do you have a little house somewhere?

COUNT: Unfortunately, no.

CHANDEL: No? Then you have a coach outside?

COUNT: Sorry—no.

CHANDEL: But you have a full purse with you, no doubt.

COUNT: Not a sou.

CHANDEL: Well, if you have neither house, nor carriage, nor money, I have nothing to say to you, and you can be sure that Duparc will have nothing to say to you either.

COUNT: (*Stamping his foot*) I'm desolate.

CHANDEL: (*To* SAMUEL) There's your unhappy man. All you had to do was pay the fee.

(*The* MARQUIS *and the* MOROSE GENTLEMAN *come in.*)

MARQUIS: So you didn't see the play when it was at Versailles? Shall I tell you the story of the plot?

GENTLEMAN: Heavens no!

MARQUIS: But it's very clever. This Molière has great wit.

GENTLEMAN: No!

MARQUIS: But you came here to see Molière in order to be entertained?

GENTLEMAN: No!

MARQUIS: Why did you come?

GENTLEMAN: Because I had nowhere else to go.

MARQUIS: (*Aside*) I must see where he sits, so that I'm not near him.

(*The* PRIEST *and* MONSIEUR TRUFFE *enter as an actress dressed as* COMEDY *walks on stage.*)

PRIEST: My dear Truffe, you asked to come to the play with all the stylish gentlemen. Here we are. You can't get out of it now.

MARQUIS: (*Aside, to* PRIEST) What the devil kind of man is that you're leading, father?

PRIEST: The kind they grow in the country.

TRUFFE: (*Who has been examining the set*) Oh, ho! They can't fool me. These are not real houses. (*He notices* COMEDY.) Is that a puppet? It's painted just like the houses.

PRIEST: To be sure, it's painted, my dear friend.

COUNT: (*Speaking low to* COMEDY) Don't budge. He thinks you're a puppet. (COMEDY *stiffens like a statue.*)

TRUFFE: (*Running his hand over* COMEDY) It's pretty all the same. It feels like a real woman. (*He feels a little too much and* COMEDY *slaps him.*) why, it's a real woman! Why did you say she was painted?

(COMEDY *runs off stage.*)

PRIEST: She is painted—but not on canvas.

(LAGRANGE, *actor–stage manager enters from wings.*)

LAGRANGE: May I present the fair ladies of Music, Dance, and Comedy who will descend from the clouds. Be seated for the prologue, please.

(MUSICIANS *begin to play.*)

TRUFFE: Bless my soul—violins and everything.

PRIEST: You happened to come on a very special day.

TRUFFE: How much do they pay those gut scrapers?

PRIEST: Fifteen sous.

TRUFFE: Too much. When I have violins, I pay five sous per bow.

VOICE FROM PIT: Be quiet.

TRUFFE: (*Looking toward audience, where the pit would be*) Well—there are people down there.

VOICE FROM PIT: Sit down. We didn't come here to see you!

COUNT: They're charming when they can't see. Is it for them that they're playing the comedy?

VOICE: Quiet!

(*The* MUSICIANS *play as the gentlemen take their seats. A prop cloud descends from above. On it are three women dressed as* COMEDY, MUSIC, *and* DANCE. *They get off, the cloud is drawn up, and the three do the prologue to* THE LOVE DOCTOR.)

COMEDY: (*Singing*)

> Let us stop our vain and foolish quarrels,
> And boasting of our talents one by one,
> For if we put our talents all together,
> Our glory will be brighter than the sun.

ALL THREE: (*Singing*)

> Let us unite,
> Sparkling and bright,
> Comedy, Music, and Dance;
> When we are three,
> There's sure to be,
> Joy that will thrill and entrance.

MUSIC: I will give the tones.

DANCE: I will add the grace.

COMEDY: I will give the words.

ALL THREE: And all will interlace.

MUSIC: I will give the beat.

DANCE: I will add design.

COMEDY: I will give it life.

ALL THREE: With joy we shall combine.

> Let us unite,
> Sparkling and bright,
> Comedy, Music, and Dance,
> When we are three,
> There's sure to be,
> Joy that will thrill and entrance.

(*The cloud descends and carries the three performers out of sight.*)

COUNT: Long live comedy!

PRIEST: Well—Monsieur Truffe is already asleep.

COUNT: Did he pay for his seat?

PRIEST: Yes.

COUNT: Very well, then—let him sleep. (*To* SAMUEL) I'm anxious to have a chat with you, my dear Samuel. Perhaps now before the play begins.

SAMUEL: (*Aside*) I see it coming. He wants to borrow money.

COUNT: (*Looking at* SAMUEL'*s hat*) What a fine feather, my friend. It's not an ostrich feather, it's a phoenix feather. Where in the devil do you bankers find the birds that you pluck? With a hat like that, you are complete. You don't need wit, and you don't need a figure.

SAMUEL: If that's a compliment—thank you. But you embarrass me.

COUNT: I don't mean to, for I have a favor to ask of you. You have a princely fortune, my dear Samuel, a cardinal's carriage, and a little hide-away worthy of a Duke. (*Admiring his sword*) And what a prodigious sword. What wonderful workmanship. Let me see it. (*He tries to draw the sword from its scabbard.*) What's wrong with your sword?

SAMUEL: There's no blade. The hilt is attached to the scabbard.

COUNT: Really?

SAMUEL: Yes. I know my quick temper and I must be careful. I would probably draw my sword for a trifle—and you know duels are forbidden.

COUNT: And so, in order not to disobey the king, you had an irremovable sword made. But as I was saying—it's very important that you lend me—

SAMUEL: What? My purse, my carriage, and my hide-away?

COUNT: Exactly, my dear Samuel. All three. I must tell you that I'm on the verge of being on very good terms with a lady of the court.

SAMUEL: You don't expect me to believe that, do you? It's not for a lady of the court that you want my purse, my carriage, and my house.

COUNT: For whom then?

SAMUEL: It's to amuse yourself with either Duparc or Ducroisy.

COUNT: And if that were true—what the devil? You can't take both of them.

SAMUEL: Why not? I'm rich enough.

COUNT: All right—use your wealth, and I'll use my talents, and we'll see who will get along.

SAMUEL: So be it. Use your talents—but you won't use my key, my coach, or my purse.

COUNT: Careful, my friend, careful. There will be a time when you beg me to take them.

SAMUEL: And you shall refuse?

COUNT: No! I'll accept. I have no hard feelings.

SAMUEL: Meanwhile the show is continuing. The curtain is going up.

(They take their places as the curtain in front of The Love Doctor *set is going up. The first scene of* The Love Doctor *begins. The scene is* SGAN-ARELLE'S *house.* SGANARELLE *is outside the house and discussing something with* AMINTA, LUCRETIA, JOSSE, *and* GUILLAUME.*)*

SGANARELLE: Ah, how strange life is, how very strange indeed. I agree with the philosopher of old who said: "He who has land, has war," and "He who has fortune, has misfortune." I had only one wife and she is dead.

GUILLAUME: How many would you have liked?

SGANARELLE: She is dead, my friend Guillaume. It was a great loss and I still can't think of it without crying. I wasn't always satisfied with her conduct, and we quarreled, but death reconciles all things.

JOSSE: Don't cry, my friend. It won't help.

SGANARELLE: She's dead, and I weep for her. If she were alive, I would argue with her.

AMINTA: Cheer up—you have your daughter.

SGANARELLE: Yes, my daughter. Of all the children that Heaven gave me, it left me only one daughter.

AMINTA: Then be thankful.

SGANARELLE: Thankful? This daughter is my greatest trouble.

LUCRETIA: Why?

SGANARELLE: Because she is overcome with a dark melancholy—a frightful sadness.

LUCRETIA: There must be some way to get her out of it.

SGANARELLE: I know of no way, because I have no idea of the cause. I'm about out of my mind, and I need good advice. Lucretia, my dear niece, Aminta, my good neighbor, and you Josse and Guillaume, my compatriots and friends—please, all of you, advise me what I should do.

JOSSE: I would say that she needs some sort of adornment—some kind of new finery. Pretty things are what delight a young girl most.

SGANARELLE: Finery, you say? Adornment? What would you suggest, Josse?

JOSSE: If I were you, I should buy her—this very day—a beautiful necklace of diamonds, rubies, and emeralds.

SGANARELLE: What do you say to that, my friend Guillaume? Do you approve, or do you have a better idea?

GUILLAUME: I have a much better idea. If I were in your place I would buy her a fine tapestry—a tranquil pastoral scene—to hang in her room. That would brighten both her vision and her spirit.

SGANARELLE: Aminta, which suggestion do you prefer?

AMINTA: Neither of them.

SGANARELLE: Neither?

AMINTA: You'd be foolish to buy either of those things. You should marry her off—and as quickly as possible—to the young man who asked her of you—so they say—not too long ago.

SGANARELLE: Oh! "They" say, do "they"? Lucretia, what do you think of that?

LUCRETIA: I don't think your daughter is fit for marriage. She has a sickly complexion, and her health is not at all good. You would be sending her to another world if you exposed her to having children in her condition. She's not made for this world, I assure you. Put her in a convent where whe will find diversions better suited to her disposition.

SGANARELLE: Well, well, all this advice is most admirable—but I do declare there's a heap of self-interest mixed in it.

ALL: What?

SGANARELLE: Self-interest, I said. Each of you gave me advice that was aimed chiefly at helping himself.

ALL: But—

SGANARELLE: You're a jeweler, my friend Josse.

JOSSE: Yes, of course. We all know that.

SGANARELLE: Well, your advice smells of a man who has some merchandise that he's waited a long time to get rid of.

JOSSE: But I assure you—

SGANARELLE: I simply said—that's the way it smells. And you, friend Guillaume, you're a dealer in tapestries.

GUILLAUME: Fine tapestries.

SGANARELLE: Of course. Fine! And you have the face of a man who is overstocked on certain of those fine items. Do you by chance have a hanging or two—with tranquil pastoral scenes—that are collecting dust in some corner?

GUILLAUME: Certainly not.

SGANARELLE: But your face looks as if you have. And you, my dear neighbor Aminta—the man you are in love with has been strongly attracted to my daughter—or so *"they"* say. I'm sure you wouldn't be at all sorry to see her become the wife of someone else.

AMINTA: How can you—?

SGANARELLE: I can—be sure of it! As for you, my dear Lucretia, my loving niece, I have no idea of marrying my daughter with anyone at all, as you well know, and I have my very good reasons. But the advice you gave to make her a nun is from a woman who would very charitably like to be my soul heir.

LUCRETIA: Uncle—

SGANARELLE: Yes—rich uncle! Well, ladies and gentlemen, I asked your advice, and you gave me the best in the world, but please permit me to follow none of it. You must admit that is the best thing to do with advice such as yours.

ALL: Well—

SGANARELLE: Here comes my daughter to take a little air. I would like to speak to her alone, if you please. Thank you all from the bottom of my heart for your help, but don't stay here on my account. (*The others all leave in a flurry.*) She doesn't even see me. She's sighing and looking towards heaven. (LUCINDA *appears.*) If heaven would only help you! Good morning, my dear Lucinda. What's the matter? How are you feeling? Huh? What? Always sad and melancholy, and you won't even tell me what troubles you? (*She shakes her head "no".*) Uncover your little heart and tell all your secret thoughts to your little papa, my pigeon. Courage! Courage! Shall I give you a big kiss? (*She shakes her head "no".*) Do you want me to die of grief without even knowing the cause of your great suffering? Tell me the reason, and I promise I will do everything possible for you. Yes, you need only tell me the subject of your sadness and I swear I will turn heaven and earth to help you. Can I say more? Are you perhaps jealous of one of your companions who might seem prettier than you? (*She shakes her head "no".*) Could there be some expensive silk that you want for a dress? (*She shakes her head "no".*) Could it be that you don't like the furnishings in your room, and you would rather have a little cabinet with inlaid mother-of-pearl, like you saw at the fair? (*She shakes her head "no".*) Not that? Would you like to study music? Shall I hire someone to teach you to play the harpsichord? (*She shakes her head "no".*) No, again? Is there someone you are in love with and want to marry?

(*She shakes her head vigorously "yes", as* DUCROISY *and* DUPARC, *both dressed identically for the role of* LISETTE, *enter.*)

THE TWO LISETTES: Well, monsieur, I see you've been questioning your daughter. Have you found the cause of her melancholy?

SGANARELLE((*Completely out of character*) Good God! What's this?

LUCINDA: (*Also out of character*) Good heavens!

DUCROISY(*To* DUPARC) I beg your pardon, mademoiselle.

DUPARC: Why are you begging my pardon?

DUCROISY: For interrupting you.

DUPARC: You're free to interrupt me, but I am free to continue. (*To* SGANARELLE *in character of* LISETTE) Well, monsieur, I see you've been questioning your daughter.

DUCROISY: (*Intervening*) Well, monsieur, I see you've been questioning your daughter.

LAGRANGE: (*Rushing on the scene*) Ladies! Ladies! Sganarelle cannot have two Lisettes.

VOICES FROM AUDIENCE: Ducroisy! Duparc! We want Ducroisy! We want Duparc!

LAGRANGE: (*To* AUDIENCE) Have patience, please, ladies and gentlemen.

VOICES: Silence! Start the play again!

LAGRANGE: Ladies and gentlemen, in the absence of Monsieur Molière, I have the honor of speaking for the troupe. These two ladies are rivals for the role, they are rivals in talent, and especially they are rivals in their desire to have the pleasure of playing before you. If ever there was an excusable interruption, this is one.

VOICES: Duparc! Ducroisy! Duparc! Ducroisy!

LAGRANGE: I am going to stop this dispute with very few words. (*Turns to the two actresses.*) Ladies, let's settle this very quickly.

DUPARC: Since I created the role at Versailles, I have the right to play it when I wish. I am the head actress.

DUCROISY: Since I was put on call for this evening, I have the right to play this evening.

DUPARC: But I am the head actress.

DUCROISY: Yes—you have seniority, but you have no talent.

DUPARC: I am the head actress.

LAGRANGE: Mademoiselle Ducroisy, your reasons are very well put.

DUCROISY: Ah, ha!

LAGRANGE: But those of Mademoiselle Duparc are more to the point. Mademoiselle Ducroisy, you will please relinquish the role.

DUCROISY: You can't do this!

LAGRANGE: Mademoiselle Duparc will continue.

DUPARC: It's the judgment of Solomon.

DUCROISY: (*In a rage*) Oh!

LAGRANGE: (*To* AUDIENCE) Ladies and gentlemen, we beg your indulgence for what has taken place. As you see, there was a small misunderstanding between the two actresses. But everything is now clarified and the performance will continue without further delay.

DUCROISY: (*As she whirls out*) Don't count on that!

(LAGRANGE *exits and* The Love Doctor *continues.*)

LISETTE (DUPARC): Well, monsieur, I see you have been questioning your daughter. Have you found the cause of her melancholy?

SGANARELLE: No! The hussy makes me mad!

LISETTE: Leave her to me. I'll sound her out a little.

SGANARELLE: It's not necessary. Since she likes this kind of stew, I have a mind to let her swim in it.

LISETTE: Let me do it, I tell you. Maybe she'll talk more freely to me than to you. Mademoiselle, you won't tell us what ails you, and you insist on afflicting everyone around you. Is that right? I don't think it is. People shouldn't act as you do, and if you have any repugance to explain yourself to your father, you ought to have none in talking to me. Tell me—do you want something of him?

(LUCINDA *shakes her head "no".*)

SGANARELLE: That's all she does—shake her head!

LISETTE: (*To* LUCINDA.) Your father has said more than once that he would spare nothing to make you happy. Does he make you stay in your room too much? (*She shakes her head "no".*) Do you crave feasts and parties? Huh? (*She shakes her head "no".*) Has anyone displeased you? Huh? (*She shakes her head "no".*) Do you have a secret yearning for someone you'd like to marry? Huh? (LUCINDA *shakes her head vigorously "yes," and smiles.*) Ah, ha! I understand! That's the thing! What the devil—why all the fuss? (*To* SGANARELLE) Sir, the mystery is discovered. She has a yearning for—

SGANARELLE: (*Cutting her sharply*) Go away, ungrateful daughter. I don't want to talk to you any longer. Go and simmer in your own obstinacy.

LUCINDA: But, father, you asked me to tell you what it was that I—

SGANARELLE: Yes, I'll discard all the affection I had for you.

LISETTE: But sir, her melancholy was—

SGANARELLE: This hussy would like to see me dead.

LUCINDA: Father, I really—

SGANARELLE: This is the recompense I get for having brought you up as I have.

LISETTE: But, sir—she—

SGANARELLE: No! I am terribly angry with her.

LUCINDA: But, father—

SGANARELLE: All the tenderness I had for you has vanished—pouf!

LISETTE: But—

SGANARELLE: She's a rascal.

LUCINDA: Listen, I—

SGANARELLE: An ungrateful slut.

LISETTE: But, sir—

SGANARELLE: She's a stubborn donkey that won't tell me what ails her.

LISETTE: It's a husband she wants.

SGANARELLE: (*Pretending not to hear*) I wash my hands of her.

LISETTE: A husband!

SGANARELLE: I hate, I hate, I hate her!

LISETTE: A husband!

SGANARELLE: I disown her as my daughter.

LISETTE: (*Yelling in his ear.*) A husband!

SGANARELLE: Don't even speak to me about her.

LISETTE: A husband! A husband!

SGANARELLE: I said not to speak to me about her.

LISETTE: (*Tries to explain with gestures.*) A hus—band!

SGANARELLE: Don't—speak—to me—about her. I don't—want—to hear.

LISETTE: (*Almost going mad, dancing around him*) A husband! A husband! A husband! You know what a husband is!

SGANARELLE: Don't even mention her name!

(*He stalks off, furious.*)

LISETTE: It's a true saying: "There are none so deaf as those who don't want to hear."

LUCINDA: Well, Lisette, I was wrong to hide things from my father, but you can see what little good it did to tell him the truth.

LISETTE: On my faith, he's a villainous rogue, and I would take great pleasure in playing him a mean trick. But tell me, mademoiselle, how comes it that you hid the cause of your distemper from me too?

LUCINDA: What good would it have done to tell you sooner? No more good than if I had kept it secret all my life.

LISETTE: What do you mean?

LUCINDA: I mean that I foresaw all that you saw just now. I knew ex-

actly what my father's sentiments were. I knew that he sent a refusal to the young man who asked for me through a friend.
Don't you think that was enough to extinguish all the hope that
was in my heart?

LISETTE: What? Is that the one? The stranger who sent a friend to
ask your father for you?

LUCINDA: Perhaps I'm not being modest to explain matters so clearly,
but I must confess that if I had but one wish I would wish for
him. We've never spoken to each other, and he has never declared the passion he has for me, but—

LISETTE: But, what?

LUCINDA: In every place where he has been able to get a glimpse of
me, his looks and his actions have always spoken so tenderly to
me. And his request to my father was so honorable that my
heart couldn't help being touched.

LISETTE: You love him then?

LUCINDA: Yes, I love him. But you see how my father's harshness
reduces that love to ashes.

LISETTE: Let me work it out. Even though I'm a little angry because
you kept your secret from me, I won't fail to help you. Provided, of course, that you have resolution enough.

LUCINDA: But what can I do against a father's authority? He's completely deaf to my wishes.

LISETTE: Do you want to be led around like a goose?

LUCINDA: But what, then?

LISETTE: There are ways to be liberated from a father's tyranny—
and without offending his honor.

LUCINDA: What shall I do?

LISETTE: What does he intend for you to do? Aren't you of age to be
married?

LUCINDA: Yes.

LISETTE: You're not made of marble are you? Or ice?

LUCINDA: Of course not. But what can we do?

LISETTE: Let me handle this passion of yours. From this moment I take full charge of all your interests. You'll see that I know a few ins and outs in this game. But be careful—your father is coming back. Go to your room, and leave me to act.

(LISETTE *hides just inside the door,* LUCINDA *exits, as* SGANARELLE *comes in, goes front and talks to audience.*)

SGANARELLE: It's good sometimes to pretend not to hear what one hears only too well. It's especially helpful when dealing with bill collectors, lawyers, or one's own children. I can't understand why parents must be subjected to such tyrannical custom. Is there anything more ridiculous and impertinent than to heap up riches with years of hard labor, to bring up a daughter with much care and tenderness, only to have both riches and daughter snatched from your hands by a man who means nothing to you? No, by thunder, that custom is a mockery. I'll keep my house, my money, and my daughter to myself.

LISETTE: (*Enters yelling, but pretends not to see* SGANARELLE.) What a misfortune! What a calamity! Poor Monsieur Sganarelle! I must find him.

SGANARELLE: Here I am! What's all this about?

LISETTE: (*Running around wildly*) My poor mistress. Poor, dear Lucinda.

SGANARELLE: (*Running after her*) What's the matter?

LISETTE: Wait till you hear the news.

SGANARELLE: Lisette! Tell me!

LISETTE: What a misfortune!

SGANARELLE: Lisette! Speak to me!

LISETTE: What a tragedy!

SGANARELLE: Lisette! Lisette! You're driving me mad! Speak!

LISETTE: Oh, sir, I can hardly speak.

SGANARELLE: You must speak! You must tell me what's the matter.

LISETTE: Your daughter—

SGANARELLE: (*Thinking the worst, tries to cry.*) Oh! Oh!

LISETTE: Don't cry like that or you'll make me laugh.

SGANARELLE: Then tell me quickly.

LISETTE: Your daughter was so shocked by your words, and by the terrible rage you were in with her, that she ran up to her room, and—

SGANARELLE: Well? Speak!

LISETTE: Full of despair, she opened the window that looks out on the river—

SGANARELLE: Well?

LISETTE: I can't go on.

SGANARELLE: You can't go on? Speak, you jade, or I'll tear you into shreds.

LISETTE: Well, she opened the window—

SGANARELLE: You said that already.

LISETTE: She lifted her eyes to heaven and said: "It's impossible for me to live with my father's hatred, and since he disowns me as a daughter, I must die."

SGANARELLE: (*Horrified*) She jumped out the window?

LISETTE: No.

SGANARELLE: What did she do?

LISETTE: She shut the window.

SGANARELLE: She shut it?

LISETTE: Yes—very gently.

SGANARELLE: And then?

LISETTE: She lay down on her bed.

SGANARELLE: Then what?

LISETTE: She started crying bitterly, and all at once her face grew pale, her eyes rolled, her heart stopped beating, and she collapsed in my arms.

SGANARELLE: Oh, my poor Lucinda! Is she dead?

LISETTE: No. I slapped her and pinched her and she revived. But she goes back into her trance every few minutes, and I don't think she'll live through the day.

SGANARELLE: Call the servants! Call everybody! Quickly! Have someone call some doctors—a lot of doctors. One can't have too many doctors in such an emergency. Oh, my poor girl, my poor girl. Call the doctors! Call the doctors!

(*The curtain of* The Love Doctor *set descends on the end of Act I*)
   (*There is a divertissement of music and dancing. Some of it might continue through the following interlude.*)

COUNT: Well, Marquis, what did you think of the first act?

MARQUIS: I think Molière is going from bad to worse.

COUNT: And to think that the King thought it was admirable.

MARQUIS: The epicureans who surround the King have perverted the taste of his Majesty.

PRIEST: And what is your opinion, Monsieur Truffe? (TRUFFE *is snoring.*) You see, gentlemen—for a country bumpkin, he's not so stupid. (*Calling*) Truffe! Truffe!

TRUFFE: What is it?

PRIEST: You can wake up now—the first act is finished.

TRUFFE: The act is finished? I'm so glad. Was it amusing?

PRIEST: Very.

TRUFFE: All I heard before I fell asleep was a lot of stilted phrases that sounded like Latin to me. I can't understand why this Molière is so popular. It won't last, I can tell you. Not one word made any sense to me.

PRIEST: Perhaps it's your curious way of listening.

TRUFFE: I don't get any pleasure from fancy language. My vocabulary has only two maxims: hunt for game on my own land, hunt for love on other people's land.

PRIEST: That was a very studied remark you made there.

TRUFFE: Was it? I don't know why it is, but some people are always about to say something stupid, while I'm always about to say something clever.

(*He sneezes.*)

PRIEST: Wit is like good fortune—it comes to you while you sleep.

TRUFFE: I had a nice nap.

PRIEST: Is that why you came to the play?

TRUFFE: No—I came for the music. But of course I like to be able to tell my friends that I've been to see Molière's troupe.

PRIEST: What do you think of Molière's troupe?

TRUFFE: I like puppet shows better.

COUNT: (*To the* MOROSE GENTLEMAN) And you?

GENTLEMAN: The only play of Molière that I like is *Oedipus Rex*.

TRUFFE: To be perfectly frank, I don't like his language. I've been told he uses the word "cuckold" just as if it wouldn't hurt anyone, but if you ask me—

(*He stretches out in his chair.*)

PRIEST: Are you going back to sleep?

TRUFFE: Not until the second act begins. Will you let me know, please? At a play, most people daydream, but I prefer to dream only when I'm asleep.

COUNT: This is a country-style philosopher you have there, Father.

PRIEST: (*To* TRUFFE) You were complaining of having to pay for your seat, but it seems you got a bed for the same price.

TRUFFE: I'm not complaining any longer. (DUCROISY *passes by.*)

MARQUIS: Are you looking for me, Lisette?

DUCROISY: No! It's Samuel I want.

MARQUIS: I see. (*Calling to* SAMUEL) Midas! Croesus! Mondor! (*Goes to* SAMUEL *and taps him on shoulder.*) My dear Samuel, I take the trouble of calling you by all your names and you don't reply.

SAMUEL: I was remarking to these gentlemen that Molière seems to have a new impertinence toward the nobility.

PRIEST: And what does that have to do with you? Turn your eyes this way and see what awaits you.

SAMUEL: (*Turns, sees* DUCROISY.) Oh, it's you, little artist. Were you asking for me?

DUCROISY: Yes, I was asking for you.

SAMUEL: Should I be happy because of it?

DUCROISY: You can be as happy as you would like to be.

SAMUEL: And what must I give for that? My purse, my land, my—

DUCROISY: That's too much and too little. I want none of that.

SAMUEL: Explain yourself. Can't you see I'm burning with curiosity?

DUCROISY: I want you to carry off Duparc.

SAMUEL: What? Carry off the leading actress of the play?

DUCROISY: Call her an actress if you like. I call her other things. I want you to carry her off.

SAMUEL: Carry her off? But to where?

DUCROISY: I don't care where! I want you to kidnap her.

SAMUEL: Oh, ho! I think I understand. You want to test me, don't you, you rascal?

DUCROISY: Test you? I?

SAMUEL: You've heard that I'm a little involved with her, and you want to know if—

DUCROISY: Heavens, I don't want to know anything. Involve yourself with her as much as you like. You have my blessing.

SAMUEL: What do you want, then?

DUCROISY: I told you.

SAMUEL: What will be my reward?

DUCROISY: You can name it yourself.

SAMUEL: I can name the reward? Let me think—

DUCROISY: As if you didn't already know.

SAMUEL: Yes—you're right—*that* will do. You may consider Duparc conveniently kidnapped—immediately after the play.

DUCROISY: It's not after the play I want her kidnapped—it's now!

SAMUEL: What do you mean—"now"?

DUCROISY: In five minutes.

SAMUEL: But in five minutes she'll be going on stage.

DUCROISY: If you kidnap her, she won't. I want you to do it before she goes on stage.

SAMUEL: Oh, ho! This is a very sudden thing.

DUCROISY: I can see you won't do it. I'll ask someone else, and someone else will get the reward.

SAMUEL: Hold on! I didn't say I won't. Let me know a little more about this kidnapping.

DUCROISY: Good heavens—a little kidnapping is not an expedition into Russia. Here is my offer—in two words: the one who carries off Duparc before the beginning of the second act will be welcome to have supper with me tonight, at my home, between eleven and midnight.

SAMUEL: Your word on it?

DUCROISY: My word.

SAMUEL: Good! I shall sacrifice myself.

DUCROISY: You have nothing to complain about. A pretty woman asks you to carry off another, and promises you a supper for your reward. You're too fortunate.

SAMUEL: Do you think so? It depends on what we have for supper.

(DUCROISY *exits, shrugging her shoulders.*)

SAMUEL: She may simply be conspiring to get rid of me. I have an idea. Count! Will you come here for a moment?

COUNT: I warn you—if you didn't call me to make honorable amends, I don't care to talk to you.

SAMUEL: Well, Count—it's true—I've reflected.

COUNT: Your choice of words is wrong. You don't mean "reflected"—you mean "calculated."

SAMUEL: Reflected is what I meant. I've decided that you were complimenting me by choosing me to be of service to you.

COUNT: Well, for the first time in your life you have said something with a tinge of common sense.

SAMUEL: So, I've decided to offer you—

COUNT: What?

SAMUEL: My purse—

COUNT: Oh!

SAMUEL: My carriage—

COUNT: Ah!

SAMUEL: And the key to my little hide-away, libertine.

COUNT: Ah! Ah! Ah!

SAMUEL: But on one condition.

COUNT: You see—I knew you had been calculating. What is the condition?

SAMUEL: It's simple. I want you to carry off Duparc.

COUNT: Carry off Duparc? That intrigues me. But when?

SAMUEL: Immediately.

COUNT: That intrigues me even more. Immediately!

SAMUEL: Before the beginning of the second act.

COUNT: It's as good as done. And now—the trifles.

(*Holds out his hand.*)

SAMUEL: My purse. (*He hands over a purse which the* COUNT *holds in his hand to feel the weight.*)

COUNT: Phew!

SAMUEL: My coach is outside. You know Grison, my coachman. He'll follow your orders. And here is the key to my little house. Grison knows where it is.

(*Hands him an enormous key.*)

COUNT: The house may be little, but the key— Where am I going to put it?

SAMUEL: Carry it, my friend, carry it. And remember—in five minutes the deed must be done.

COUNT: Rest easy. In five minutes Duparc will evaporate.

(COUNT *exits.*)

SAMUEL: Now—where can I hide so that my fair lady will think I'm at work?

(CHANDEL *enters from wings.*)

CHANDEL: Monsieur Samuel—look what the Count just gave me. He must have come into a fortune.

(*He shows the money.*)

SAMUEL: He's a liberal man. Chandel, I was just going to look for you. I need a favor.

CHANDEL: Two if you like.

SAMUEL: I want you to hide me somewhere.

CHANDEL: But, where?

SAMUEL: Where I can see without being seen.

CHANDEL: I can put you in the house on the stage.

SAMUEL: That won't do—Ducroisy will see me.

CHANDEL: I have an idea. I'll put you up in the clouds with Comedy, Music, and Dance. You won't be in such bad company, eh?

SAMUEL: In the clouds? What are you talking about?

CHANDEL: Up there! You saw it in the prologue. It will be down again for the finale. What do you think about that?

SAMUEL: I would prefer to stay on the ground, but no matter—I'll risk it.

CHANDEL: You know that when you move into a new home you have to pay in advance.

SAMUEL: Gladly. (*Starts to reach for his purse.*) Oh, the Count has my purse.

CHANDEL: Too bad! No money—no cloud.

SAMUEL: Do you mean you refuse to give me credit?

CHANDEL: Not without some security.

SAMUEL: All right, bandit. Here!

(*He takes off a ring and gives it to* CHANDEL.)

CHANDEL: (*Going towards the wings, passes* MARQUIS.) Who would ever have thought I would wear a diamond on my little finger like a Marquis?

MARQUIS: (*Holding his ring next to* CHANDEL'*s*) One exception, friend. Yours is real while ours is false.

CHANDEL: (*Motioning above his head*) Well! Come on down with the cloud. (*The cloud descends with the three girls on it.*) Here's your little flock, Samuel—be a good shepherd. (SAMUEL *gets on the cloud.*) Take good care of our banker, girls. (*The cloud is drawn out of sight. There are three knocks on stage which signify that the play is about to resume. Everyone takes his seat. The curtain goes up on* The Love Doctor *set.*)

PRIEST: My friend, Truffe, you can go back to sleep. The act is about to begin.

TRUFFE: Good night.

(LAGRANGE *comes rushing on stage.*)

LAGRANGE: Where is Lisette? We can't find Lisette.

PRIEST: She was here a few minutes ago.

LAGRANGE: (*Calling*) Mademoiselle Duparc!

VOICE IN WINGS: Mademoiselle Duparc!

GENTLEMAN: What's going on?

MARQUIS: Where is the Count?

PRIEST: Where is Samuel the banker?

VOICE IN WINGS: Mademoiselle Duparc!

LAGRANGE: Ladies and gentlemen, we can't find Mademoiselle Duparc, but we will look for her. Be patient. (CHANDEL *comes to him, whispers.*) What did you say, Chandel? Speak up.

CHANDEL: I was told that Duparc fell through a trap-door that wasn't bolted down.

LAGRANGE: Is she below the stage then?

CHANDEL: I went down there—I looked, and I called her name, but she wasn't there.

LAGRANGE: What can we do?

CHANDEL: If Ducroisy is still here, and if she is willing—

LAGRANGE: Go and see quickly. (CHANDEL *dashes off.*) Ladies and gentlemen, I don't know how to tell you this new development, but Mademoiselle Duparc has—well, she has disappeared. Nevertheless, we hope to continue with the performance without further interruption if Mademoiselle Ducroisy can be located. We feel certain that she will do us the honor of assuming the role of Lisette for the duration of the play. (CHANDEL *comes in, whispers.*)

Ladies and gentlemen, I have good news. Ducroisy was in her dressing room, and will make her entrance as soon as she has time to put on her costume and prepare herself. Be good enough to take a short intermission. Thank you for your indulgence.

(The Love Doctor *curtain and the main curtain are both lowered.*)

Intermission

Act II

(We hear three knocks and a voice backstage saying "places, please." The stage audience takes seats as the curtain rises on Act Two *of* The Love Doctor.*)*

(The scene is a room in SGANARELLE's *house. He is pacing the floor.* LISETTE *is watching him.)*

LISETTE (DUCROISY): But sir, why did you insist on four doctors? Isn't one enough to kill a person?

SGANARELLE: Hold your tongue! Four minds are better than one.

LISETTE: With doctors, you mean equal to one.

SGANARELLE: Hold your tongue, I said.

LISETTE: Can't your daughter die well enough without the assistance of those quacks?

SGANARELLE: Are you trying to say that physicians kill people?

LISETTE: Without even trying! I knew a man who proved with good reasoning that we should never say "So and so is dead of a fever or pneumonia," but "She is dead of four doctors and two apothecaries."

SGANARELLE: Hush! Don't offend the physicians. They'll be coming back in soon.

LISETTE: Monsieur, our cat has just recovered from a fall she had from the top of the house to the street. She went three days without eating, and she couldn't so much as lift a paw, but lucky for her there are no cat-doctors or she would have been done for. They would have purged her and bled her to death.

SGANARELLE: Shut up! My daughter is not a cat! Stop being impertinent. Here they are.

LISETTE: Take care! You're going to be well instructed. They'll tell you in Latin that your daughter is sick.

(*Doctors* TOMES, FONANDRES, MACROTON, *and* BAHYS *come in.*)

SGANARELLE: Well, gentlemen?

TOMES: We have examined the patient thoroughly and we have found a great many impurities in her.

SGANARELLE: What? My daughter is impure?

TOMES: I mean there is much impurity in her body—a large quantity of corrupt vapors.

SGANARELLE: I understand—but not very well.

TOMES: We are now going into consultation.

SGANARELLE: Sit down, won't you please?

LISETTE: Well, Doctor Tomes, we meet again.

SGANARELLE: How do you know the doctor?

LISETTE: I saw him the other day at a friend of your niece's. He was attending her coachman.

TOMES: How is her coachman doing?

LISETTE: Very well! He's dead.

TOMES: Dead?

LISETTE: Yes.

TOMES: That can't be.

LISETTE: I don't know if it can be or not, but I know that it *is*.

TOMES: He can't be dead, I tell you.

LISETTE: It's too bad, then, because they buried him.

TOMES: You're mistaken.

LISETTE: I saw it.

TOMES: It's impossible. Hippocrates says distinctly that illnesses such as his don't terminate until the fourteenth or twenty-first day, and he fell sick just six days ago.

LISETTE: You tell Hippocrates that the coachman is dead. Maybe he didn't know how to count.

SGANARELLE: Silence, babbler! Let us leave the good doctors alone. Gentlemen, I beg you to consult in the best manner. Although it's not my custom to pay in advance, still, for fear I should forget it, here—

(*He pays each one, and each makes a different gesture on receiving the money.* LISETTE *and* SGANARELLE *then leave the room. The doctors sit down and spend time clearing their throats.*)

FONANDRES: Paris is getting so large these days that house calls barely pay.

TOMES: I have an admirable mule to get around on. It's hard to believe how far I make him go every day.

FONANDRES: I have a wonderful horse that is indefatigable.

TOMES: Do you know where my mule has gone today? First, over by the Arsenal, from the Arsenal to Saint-Sulpice, then to the very end of the Rue Clichy, and back to Montparnasse. From there to Saint-Denis and from Saint-Denis to Faubourg Saint-Jacques, from Faubourg Saint-Jacques to Colombes, from Colombes to the Place Royale, from the Place Royale to here. And I still must go to the Place des Vosges.

FONANDRES: My horse has done more than that today, and besides I dropped off at Dampierre to see a patient.

TOMES: By the way, which side do you take in the dispute between the two doctors, Theophratus and Artemius? It's an affair that has divided the whole profession.

FONANDRES: I'm for Artemius.

TOMES: I likewise. Not that his advice didn't kill a patient. Theophratus was certainly the better, but he was wrong under the circumstances, and he ought not to have held a different opinion than his senior. What do you say?

FONANDRES: Without a doubt. The formalities should always be observed whatever happens.

TOMES: I'm strict as the devil in that respect unless I'm among friends. The other day three of us were called in to consult with a physician from outside. I stopped the whole business and would not allow them to give opinions unless things were in order. The people of the house did what they could, but the patient got worse. I refused to budge an inch, and he died bravely during the dispute.

FONANDRES: It's good to give people something to think about now and then, and to show them their mistakes.

TOMES: A dead man is only a dead man, and he is of no great consequence, but one neglected formality can prejudice the entire body of physicians.

(SGANARELLE *enters.*)

SGANARELLE: Doctors, my daughter's oppression is increasing. Please tell me quickly what you have decided.

TOMES: (*To* FONANDRES) Tell him, sir.

FONANDRES: No, sir, you speak first if you please.

TOMES: You must be jesting.

FONANDRES: I will not speak first.

TOMES: Well, sir!

FONANDRES: Well, sir!

SGANARELLE: Please, gentlemen, drop the ceremonies and remember my daughter is dying.

TOMES: Your daughter's illness—

FONANDRES: Our opinion is—

MACROTON: After having consulted—   (*They all speak at same time.*)

BAHYS: In order to reason—

SGANARELLE: I pray you, gentlemen, speak one at a time if you please.

TOMES: Sir, we have consulted upon your daughter's condition, and my studied opinion is that it proceeds from a great heat of the blood. So I'd have her bled immediately.

FONANDRES: And I say that her illness is a putrefaction of vapors, caused by too great a repletion. I prescribe an immediate emetic.

TOMES: I maintain that an emetic will kill her.

FONANDRES: And I am sure that bleeding will be the end of her.

TOMES: It's like you to make yourself the competent judge.

FONANDRES: Yes, it's like me. And I'll match you in all kinds of learning.

TOMES: Oh, ho! Do you remember the man you killed a few days ago?

FONANDRES: Do you remember a kind little woman you sent into another world last week?

TOMES: (*To* SGANARELLE) I have told you my opinion.

FONANDRES: I have given you my thoughts on the matter.

TOMES: If you don't bleed your daughter immediately, she's a dead woman.

(*He leaves the house.*)

FONANDRES: If you do bleed her, she won't be alive fifteen minutes from now.

(*He leaves.*)

SGANARELLE: (*To the other two doctors*) Which of the two am I to believe? How am I supposed to act on two such contrary opinions? Gentlemen, I beg of you to decide for me, and to tell me without passion what you think is the proper way to give my daughter relief.

MACROTON: (*Drawing out his words*) Sir, in these mat-ters, we must pro-ceed with cir-cum-spect-ion, and do noth-ing hast-i-ly, for the dam-age which might be com-mit-ted in this case, acc-ord-ing to our mas-ter Hipp-hipp-oc-rat-es might have dan-ger-ous con-se-quences.

BAHYS: (*Spitting out his words like a machine gun*) It's true, it's true. We must be careful of what we do. This isn't child's play, you know, not child's play, and once we've made a slip it isn't easy to repair the mistake and re-establish what we have spoiled. *Experimentum periculosum.* That is why it's a question of reasoning things out first, weighing them carefully, considering the constitution of the patient, examining the causes of the malady, and seeing what remedies ought to be applied.

SGANARELLE: (*Aside*) One goes like a tortoise and the other like a race-horse.

MACROTON: Now, sir, to be fact-u-al, I find that your daugh-ter has a chron-i-cal dis-ease, and she can be en-dang-ered if she is not giv-en ass-iss-tance im-med-i-ate-ly be-cause the symp-toms that she has are in-dic-a-tive of a ful-ig-in-ous and mor-di-cant va-por which pen-e-trates the mem-branes of the cer-e-bel—the cer-e-bel—the brain. Now this va-por which in Greek is called At-mos, is caused by ten-a-cious and con-glu-tin-ous con-glom-er-ations which are con-tained in the low-er ab-do—ab-do—stomach.

BAHYS: And as this conglomeration has been engendered by a long succession of time, it has been over-cooked and has acquired this vaporization which fumes toward the region of the brain.

MACROTON: So, then, in or-der to draw a-way, loo-sen, ex-pel, and e-vac-u-ate the said con-glom-er-a-tion, there must be a vig-o-rous pur-ga-tion. But first, I think it prop-er and not at all in-con-ven-ient to u-til-ize some lit-tle an-o-dyne rem-e-dies, that is to say, some e-mol-li-ent en-e-mas of ju-lep and syr-up. Very re-fresh-ing.

BAHYS: After that we come to the purgation and the bleeding, which, let me reiterate, will be done only if needed.

MACROTON: That is not to in-fer that with all our care, your daugh-ter can-not die. But at least you will have done some-thing, and you will have the con-so-la-tion that she died according to form.

BAHYS: It's better to die by the rules than to recover contrary to them.

MACROTON: We have told you our thoughts in all sin-cer-i-ty.

BAHYS: We've spoken to you just as we would to our own brother.

SGANARELLE: (*To* MACROTON, *mimicking him*) I ren-der my most humble app-re-ci-a-tion, and thank you for bring-ing us your ass—
iss-tance. (*To* BAHYS, *racing his words*) And I might say that I'm
infinitely obliged to you for the prodigious pains you have put
forth on the part of the poor patient. (*He spits the words with "p"
right at* BAHYS.) Good-day, gentlemen. (*The two doctors leave.*)
Here I am just a little more uncertain than I was before. But I
have a little idea in my head. I'll go buy some Orvietan and
make her take some of it. Orvietan is a remedy that many people find quite beneficial. (*He goes out of house and is seen again in
the street, calling to a* VENDOR *who has a push-cart.*) Ho there,
fellow—give me a box of your Orvietan which I'll pay you for.

(*The* VENDOR *turns towards him.*)

VENDOR: (*Singing*)

> The gold in all climates and under the sea,
> Is not worth this potion that I have with me;
> My remedy cures you, with never a fear,
> Of all of the ills you can catch in a year.
>
> The scabs and the pox,
> And the grippe and the gout,
> The measles, the fever,
> Without any doubt.
> There's no kind of sickness
> That's been known to man,
> That won't disappear if you take Orvietan.

SGANARELLE: Sir, I frankly believe that all the gold in the world is not
sufficient to pay for your medicine, but here are twenty sous
which you may take if you please.

VENDOR: (*Singing*)

> My heart's filled with goodness; for twenty small pence,
> This marvellous treasure my hands will dispense;
> And you can be certain that by morning's dawn,
> The plagues that now curse you will long have been gone.
>
> The colic and scurvy,
> The dropsy, the itch,

Or plain constipation,
It's no matter which.
There is no elixir
Since time first began,
That equals the wonders of my Orvietan.

(*The curtain goes down on the second act of* The Love Doctor, *and there is a divertissement with several Trivelins and Scaramouches, as the following dialogue continues.*)

SAMUEL: (*Calling from above*) Chandel! Chandel!

CHANDEL: (*Looking up*) At your service.

SAMUEL: Chandel, I don't need to hide any longer. Let me down. I'm getting dizzy up here.

CHANDEL: It's not possible until the end of the play.

SAMUEL: What do you mean?

CHANDEL: It's my orders. You can't come down until the finale. Be patient—there's just one more act.

MARQUIS: Be quiet! You're disturbing the ballet.

(*The ballet finishes and there are three knocks signifying the start of Act III of* The Love Doctor. *The scene is the same as Act II. The doctors* TOMES *and* FONANDRES *are discovered, talking to* LISETTE, *played by* DUCROISY.)

LISETTE (DUCROISY): What! You gentlemen are here again? And are you not giving a thought to repairing the harm that has been done to medicine?

TOMES: What? What's the matter?

(*Suddenly,* DUPARC, *in costume of* LISETTE, *rushes in, out of breath, and takes up the lines.*)

LISETTE (DUPARC): You haven't heard? An insolent fellow who had the effrontery to encroach upon your profession? He just killed a man with a sword thrust through his heart, and without having a prescription from you.

DUCROISY: Mademoiselle Duparc, I would like to know where you came from.

DUPARC: Where I came from? You know very well. You're the one who had me carried away by your lover.

PROMPTER: "You make a jest of it now, but you'll pass into our hands someday."

DUCROISY: My lover? Is Samuel my lover by any chance?

DUPARC: It wasn't Samuel who carried me off—it was the Count.

DUCROISY: The Count? (*Calling*) Monsieur Samuel! Monsieur Samuel!

PROMPTER: "You make a jest of it now."

MARQUIS: Be quiet, prompter—you're preventing our hearing what the ladies are saying.

GENTLEMAN: Pardon me, but we came to see *The Love Doctor*. We would like to hear Molière's play, as bad as it is, and not discussions about the actresses' lovers.

MARQUIS: What did you say?

GENTLEMAN: I say what I please.

MARQUIS: Would it please you to meet me in the street?

GENTLEMAN: Gladly.

MARQUIS: After you, monsieur.

(*They both leave.*)

DUPARC: I would like to speak to the audience.

DUCROISY: I also.

DUPARC: I want them to know how I've been treated.

DUCROISY: I want them to know how I've been humiliated.

BOTH TOGETHER: Ladies and gentlemen—

DUPARC: Monsieur Lagrange! (LAGRANGE *comes running in.*) As leading actress, I demand the right to speak. Do your duty.

LAGRANGE: Ducroisy—

DUCROISY: No!

LAGRANGE: Mademoiselle Ducroisy!

DUCROISY: No, no, no! I was told to get into costume. I was told to play the scene. I will play it in spite of you, in spite of her, in spite of everybody.

LAGRANGE: Mademoiselle, I shall be forced to call the guard.

DUCROSIY: (*Enraged*) Oh!

DUPARC: (*To audience*) Ladies and gentlemen, in order to have the honor of appearing before you tonight, I was forced to leave my elderly aunt on her death-bed—an aunt whose sole heir I am.

DUCROISY: The liar! The only bed she left was the one she was in with the Marquis.

DUPARC: (*Continuing, to audience*) You have seen how insistent I was to play before you tonight.

DUCROISY: Before the Count, she means.

DUPARC: Shut up, you goose!

DUCROISY: Oh! Goose!

DUPARC: Justice has been done, and the role has been returned to me. Thank you for your kind acknowledgment of my feeble talent during the first act.

DUCROISY: Oh, if I only knew how to hiss!

DUPARC: Encouraged by your indulgence, I was preparing to come on stage for the second act, but in walking over a trap-door, I felt the opening give way and I suddenly found myself below, where three men were waiting for me—three rapists, three kidnappers hired by my rival.

DUCROISY: It's a lie. I hired no rapists.

DUPARC: Quiet! (*To audience*) I tried to cry out, but they dragged me out, threw me in a carriage, where I found—(*Looks around for the* COUNT.) Count—be my witness—tell them what I found.

COUNT: Why—you found me.

DUPARC: Immediately, the order was given to the coachman to leave.

I struggled, I cried out—Count, you are witness to the resistance I made.

COUNT: An unbelievable resistance—and a great deal of noise—it's true, ladies and gentlemen.

DUPARC: At last the Count began to realize he had done wrong. He made excuses, and I forgave him on condition that he would bring me back—and here I am. Count, isn't that exactly the way it happened?

COUNT: Well—true, true. (*Low to* DUPARC) Except for one small detail you're forgetting.

DUPARC: (*Gives* COUNT *a quick kick in the shin which makes him recoil, then to audience.*) There you are, ladies and gentlemen—a perfectly truthful account of the horrible event that deprived me of your applause for many long minutes.

VOICES IN PIT: Hurrah! Duparc! We want Duparc!

LAGRANGE: (*To* DUCROISY) Have you anything to reply?

DUCROISY: If the Count sides with her, I have nothing to say. But the evening is not ended. (*In a huff, aside*) Duparc and Samuel will pay for this. (*Calling*) Monsieur Samuel! Samuel!

SAMUEL: (*Above the stage*) Did someone speak my name?

LAGRANGE: Silence, please. Let us start from the beginning of the act. Places, please.

(DUCROISY *goes off. Act III of* The Love Doctor *begins again.*)

LISETTE (Duparc): What! You gentlemen are here again? And are you not giving a thought to repairing the harm that has been done to medicine?

TOMES: What? What's the matter?

LISETTE: You haven't heard? An insolent fellow who had the effrontery to encroach upon your profession? He just killed a man with a sword thrust through his heart—

(*The* MARQUIS *comes in, sword still in hand.*)

MARQUIS: Yes—I killed the bastard.

LISETTE: (*Continuing without looking at* MARQUIS *who takes his seat*)—and without having a prescription from you.

TOMES: You make a jest of it now, but you'll pass into our hands someday.

LISETTE: You mean "pass away" in your hands! I'll permit you to kill me when I'm forced to call you to cure me.

(*The* DOCTORS *go out and* CLITANDRE, *in doctor's garb, enters, getting dark looks from the departing physicians.*)

CLITANDRE: Well, Lisette, what do you say to my masquerade? Do you think it will fool the old man?

LISETTE: Anything would fool him.

CLITANDRE: How do you like me in this costume?

LISETTE: Very fetching! You look like the best doctor in the world. But now we must talk. I've been waiting impatiently for you.

CLITANDRE: Tell me your plan.

LISETTE: You see, heaven has made me one of the most humane creatures in the world. I can't see two lovers sigh for each other without being overcome with a profound tenderness, and a desire to relieve the pains that they suffer.

CLITANDRE: It sounds wonderful. Go on.

LISETTE: I'm determined—at all costs—to deliver Lucinda from the tyranny she is under, and put her in your power.

CLITANDRE: But why should you want to help *me*?

LISETTE: Didn't I already tell you?

CLITANDRE: But you scarcely know me.

LISETTE: But I know men very well. You pleased me from the very first. I know that Lucinda couldn't have made a better choice.

CLITANDRE: I'm very flattered.

LISETTE: Flattering you is not part of this. My plan is to help Lucinda.

CLITANDRE: But will your scheme work?

LISETTE: Love ventures on strange adventures. Our stratagem is planned, our measures are taken. Perhaps we shall succeed.

CLITANDRE: If we can only fool him.

LISETTE: He's not what you would call brilliant. But if this adventure fails, we'll find a thousand others that will work the same result. Wait for me a moment and I'll come back with the tyrant.

(CLITANDRE *retires to side of stage,* LISETTE *goes out and returns with* SGANARELLE.)

SGANARELLE: What do you want with me?

LISETTE: I want to tell you of joy—overwhelming joy!

SGANARELLE: What's the matter?

LISETTE: Rejoice, master, rejoice.

SGANARELLE: For what?

LISETTE: Rejoice, I tell you.

SGANARELLE: But I can't rejoice unless you tell me why I should rejoice.

LISETTE: No! I want you to rejoice beforehand. I want you to sing and dance.

SGANARELLE: On what account?

LISETTE: On my word.

SGANARELLE: Come, then. (*He does a stiff dance.*) La, la, la, la, lera, la. (*Stops abruptly.*) What the devil am I doing?

LISETTE: Master, your daughter is as good as cured.

SGANARELLE: My daughter is cured?

LISETTE: Yes! As good as cured! I have brought you a doctor.

SGANARELLE: Another doctor?

LISETTE: But what a doctor this is. He is not like any other doctor. He is a doctor of importance, of great renown. He makes marvellous cures.

SGANARELLE: He does?

LISETTE: He never fails. And what is more—he hates other doctors as much as you do.

SGANARELLE: I like him already. Where is he?

LISETTE: I'll bring him in.

SGANARELLE: I must see if he'll do more than those other horrible doctors.

LISETTE: (*Beckoning to* CLITANDRE.) Here he is.

SGANARELLE: A doctor without a beard?

LISETTE: Any idiot can wear a beard—and most of them do. Knowledge isn't measured by the beard. This doctor's healing power isn't in his chin.

SGANARELLE: Sir, I'm told that you have wonderful remedies. Are they like those of the other doctors that do nothing but make a person go to the toilet?

CLITANDRE: Sir, my remedies are different from those of any other doctor. They have enemas, purges and emetics, and bleedings. But I cure by words, sounds, letters, talismans, and rings.

LISETTE: Didn't I tell you?

SGANARELLE: This is a great man.

LISETTE: Sir, your daughter is dressed. I'll bring her to you.

SGANARELLE: Yes, do.

(LISETTE *goes out.*)

CLITANDRE: Give me your hand. I want to take your pulse.

SGANARELLE: I'm not sick.

CLITANDRE: Give me your hand! (SGANARELLE *extends hand.* CLITANDRE *listens to his pulse.*) Your daughter is a very sick girl.

SGANARELLE: Can you tell that here?

CLITANDRE: Of course—by the sympathy that there is between father and daughter.

SGANARELLE: I'm amazed.

(LISETTE *enters with* LUCINDA *who sits.*)

LISETTE: Doctor—take this chair next to her. (*To* SGANARELLE) Come—we must leave them.

SGANARELLE: Why? I want to stay here.

LISETTE: You're joking. We must leave them alone. A doctor has a hundred things to ask a girl that a man shouldn't hear.

SGANARELLE: All right—we'll go over here so they can talk privately.

(*He goes far to one side with* LISETTE.)

CLITANDRE: (*Speaking to* LUCINDA *but with manner of a doctor, feeling her forehead, taking her pulse et cetera*) Oh, Lucinda, what a great moment for me. I really don't know how to begin to speak to you. When I spoke to you only with my eyes, it seemed I had a thousand things to say, and now that I have the joy of speaking to you, I am at a loss for words, because my happiness stifles me.

LUCINDA: I might say the same thing. My great joy prevents my telling you my thoughts.

CLITANDRE: Lucinda, how happy I would be if it were true that you felt all that I feel, if I could judge of your heart by my own. But may I at least believe that it is to you that I owe the thought of this happy plan which allows me to be near you?

LUCINDA: If you don't owe me the thought, you are at least obliged to me for approving the plan.

SGANARELLE: (*Whispering to* LISETTE) He talks mighty close to her.

LISETTE: He's examining her, and studying her face.

CLITANDRE: Will you be constant in the favors that you show me?

LUCINDA: Will you be firm in the resolutions you have made?

CLITANDRE: Until death. I want nothing so much as to be yours, and I'll prove it by what you are going to see me do.

SGANARELLE: (*Breaks away from* LISETTE *and approaches* CLITANDRE.) How's the sick one, doctor? She seems a little brighter.

CLITANDRE: It's because I have already tried one of the remedies that my art teaches.

SGANARELLE: What is that?

CLITANDRE: The mind is sovereign of the body, and since it is often the cause of disorders, my custom is first to cure the mind before I come to the body.

SGANARELLE: How did you do it?

CLITANDRE: I observed her looks, her features, and the lines of her hands, and by the science that heaven has given me, I discovered that her mind is the part in which she is sick.

SGANARELLE: Her mind? Do you mean she is mad?

CLITANDRE: Not at all. Her illness comes from a disordered imagination, from a depraved desire to be married.

SGANARELLE: Married?

CLITANDRE: Yes. Ridiculous, isn't it? I see nothing sillier than this urge that people have for matrimony.

SGANARELLE: You're a wise doctor.

CLITANDRE: I have, and always will have, a horrible aversion to marriage.

SGANARELLE: A *great* doctor!

CLITANDRE: But we must flatter the imagination of our patient, and since she has an alienation of mind which will prove dangerous if not cured promptly, I have resorted to a little trick—a ruse.

SGANARELLE: A ruse?

CLITANDRE: Yes. (*Very confidentially, in a faked whisper*) I told her that I had come here to ask for her hand in marriage.

SGANARELLE: Clever! What did she say?

CLITANDRE: Suddenly her countenance changed, her complexion cleared, her eyes brightened, her pulse became steady, and if you can only hold her under this misapprehension for a few days, you'll see that we shall withdraw her entirely from the sad state in which she has been.

SGANARELLE: We'll do it, by all means.

CLITANDRE: Afterwards, we'll use other remedies to cure her wholly of her fantasy.

SGANARELLE: That's the best I've heard. Well, my girl, this gentleman has a mind to marry you, and I've told him that I am willing.

LUCINDA: Is it possible?

SGANARELLE: Yes.

LUCINDA: Really?

SGANARELLE: Yes, yes!

LUCINDA: (*To* CLITANDRE) You want to be my husband?

CLITANDRE: Yes, mademoiselle.

LUCINDA: And does my father consent to it?

SGANARELLE: Yes, daughter, I consent with all my heart.

LUCINDA: Oh, how happy I am if it's true.

CLITANDRE: Don't doubt it, mademoiselle. It was only today that I began to love you, and burned with a desire to be your husband. I came here only for that. And if you want me to tell you things just as they are, this costume is nothing but a mere pretense. I played the part of a doctor only to be able to get near you—to obtain what I desired.

(*He gives a sly wink to* SGANARELLE.)

SGANARELLE: (*Aside, laughing*) What a story!

LUCINDA: You seem to have a very tender love for me, and I am deeply moved.

SGANARELLE: (*Aside, roaring with laughter*) Oh, the silly girl! The poor, silly girl! What a trap! And she fell right in.

LUCINDA: (*To her father*) Then, dear father, do you give me this gentleman for a husband?

SGANARELLE: Yes. Give me your hand. (*To* CLITANDRE) Give me yours too.

CLITANDRE: (*Holding back*) But, sir—

SGANARELLE: No, no, it's only to—(*Whispering, and stifling a laugh*) to calm her mind. (*Aloud*) Come, take hands. There!

(*He puts their hands together.*)

CLITANDRE: As a pledge of my faith, I give you this ring. (*To* SGAN-ARELLE) This is an astrological ring that cures distractions of the mind.

SGANARELLE: Good! I like that!

LUCINDA: Prepare the marriage contract so that nothing is lacking.

CLITANDRE: Oh, yes, the contract. With all my heart, mademoiselle. (*Low, to* SGANARELLE) What's her name?

SGANARELLE: Lucinda. That's funny! You didn't even know her name.

CLITANDRE: I'll get a man who writes my prescriptions, and we'll make her believe he's a notary.

SGANARELLE: That's good! I like that!

CLITANDRE: (*Calling out window*) Ho, there! Send up the notary I brought with me.

LUCINDA: What? You brought a notary?

CLITANDRE: Of course.

(*He jabs* SGANARELLE *who roars with laughter.*)

LUCINDA: I'm delighted.

SGANARELLE: (*Aside*) Oh, the silly girl! What a fool of a daughter I raised.

(NOTARY *comes in and* CLITANDRE *whispers to him.*)

SGANARELLE: (*To* NOTARY) Notary, you are to make up a contract for two people. Write! (*To* LUCINDA) The contract is being written, my dear daughter. (*He laughs in his hand as he goes to* NOTARY.) Put in it that I give her twenty thousand as a dowry. Write!

LUCINDA: I thank you, father.

NOTARY: It's done. All you have to do is sign it.

SGANARELLE: That was a contract made in a hurry.

CLITANDRE: (*Low, to* SGANARELLE) You needn't sign it.

SGANARELLE: Why not? It will be amusing. (*To* NOTARY) Let's have the pen so we can sign. (NOTARY *hands pen to* CLITANDRE *who signs.*)

You too, Lucinda—sign—sign— Then give me the contract. I'll sign it later.

LUCINDA: (*Signing*) No, no—I want the contract in my own hands, and I want it signed.

SGANARELLE: Have it your way. (*He signs the contract and hands it to* LUCINDA.) Well—take it. Are you satisfied?

LUCINDA: Even more than you can imagine.

SGANARELLE: (*To* CLITANDRE) The poor girl swallowed it all. Everything worked out fine. She looks cured already.

CLITANDRE: I not only took the precaution of bringing a notary, I also brought several dancers and musicians to celebrate the event. I'll call them in. (*Motions at window.*) These are people I keep with me and whom I use daily to pacify disturbances of the mind with their harmony and their dances.

(*The group of* ENTERTAINERS *comes in, all in colorful costumes. As they start their frolic, they engage* SGANARELLE *in their antics while* CLITANDRE *picks up* LUCINDA *and carries her off.*)

SGANARELLE: This is a pleasant way of curing people. (*He enjoys the frolic a great deal as the merriment continues. Finally, he stops and looks around.*) Where is my daughter? And the doctor?

LISETTE: They've gone to conclude the rest of the marriage.

SGANARELLE: What marriage?

LISETTE: The marriage you believed was a jest. But it turned out to be in truth. The bird has been caught.

(SGANARELLE *tries to run out but the* DANCERS *hold him back.*)

SGANARELLE: What the devil! Let me go! Let me go, I say!

LISETTE: Dance! Dance!

SGANARELLE: Again? A plague on you all.

(*The* DANCERS *push* SGANARELLE *around in great merriment. The cloud begins to descend from above as* DUCROISY *comes in and talks to the* COUNT *who takes her hand, kisses it, then walks with her, arm in arm, towards the exit.*)

MARQUIS: (*To* SAMUEL *who is on the cloud in mid-air*) Samuel, what the devil are you doing up there?

SAMUEL: Mademoiselle Duparc! Ducroisy is taking away your Count, and the Count is taking away Ducroisy.

MARQUIS: Duparc is still backstage.

SAMUEL: Count! Count! What about me? What about me?

COUNT: (*Turning*) Don't worry about a thing, Samuel. I have the carriage and the key. I'll return them tomorrow—with your empty purse.

(*Exits with* DUCROISY *and waves to* SAMUEL.)

SAMUEL: Damn! Damn! Damn!

(*The cloud finally touches the stage floor and* SAMUEL *jumps off, running after the* COUNT *and* DUCROISY. COMEDY, MUSIC, *and* DANCE *get off the cloud and perform the epilogue of* The Love Doctor.)

COMEDY, MUSIC, DANCE: (*Singing*)

> Without us all the human race
> Would full of illness be;
> But you will find in our embrace,
> Complete salubrity.

> The knowledge of Hippocrates
> Will never cure your ills;
> Just lead with us the life of ease,
> And throw away your pills—
> With Comedy, Music, Dance.

(*They dance as the stage* AUDIENCE *gets up to leave.* TRUFFE *remains snoring.* SUBTIL *comes by and sees him. He turns to the* PRIEST *who has already started out.*)

SUBTIL: You've forgotten your friend.

PRIEST: Let him be. He'll be the first here for tomorrow's performance.

(PRIEST *goes out.* SUBTIL *begins to snuff out candles as the main curtain goes down.*)

The End